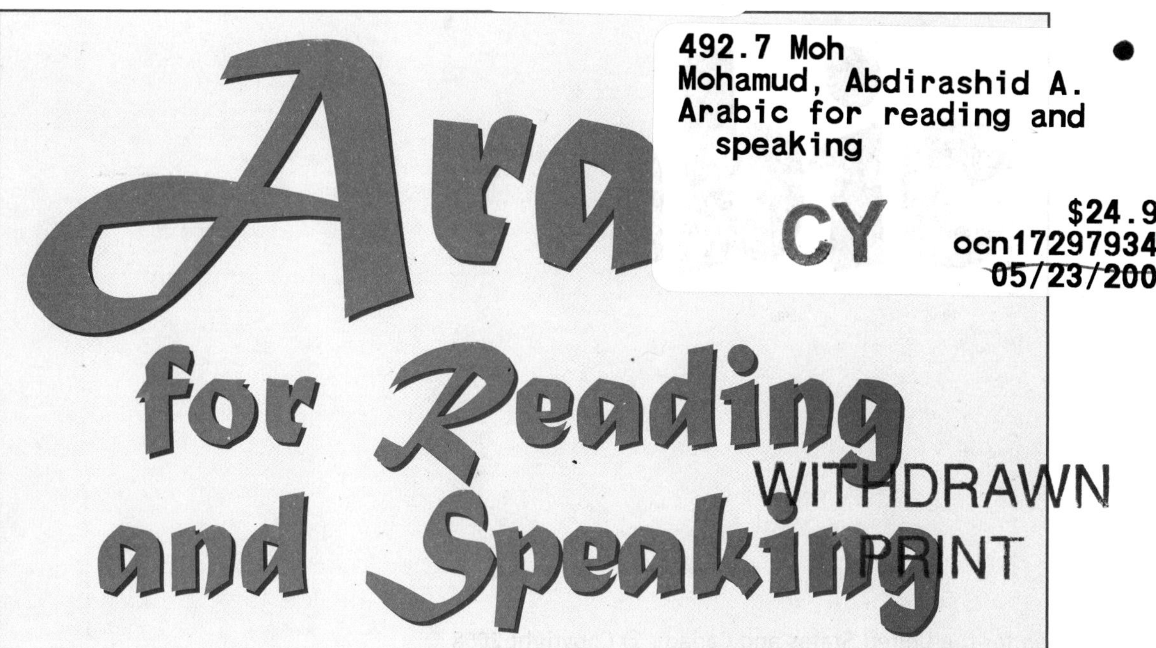

Abdirashid A. Mohamud

Title of the original German edition: **PONS lernen & üben Arabisch.**

Author: **Abdirashid A. Mohamud**
English translation: **Kathleen Luft**

All inquiries should be addressed to:
Barron's Educational Series, Inc.
250 Wireless Boulevard
Hauppauge, NY 11788
http://www.barronseduc.com

ISBN-13: 978-0-7641-3908-6 (book only)
ISBN-10: 0-7641-3908-8 (book only)
ISBN-13: 978-0-7641-9427-6 (book & CD package)
ISBN-10: 0-7641-9427-5 (book & CD package)

Library of Congress Control Number 2007928253

Printed in the United States of America
9 8 7 6 5 4 3 2 1

Welcome ...

to the direct way of language learning. Are you currently learning Arabic and interested in additional ways of improving your knowledge of the basics, by focusing on certain key areas and practicing them?
Then this book, *Arabic for Reading and Speaking*, is exactly right for you.

About This Book

An introduction to the language will first give you interesting background information about Arabic and tips to help you learn this language more easily.

The section titled Alphabet and Pronunciation (A) will familiarize you with the script and the sound system. The Vocabulary (V) section will provide you with a basic Arabic vocabulary, arranged according to theme. In the Grammar (G) section, major aspects of Arabic grammar are discussed in a way suitable for beginners as well as for those who want a review. The section titled Communication (C) repeats words and phrases from the Vocabulary section and provides practical building blocks to help you communicate in everyday situations.

In these four sections—A, V, G, and C—each spread, or unit of two facing pages, contains a learning unit: On the left-hand page, a topic or a grammatical phenomenon is explained in a readily comprehensible way; on the right-hand page, it is drilled in a wide variety of exercises. You can use the key in the Answers section to check your work. Marginal references to sections A, V, G, and C provide links to material elsewhere in the book and help you move around quickly among related topics.

The tables provide you with an overview of the different conjugated forms of the most important verb stems. In the Arabic-English mini-dictionary, you will find a list of all the words used in the book, with their English meanings.

An audio CD is included to support and reinforce your learning process. Numerous listening comprehension exercises dealing with the alphabet and pronunciation, as well as mini-dialogues from the Communication section of the book, will train your ear as you acquire listening skills.

Symbols

7 This explanation or exercise is recorded on the CD.
The number indicates the track number on the CD.

V3
–
V6 These letters and numbers refer you, for example, to the Vocabulary section, Chapters 3–6, and to Chapter 8
G8 in the Grammar section.

In Arabic ... — In the info boxes, you'll find additional information about exceptions to rules, learning tips, or regional and cultural matters.

We wish you success, as well as lots of fun, as you learn Arabic!

Contents

Introduction to the Language

Arabic Today

Arabic is the mother tongue of approximately 240 million people and a second language for some 60 million. It is the official language of twenty-five countries: in the Arabian Peninsula (Saudi Arabia, Oman, United Arab Emirates, and others), in the states of the Levant (for example, Syria and Lebanon), and in the countries of North Africa (Egypt, Sudan, Libya, Tunisia, Algeria, Morocco, and Mauretania). So-called Modern Standard Arabic (MSA) is a connecting link among the numerous Arabic dialects, which differ from one another primarily in terms of daily vocabulary. Modern Standard Arabic is the literary standard, used in formal writing and in the media.

In addition, Arabic is used as a liturgical language by Muslims in countries such as Turkey, Iran, Pakistan, some states of the former Soviet Union (such as Uzbekistan and Kyrgyzstan), Indonesia, and Malaysia.

After the Roman, or Latin, alphabet, the Arabic alphabet is the most widely used alphabetic writing system in the world today. Turkish was written with a version of the Arabic alphabet until 1929, as was Swahili until about 1920. Persian (Farsi), Urdu, and Haussa, among others, continue to use Arabic script today.

History of the Arabic Language

Arabic, along with Hebrew, Amharic, and other Afro-Asiatic languages, belongs to the Semitic language group.

Arabic script developed from Nabataean Aramaic. The oldest archeological find that bears an inscription in the Arabic language and Nabataean script is a tombstone from the Syrian Desert, dated 328 A.D. Later finds from the sixth century A.D. indicate that the script already had begun to evolve.

Originally, however, Arabic was primarily a spoken language. Pre-Islamic Arabia is known as *al-jāhiliya* ("Ignorance"), and the people who lived there were called *al-ummijūn* (people unable to read or write). This era is famed for its poets. Poets such as Imra ul-Qais and Antara Ibn Shaddad read their poems aloud at an annual poetry festival in Ukaz, a market town near Mecca, and at other important gathering places in the Arabian Peninsula. In this way they were transmitted orally from one generation to the next. To this day, poems (now in written form) remain a major point of reference for speakers of Arabic.

Following 622 A.D., with the spread of Islam by the Prophet Mohammed, Arabic developed into a written language. The *Koran*, the holy text of Islam, was written in Arabic. It is the first great written document in Arabic, and, in addition to poetry, it became the most important source for the written and spoken language. Toward the end of the seventh century, Caliph Abd al-Malik declared the classical Arabic of the Koran the official administrative language of the Islamic empire. Arabic grammarians in the Middle Ages used the Koran as the basis for standardization of classical Arabic.

The works of Islamic scholars—including the two great Aristotelians of Islamic philosophy, Avicenna (who died in 1037) and Averroes (who died in 1198)—also helped to advance science in medieval Europe. Avicenna's medical writings, for example, were considered authoritative for centuries to come. Both men translated Greek philosophy into Arabic. Their works, in turn, were translated into Latin. This process of translation, interpretation, and retranslation not only promoted an intellectual exchange between Christendom and Islam, but also made a substantial contribution to the development of classical Arabic.

The development of regional Arabic dialects began in the thirteenth century and continued into the eighteenth century. Classical Arabic retained its role as the literary language.

Modern Standard Arabic

In the late eighteenth century, as the literacy rate increased among larger segments of the population, Modern Standard Arabic began to develop, taking the form used today in literature and in the media. It evolved from the classical Arabic of the Koran and is very similar to it in terms of its grammatical structures, although it differs markedly in style.

Modern Standard Arabic coexists with the numerous Arabic dialects (for example, those of the Gulf States, the western Arabian Peninsula, western North Africa, Egypt, and the Sudan) as a written language, and it is also used in communication between people from far-flung regions. In addition, great weight is attached to it in the educational system of the Arab countries. It is taught in schools as a standard written language.

Distinctive Features of Arabic

Arabic presents a challenge to language learners, above all because of the script and the often unfamiliar sounds (such as the guttural sounds). Arabic is also characterized by several grammatical structures that seem unusual and by a flowery, poetic mode of expression.

In contrast to Indo-European languages, which include a great many words of Latin or Greek origin, Arabic contains almost no words that learners can derive from their own mother tongue or from foreign languages. Conversely, however, many Indo-European terms from the fields of mathematics, medicine, astronomy, and botany are derived from Arabic. Arabia was an important center for philosophy and the natural sciences in the Middle Ages, and the Arabic language gave us terms such as *al-kīmiya* الكِيْمِيَاء (chemistry) and *al-jabr* الجَبْر (algebra).

Arabic grammar, in spite of numerous exceptions and peculiarities, is to a great extent systematic and clear. It also exhibits a few structures similar to English grammar, for example. These aspects of the language will be easier for you to become familiar with, and they will help you gain confidence in dealing with the structures that initially seem strange.

- **Arabic Script**

Arabic is a cursive script; that is, both printed and written letters (with a few exceptions) connect directly to the letter that follows. Arabic is written from right to left. No distinction is made between uppercase and lowercase. The individual characters in a word change their appearance, depending on their position in the word. For example, the letter *bā* ب can take the following forms:

final	medial	initial	isolated
ـب	ـبـ	بـ	ب

		final			medial			initial
to write	*kataba*	كَتَبَ	big	*kabīrun*	كَبِيرٌ	(a) house	*baytun*	بَيْتٌ

- **Consonants and Vowels**

Arabic script is based on a consonantal alphabet (abjad). It has three long vowels (*ā*, *ī*, *ū*), of which two represent semiconsonants and/or semivowels. *yā* ي can represent the consonant *y* or the vowel *ī*, and *wāw* و the consonant *w* or the vowel *ū*. The letter *alif* ا represents the long vowel *ā*.

The short vowels *a*, *i*, *u* are expressed with vowel signs that appear above or below a consonant. The vowel signs *fatḥa* ـَ, *kasra* ـِ and *ḍamma* ـُ thus give the vowel sound *a*, *i*, or *u* to a consonant.

bu	بُ	*bi*	بِ	*ba*	بَ

• **Diacritical Marks**

In addition to the vowel signs *fatḥa* ـَ, *kasra* ـِ, and *ḍamma* ـُ, Arabic also uses other so-called diacritical marks (small marks specifying a distinctive sound value). If a consonant is not followed by a vowel or if a word ends in a consonant, *sukūn* ـْ is used to indicate the absence of the vowel signs (for the short vowels).

east *mash**r**iq* مَشْرِق

The doubling of a consonant's sound is indicated by the diacritic *shadda* ـّ, which appears above the corresponding letter.

love *ḥu**bb**un* حُبٌّ

The diacritical marks known as *tanwin*—represented by a double *fatḥa* ـً, *kasra* ـٍ and *ḍamma* ـٌ—indicate the indefinite (indeterminate) state of nouns, adjectives, and adverbs.

man *raju**lun*** رَجُلٌ *raju**lin*** رَجُلٍ *raju**lan*** رَجُلاً

The diacritical marks play an important role for anyone learning Arabic because they make a text easier to read. In addition, the meaning of a word frequently is determined by the sequence of long and short vowels. Note, however, that the diacritical marks generally are used only in textbooks, in the Koran, and in poetry. They do not appear in newspapers, books, letters, and so forth; only consonants and long vowels are used there. For experienced readers, the meaning of individual words is derived from the context.

• **Sounds**

Basically, there is a direct correspondence between sound and symbol in Arabic: A sound is expressed with a single letter, never with a combination, as in English "sh" or "ch," for example.

Arabic has several sounds that have no English counterpart. These include the typical guttural sounds of the consonants *ḥā* ح, *'ain* ع and *qāf* ق as well as the emphatically velarized sounds (such as those of the consonants *ṣād* ص and *ḍād* ض), which are produced by retracting the back part of the tongue toward the soft palate.

Some consonants, however, closely resemble English sounds (such as *bā* ب for *b*, *tā* ت for *t*, *dāl* د for *d*, *thā* ث for *th*, etc.). The glottal stop, or *hamza* ء, a type of consonantal sound at the beginning of a syllable, appears in English words such as "uh-uh" or "uh-oh." The positioning of the *hamza*, which is subject to manifold rules, is a major feature of Arabic, however.

• **Gender of Nouns**

Arabic has two genders, masculine and feminine. In most instances, they can be easily recognized by the endings of the nouns.

(a) man *raju**lun*** (m. sing.) رجُلٌ

(a) woman *imra'**atun*** (f. sing.) إمرأةٌ

Here we differentiate between nouns that refer to animate beings and nouns that refer to things. This distinction is reflected, for example, in the use of pronouns: For plural nouns referring to things, the 3rd person feminine singular form of the pronouns is used.

- **Number of Nouns**

In addition to the singular and the plural, Arabic has a third grammatical number: the dual. A noun is in the dual if it refers to precisely two persons, animals, or things.

(a) car	*sayyār**atun*** (f. sing.)	سَيَّارَةٌ
two cars	*sayyār**atāni*** (f. dual)	سَيَّارَتَانِ

In the plural, a distinction is made between the sound (external) plural and the broken (internal) plural. The latter exhibits irregular plural forms.

cars	*sayyār**ātun*** (f. pl., sound)	سَيَّارَاتٌ
(a) newspaper	*jarī**datun*** (f. sing.)	جَرِيدَةٌ
newspapers	*jar**ā'idun*** (f. pl., broken)	جَرَائِدُ

- **Article**

Arabic has a definite article, the article *al* ال. It lacks an indefinite article (as in English "a car"). The indefinite state of a noun is expressed in the word ending.

the teacher	*al-muʿalim**u*** (m. sing.)	المعلمُ	(a) teacher	*muʿalim**un*** (m. sing.)	معلمٌ

- **Case**

Arabic has three cases: nominative, genitive, and accusative. They are indicated by the vowel signs *ḍamma* ـُ (nominative), *kasra* ـِ (genitive) and *fatḥa* ـَ (accusative).

the man	*ar-rajul**u*** (nom. m. sing.)	الرَّجُلُ
of the man, the man's	*ar-rajul**i*** (gen. m. sing.)	الرَّجُلِ
the man	*ar-rajul**a*** (acc. m. sing.)	الرَّجُلَ

Possession is indicated in Arabic with the genitive construction (*idafa*) by linking two or more nouns.

the teacher's book/ the book of the teacher	*kitābul-muʿalimi*	كِتَابُ الْمُعَلِّمِ

- **Noun and Adjective**

In Arabic, the adjective always follows the noun it modifies. Adjectives generally agree with the noun in gender, number, state, and case, and thus they have the same endings as the noun they modify.

(a) diligent student (m.)	*ṭālib**un** mujtahid**un***	طَالِبٌ مُجتَهِدٌ
(a) diligent student (f.)	*ṭālib**atun** mujtahid**atun***	طَالِبَةٌ مُجتَهِدَةٌ

- **Verbs**

Every Arabic verb has a basic form in the past (perfective) tense and in the present (imperfective) tense. The third tense, the future, is constructed with the basic form of the present tense.

The moods of the verb are indicative (objective statement), subjunctive (hypothetical action/condition), jussive (negation of the past tense form and the imperative), and imperative (command). These moods are rendered only in the present and are derived from the present tense form of the verb.

A verb is conjugated according to gender and number. The various inflectional characteristics take the form of prefixes, suffixes, or changes in the vowel pattern. Therefore there is no need for the subject of the verb to be mentioned separately.

We watched a film.	*shāhad**nā** filman.*	شَاهَدنَا فِلماً.
We're watching a film.	***nu**shāhidu filman.*	نُشَاهِدُ فِلماً.

• **Word Stems**

In Arabic, words are formed on the basis of word stems. The root consonants of the word stem are the signifiers, the elements that convey meaning. Adding other consonants or vowels can expand meanings or give the word an entirely different meaning.

to write	*kataba*	كَتَبَ
book	*kitābun*	كِتَابٌ

The basic stem of a word can be derived with the help of various stem patterns.

• **Word Order**

Arabic has nominal sentences and verbal sentences. The dominant word order, as in English, is subject - verb - object (SVO). The adjective, however, is placed after the subject. A nominal sentence has the structure subject - predicate and dispenses with the verb.

"The room large." (= The room is large.)	*al-ġurfatu wāsiʿatun.*	الغُرفَةُ واسِعَةٌ.

The word order of a verbal sentence is predicate - subject or predicate - subject - object. The subject is expressed in the conjugated verb ending.

"Traveled." (= I traveled.)	*sāfar**tu**.*	سَافَرتُ.

An independent subject, for example, a personal pronoun, usually is used only if emphasis is being placed on the agent of an action.

I bought it.	***'ana** ishtaray**tu**hu.*	أَنَا اِشتَرَيتُهُ.

Tips for Learning Arabic

• **Reading and Writing**

The point of departure for learning Arabic is the script. Therefore, you first need to concentrate on the Alphabet and Pronunciation section of this book and practice the script in reading and writing drills. Also central here is gaining an understanding of the diacritical marks, such as the vowel signs, because they determine a great many grammatical structures.

When learning the script, try to use the transcription in the book as a helpful backup, not as an actual text. That is, always read the Arabic text first and look at the transcription only for verification or for help if difficulties arise.

Promote the learning process by trying from the very outset to read texts in Arabic. At first, try to decipher simple characters, for example, on food product labels or—if you're on a trip—street signs or store signs. Gradually work your way into short articles in magazines and newspapers or on the Internet. Short stories (or even children's books) can provide you with an additional and interesting way of gaining access to the language and culture.

- **Oral Comprehension and Speaking**

When you learn new words, pay attention not only to their meaning and spelling, but also to their pronunciation. Say the new words aloud. You can improve your level of auditory comprehension by tuning in to Arabic-language television and radio stations and by listening to Arabic music.

Don't miss any opportunity to speak Arabic. The best opportunities, of course, will come when you travel in Arabic-speaking countries. You can practice your Arabic in your own country too, however, possibly by going to a restaurant that specializes in Arabic cuisine or shopping in an Arabic store. Even if your vocabulary is limited and you know only very simple grammatical structures, you'll quickly see that you can make yourself understood and get a positive response from the person you're talking to. You can also look for people who speak Arabic at local gatherings such as Arabic roundtables for students, or find a tandem partner to work with.

- **Grammatical Structures**

Don't limit yourself to learning only the basic form of a new word. Besides the singular, always memorize the plural of a noun because most Arabic nouns have a broken, or irregular, plural. In addition, learn the masculine and feminine forms of adjectives, and keep in mind that adjectives and some pronouns also agree with the noun in gender, number, and case. Memorize the various case endings of nouns and the conjugational prefixes or suffixes of verbs, and become familiar with the different verb stems and various stem patterns. Remember also that prepositions and some adverbs always take a certain case.

- **Working with the Dictionary**

To work with a dictionary, it's important to familiarize yourself with Arabic word stems. The main entry in a dictionary is almost always the basic stem of the word. If you want to look up a word that is not in that form, you first need to derive it by using the templates. Gradually you can memorize the patterns for the various basic stems and expanded stems.

Specific Features of This Book

This book will provide you with knowledge of Modern Standard Arabic (MSA). A deliberate decision was made not to include regional variants and dialects. Learning Modern Standard Arabic will give you a solid foundation for confident handling of the written language and for communication in Arabic-speaking countries. From this point of departure, you can eventually feel your way into regional dialects.

The most difficult hurdle for anyone learning Arabic is the script. To help you overcome that obstacle, this book provides a transcription of the Arabic words and sentences in all the teaching units. The transcription system is presented in section A1. There, on facing pages, you will find the entire alphabet in an easy-to-use table.

To enhance the readability of the Arabic text, it is vocalized in almost every instance, as is usual in textbooks. That is, all the diacritics are supplied. Keep in mind that this by no means reflects common practice, but it is a useful support for people learning the language.

The Arabic text in the lesson and exercise sections is read throughout from right to left. To retain this order, the translations of the Arabic target words and sentences usually are not placed directly next to the actual entry but beneath it or to the left of the exercise.

Alphabet / Numbers

Alphabet حُروف الأبجَدِية

A2

The Arabic alphabet consists of 28 letters. Columns 1 and 2 of the table contain the English and Arabic names of the letters. Columns 3 to 6 show how the letter looks, depending on its position in a word. In column 7, you can see how the letters are represented in the system of Romanized transcription used in this book. Column 8, the phonetic value, shows in phonetic symbols how the letters are pronounced. As an additional pronunciation aid, examples and explanations are given in column 9.

1
A2
A3
A6
A7
A10
A17

1 Name	2 Arabic Name	3 Isolated	4 Initial	5 Medial	6 Final	7 Transcription	8 Phonetic value	9 Example
alif	ألف	ا	ا	ـا	ـا	*ā*	[ɑː]	*a*, as in f*a*ther
bā	باء	ب	بـ	ـبـ	ـب	*b*	[b]	*b* as in *b*oy
tā	تاء	ت	تـ	ـتـ	ـت	*t*	[t]	*t* as in *t*oy
thā	ثاء	ث	ثـ	ـثـ	ـث	*th*	[θ]	*th* as in *th*ink
jīm	جيم	ج	جـ	ـجـ	ـج	*j*	[ʤ]	*j* as in *j*am
ḥā	حاء	ح	حـ	ـحـ	ـح	*ḥ*	[ħ]	gutturally aspirated *h*
hā	خاء	خ	خـ	ـخـ	ـخ	*kh*	[x]	*ch* as in Scottish lo*ch*
dāl	دال	د	د	ـد	ـد	*d*	[d]	*d* as in *d*og
dhāl	ذال	ذ	ذ	ـذ	ـذ	*dh*	[ð]	*th* as in *th*is
rā	راء	ر	ر	ـر	ـر	*r*	[r]	slightly trilled, like Spanish *r*
zāy	زاي	ز	ز	ـز	ـز	*z*	[z]	*z* as in *z*ebra
sīn	سين	س	سـ	ـسـ	ـس	*s*	[s]	*s* as in *s*ee
shīn	شين	ش	شـ	ـشـ	ـش	*sh*	[ʃ]	*sh* as in *sh*ip
ṣād	صاد	ص	صـ	ـصـ	ـص	*ṣ*	[s̴]	emphatically velarized *s*, with tongue against lower palate
ḍād	ضاد	ض	ضـ	ـضـ	ـض	*ḍ*	[d̴]	emphatically velarized *d*, with tongue against front of palate
ṭā	طاء	ط	طـ	ـطـ	ـط	*ṭ*	[t̴]	emphatically velarized *t*, with tongue against palate
ẓā	ظاء	ظ	ظـ	ـظـ	ـظ	*ẓ*	[ð̴]	emphatically velarized *dh*, with tongue tip against front of palate
ʿain	عين	ع	عـ	ـعـ	ـع	*ʿa* or *ʿ*	[ʕ]	voiced equivalent of *ḥ*, like an *a* squeezed out of the throat
ġain	غين	غ	غـ	ـغـ	ـغ	*ġ*	[ɣ]	gargling sound, like an untrilled uvular flap
fā	فاء	ف	فـ	ـفـ	ـف	*f*	[f]	*f* as in *f*all
qāf	قاف	ق	قـ	ـقـ	ـق	*q*	[q]	*q* as in *q*ueen, guttural
kāf	كاف	ك	كـ	ـكـ	ـك	*k*	[k]	*k* as in *k*it
lām	لام	ل	لـ	ـلـ	ـل	*l*	[l]	*l* as in *l*ook

1 Name	2 Arabic Name	3 Iso-lated	4 Initial	5 Medial	6 Final	7 Trans-crip-tion	8 Pho-netic value	9 Example
mīm	ميم	م	مـ	ـمـ	ـم	*m*	[m]	*m* as in *mat*
nūn	نون	ن	نـ	ـنـ	ـن	*n*	[n]	*n* as in *not*
hā	هاء	ه	هـ	ـهـ	ـه	*h*	[h]	*h* as in *hit*
wāw	واو	و	و	ـو	ـو	*w* or *ū*	[w]	*w* as in *water* *u* as in *June*
yā	ياء	ي	يـ	ـيـ	ـي	*y* or *ī*	[j]	*y* as in *yet* *i* as in T*i*na

Numbers أعداد

	tisʿatun	*thamāniyatun*	*sabʿatun*	*sittatun*	*khamsatun*	*arbaʿatun*	*thalāthatun*	*ithnāni*	*wāhid*	*ṣifir*
1	٩	٨	٧	٦	٥	٤	٣	٢	١	٠
2	9	8	7	6	5	4	3	2	1	0
3	IX	VIII	VII	VI	V	IV	III	II	I	

V6
G29

The numerals used in Arabic (row 1 of the table) originated in India in the sixth and seventh centuries. Arab mathematicians introduced them in a slightly modified form (row 2) in Spain in the tenth and eleventh centuries. From there, the "Arabic" numerals spread through the rest of Europe and replaced Roman numerals (row 3) in the fifteenth century.

Multidigit numbers, unlike letters, are written from left to right in Arabic, as here:
٣٧٨ = 378

When giving the date, however, the distinct number groups are arranged from right to left:
٢٠٠٦/٧/١٥ = 15 July 2006

Script

Arabic is a cursive script; that is, the successive letters (with a few exceptions; see later) are joined together, even in print. The difference between the printed script and the handwritten script is that many letters are represented in simplified form in handwriting. The present textbook is concerned with the printed form of the
A6 letters. They can also be used for writing.

A7

A10 Arabic is written from right to left. No distinction is made between uppercase and lowercase letters. The
A17 individual letters in a word change their appearance in accordance with their position in the word, as illustrated here in the example of the letter *ʿain* ع:

Final	Medial	Initial	Isolated
ـع	ـعـ	عـ	ع

In the context of a word, here is how *ʿain* ع looks:

Final	Medial	Initial	Isolated
she hears	teacher	flag	he sold
tasmaʿu تسمع	*muʿalimun* معلم	*ʿalamun* علم	*baʿa* باع

There are six letters, however, that can be joined only with a preceding letter, not with a following one:

rā	ر	*alif*	ا
zāy	ز	*dāl*	د
wāw	و	*dhāl*	ذ

In a word, this looks as follows:

Adam	*ādam*	ادم
store	*dukānun*	دكان
fly (insect)	*dhubābun*	ذباب
letter	*risālatun*	رسالة
oil	*zaytun*	زيت
face	*wajhun*	وجه

If one of these six letters is preceded by a letter that also cannot be joined to the left, both remain unconnected in their basic form (isolated):

to study	*darasa*	درس

If, at the end of a word, one of the letters just listed is followed by a letter that actually can be joined on both sides, then it too appears in its basic form (isolated):

man's name	*sulaymān*	سليمَان

The letter *nūn* ن in final position is preceded by *alif* ا; that is, *nūn* ن appears in its basic form.

1 Look at the individual letters and decide whether the statements next to them are true or false. To answer correctly, first take another look at the table in A1.

correct	incorrect		
☐	☐	1. *sīn* in initial position (beginning of word), joined with a following letter.	سـ
☐	☐	2. *sīn* in medial position (middle of word), joined on both sides.	ـسـ
☐	☐	3. *sīn* in its basic form (isolated).	س
☐	☐	4. *tā* in final position (end of word), joined with a preceding letter.	ـتـ
☐	☐	5. *tā* in its basic form (isolated).	ت
☐	☐	6. *kāf* in medial position, joined on both sides.	ـكـ
☐	☐	7. *wāw* in medial position, joined on both sides.	ـو
☐	☐	8. *dāl* in initial position in its basic form (isolated).	د

2 Connect the letters. The table in A1 can help you with this exercise.

minister	وزير	=	و + ز + ي + ر	1
store	__________	=	د + ك + ا + ن	2
principal	__________	=	م + د + ي + ر	3
rounds	__________	=	أ + د + و + ا + ر	4
time	__________	=	ز + م + ا + ن	5
Adam	__________	=	ا + د + م	6
cyclical	__________	=	د + و + ر + ي	7
he visits	__________	=	ي + ز + و + ر	8

3 Fill in the individual letters at the end of the chain of letters. The letters to be filled in are given in their basic form (isolated). The table in A1 can help you with this exercise.

Sumaya	__________	=	+ ا	سميـ	6	flag	علم	=	+ م	علـ	1
radiance	__________	=	+ ع	لـ	7	stingy	__________	=	+ ل	بخيـ	2
gazelle	__________	=	+ ل	غزَا	8	he visits	__________	=	+ ر	يزو	3
to cook	__________	=	+ خ	طبـ	9	harvest	__________	=	+ د	حصا	4
camel	__________	=	+ ل	جمـ	10	to greet	__________	=	+ ب	رحـ	5

Vowels: Long Vowels / Short Vowels

Long Vowels حُرُوف العِلَّة

A6 Arabic script is a consonantal script. The letters *yā* ي and *wāw* و, however, represent semiconsonants or
A7 semivowels. That is, depending on their position in a word, they serve as consonants or as long vowels
A11 (*ḥurūf 'al-'illa*). *yā* ي becomes the long vowel *ī* and *wāw* و becomes the long vowel *ū*. *alif* ا represents the long
A16 vowel *ā* (as in f*a*ther):

woman's name	*sumayā*	سميا
man's name	*mālik*	مالك

yā ي in final position and in some cases in medial position becomes the long vowel *ī* (as in T*i*na):

my mother	*ummī*	أمي
darling	*ḥabīb*	حبيب

yā ي in initial position and in some cases in medial position becomes the consonant *y* (as in *y*et):

he plants	*yazraʿu*	يزرع
to be driven	*suyyira*	سُيِّرَ

wāw و in final position and in some cases in medial position becomes the long vowel *ū* (as in J*u*ne):

Eat!	*kulū*	كُلُوا
he gets up	*yaqūmu*	يقوم

wāw و in initial position and in some cases in medial position becomes the consonant *w* (as in *w*ater):

minister	*wazīr*	وزير
streets	*shawariʿ*	شوارع

Short Vowels حركات

For the short vowels *a*, *i*, and *u*, Arabic has no independent letters. Instead, they are expressed by diacritical marks that represent vowel sounds (*ḥarakāt* = "movements"). The diacritics *fatḥa* ـَ, *kasra* ـِ and *ḍamma* ـُ can be placed above or below any letter of the alphabet to indicate the corresponding vowel sound.

1. *fatḥa* ـَ is a small diagonal line that is always placed above a letter and represents a short *a*.
2. *kasra* ـِ is a small diagonal line that is always placed under a letter and represents a short *i*.
3. *ḍamma* ـُ is a small curl-like diacritic that resembles a small *wāw* و. It is always placed above a letter and represents a short *u*.

The phonetic value of a letter thus changes as follows:

bu بُ *bi* بِ *ba* بَ

1 In this exercise, you will hear each sound twice in succession, followed by a sample word from the lesson. Repeat the sounds during the pause, and then repeat the word.

2

3	و	*ū*	يقوم		2	ي	*ī*	حبيب	1	ا	*ā*	مالك

2 Match the Arabic with the transcription.

1 دَا	A *ba*
2 جَ	B *dā*
3 بَ	C *tā*
4 رَا	D *ja*
5 تَا	E *rā*

3 Identify *fatḥa*, *kasra* and *ḍamma* above or below the following letters, and write the letters with diacritical marks in the appropriate column.

قُ يَ وَ سِ حُ عِ نَ زِ رُ دَ جُ بِ تَ مِ لُ

1. Letters with *fatḥa*	2. Letters with *kasra*	3. Letters with *ḍamma*
______	______	______
______	______	______
______	______	______
______	______	______
______	______	______

4 Listen to the words and decide whether they contain a short vowel or a long one. Mark the correct box, as in the first example.

3

	short vowel	long vowel
1	☐	☒
2	☐	☐
3	☐	☐
4	☐	☐
5	☐	☐
6	☐	☐

Diacritical Marks: *sukūn*, *shadda*, and *tanwin*

A3 In Arabic, the marks *fatḥa*, *kasra*, *ḍamma* (vowel signs), *tanwin*, *shadda*, and *sukūn* serve as so-called diacritical marks (orthographic aids), which are intended to make a text easier to read. Generally, however, they are used only in the Koran, in poetry, and in textbooks. They do not appear in newspapers, books, and other texts, where only consonants and long vowels are represented.

sukūn ـْـ سُكُون

The diacritical mark *sukūn* ـْـ ("no vowel") resembles a small zero. It is placed above a consonant when no vowel follows it or when a word ends in a consonant. *sukūn* ـْـ therefore indicates the absence of vowel signs (for the short vowels).

glance	*naẓratun*	نَظْرَةٌ
east	*mashriq*	مَشْرِقْ

In the first example, *sukūn* ـْـ is placed on *ẓā* ظ, which is directly followed by *rā* ر. In the second example, *sukūn* ـْـ is placed on the letter *qāf* ق, in which the word ends.

shadda ـّـ شَدَّة

In Arabic, the doubling of consonants is also indicated by a diacritical mark. When *shadda* ـّـ ("strengthening") is placed above a letter, it extends the length of the sound, but the letter is not written twice.

love	*ḥu**bb**un*	حُبٌّ
to run away	*fa**rr**a*	فَرَّ

When *shadda* ـّـ is placed on the consonant *bā* ب or *rā* ر, it extends the length of the sound.

If *shadda* ـّـ is accompanied by the short vowels *fatḥa* ـَـ and *ḍamma* ـُـ they are placed above *shadda* ـّـ. The vowel sign *kasra* ـِـ, however, which normally is placed below a letter, in this case appears directly below *shadda* ـِّـ, that is, above the letter.

tanwin ـٌـ, ـٍـ, ـًـ تَنوين

Arabic has no indefinite article such as the English "a" / "an." Instead, indefinite nouns, adjectives, and adverbs
G4 are expressed by nunation, with the help of the *tanwin* diacritics. By doubling the vowel signs *fatḥa* ـَـ, *kasra* ـِـ
G8 and *ḍamma* ـُـ the final *n* of the letter *nūn* ن is added to a word. Depending on the grammatical case, the final sound changes.

1. ـًـ adds the final sound *an* to a letter. The word is in the accusative.
2. ـٍـ adds the final sound *in* to a letter. The word is in the genitive.
3. ـٌـ adds the final sound *un* to a letter. The word is in the nominative.

tanwin also can be placed above every letter of the alphabet, changing the phonetic value as follows:

bun بٌ *bin* بٍ *ban* بًا

(a) man *rajulun* رَجُلٌ *rajulin* رَجُلٍ *rajulan* رَجُلًا

1 Listen to the words from the lesson and repeat them.

(example of *sukūn*)	نَظْرَة 1	(example of *tanwin*)	رَجُلاً 5
(example of *sukūn*)	مَشْرِق 2	(example of *tanwin*)	رَجُلٍ 6
(example of *shadda*)	حُبّ 3	(example of *tanwin*)	رَجُلٌ 7
(example of *shadda*)	فَرَّ 4		

2 Match the following.

1 The letter *rā* with *sukūn*.
2 The letter *tā* with *kasra*.
3 The letter *bā* with *fatḥa*.
4 The letter *dāl* with *sukūn*.
5 The letter *mīm* with *tanwin* (double *kasra*).
6 The letter *thā* with *shadda*.
7 The letter *jīm* with *kasra*.
8 The letter *zāy* with *tanwin* (double *ḍamma*).
9 The letter *nūn* with *sukun*.
10 The letter *wāw* with *shadda*.
11 The letter *hā* with *fatḥa*.
12 The letter *tā* with *tanwin* (double *fatḥa*).

A بَ
B جِ
C مٍ
D تِ
E وّ
F تاً
G رْ
H حَ
I دْ
J زٌ
K ثّ
L نْ

3 Enter the words in the appropriate column.

فَرَّ	شَجَرَةٍ	إبْنَة	مُعَلِّم	كُلّ	مِصْبَاح	بَنْك	قَلَمٌ
to race	tree	daughter	teacher	everything	lamp	bank	pen
	فُرْشَة الأسْنانِ	دُبّ	رَجُلاً	جَرَّ	رَجُلٌ	مَزَّق	مَسْرَح
	toothbrush	bear	man	to pull	man	to tear	theater

3. Words with *tanwin*	2. Words with *shadda*	1. Words with *sukūn*

4 Listen to the words and fill in *sukūn*, *shadda*, and *tanwin* in the appropriate place. Caution: Some words have both *sukūn* and *tanwin* or *shadda* and *tanwin*. You will hear each word twice.

(for a) long (time)	طَويلا 1	coffee	قَهوَة 4
month	شَهر 2	six	سِتَة 5
to give back	رَد 3	sand	رَمل 6

Syllables / Stress

Arabic syllables can be classified as short, long, and extra-long. Stress placement is determined by the various types of syllables.

Short Syllables

A3 Short (weak, light) syllables consist of a consonant and a short vowel:

bu بُ *bi* بِ *ba* بَ

Long Syllables

A3 Long (strong, heavy) syllables can consist of two different consonant-vowel combinations:

consonant – long vowel: *thū* ثُ و *tī* تِ ي *bā* بَ ا

or

consonant – short vowel – consonant: *lum* لُم *rib* رِب *tab* تَب

Extra-Long Syllables

Extra-long (superheavy) syllables consist of this combination: consonant – long vowel – consonant. They occur only at the end of a word: *nūn* نُون *tīn* تِين *bāb* بَابْ

Stress

The stress of Arabic words follows rules that are based on the syllabic structure of each word. Generally, these rules apply:

- To determine which syllable bears the stress, always start with the last syllable of the word.
- The last syllable of a word is never stressed.
- If a word has two syllables, the first is always stressed:

they said	***qā**lū*	قَالُوا	this	***hā**dhā*	هَذَا
what	***mā**dhā*	مَاذَا	he	***hu**wa*	هُوَ
he came	***jā**'a*	جَاءَ	to	***'i**lā*	إِلَى

- If a word has more than two syllables, the stress always falls on the next-to-last (penultimate) syllable, provided it is a strong (long) syllable.

sailor	*mal**lā**ḥun*	مَلاَّحٌ
witness	*shu**hū**dun*	شُهُودٌ
they (f. pl.) write	*yak**tub**na*	يَكْتُبْنَ
they (m. pl.) taught him	*darra**sū**hu*	دَرَّسُوهُ
they (f. pl.) eat	*y'a**kul**na*	يَأْكُلْنَ

- If the next-to-last syllable is weak, that is, short, then the stress falls on the third-from-last (antepenultimate) syllable.

library	*mak**ta**batun*	مَكْتَبَةٌ
Germany	*'al**mā**niyā*	أَلْمَانِيَا
all (m. pl.)	***kul**luhum*	كُلُّهُم
he discusses	*yu**ḥā**wiru*	يُحَاوِرُ

1 Listen to the syllable groups and repeat them during the pause.
Then repeat the word.

to sell	= بَاعَ	بَا /عَ	1
pen	= قَلَمٌ	قَ /لَ /مٌ	2
to be rewarded	= ثُوِّبَ	ثُ /وِ /بَ	3
glance	= نَظْرَةٌ	نَ ظْ /رَ /ةٌ	4
hearts	= قُلُوبٌ	قُ /لُ وْ /بٌ	5

2 Divide the words into syllables.

to give back	_____/_____ =	رَدَّ	1
he	_____/_____ =	هُوَ	2
this	_____/_____ =	هَذَا	3
what	_____/_____ =	مَاذَا	4
they write (f.)	_____/_____/_____ =	يَكْتُبْنَ	5
she	_____/_____ =	هِيَ	6
they said (m.)	_____/_____ =	قَالُوا	7
on	_____/_____ =	عَلَى	8

3 In the middle column, underline the part of the word that bears the stress. Decide in advance how many syllables the word has.

grandfather	*jaddun*	جَدٌّ	1
to come	*jā'a*	جَاْءَ	2
sailor	*mallāḥun*	مَلَّاحٌ	3
they eat (f.)	*y'akulna*	يَأْكُلْنَ	4
they all	*kulluhum*	كُلُّهُم	5
Germany	*'almāniyā*	أَلْمَانِيَا	6
they went (m.)	*dhahabū*	ذَهَبُوا	7
wise woman	*ʿāqilatun*	عَاقِلَةٌ	8

Vowels: *alif* ا (1)

A2 *alif* ا is one of the six letters of the alphabet that are joined only with a preceding letter, never with a following one. This means that its form scarcely changes in different word positions:

Final	Medial	Initial	Isolated
ـا	ـا	ا	ا

alif ا thus is joined only to the right (in the following example, only with the letter *bā* ب but not with the following letter *ḥā* ح):

lamp	*miṣbāḥun*	مِصباحٌ

If *alif* ا is preceded by a letter that also can be joined only with a preceding letter, however, then *alif* ا appears in its basic form (isolated):

man's name	*murād*	مُرَاد

Long Vowel *ā* أَلِف طَويلة

The basic form of the letter *alif* ا is *alif ṭawīla*, the long vowel *ā* (as in f**a**ther). In this form, *alif* ا usually occurs
A3 in medial or final position in a word. But if *alif* ا is the first letter of a word, it does not represent a long vowel;
A8 instead, it carries the syllable-opening consonantal diacritic *hamza* ء. In this case, one of the short vowels,
A9 *fatḥa* ـَ, *kasra* ـِ, or *ḍamma* ـُ appears above or below *alif* ا, and the pronunciation changes according to the short vowel signs:

father	*'abun*	أَبٌ
woman	*'imra'atun*	إمرأةٌ
feminine	*'unthā*	أُنثى

lām alif لام أَلِف

If the long vowel *alif* ا follows the letter *lām* ل, then *alif* ا is placed in the curve of *lām* ل. This special ligature,
A17 called *lām alif*, sometimes is counted as the twenty-ninth letter of the alphabet:

player	*lāʿibun*	لاعِبٌ
countries	*bilādun*	بِلادٌ
"Hello" / "Welcome"	*'ahlan*	أَهلاً

alif qaṣīra أَلِف قَصيرة

An additional variant of the letter *alif* ا is *alif qaṣīra* (the short *alif*). The pronunciation remains unaltered (long vowel *ā*), but the spelling changes: Here a short *alif* "hangs" over the preceding letter. In most Arabic texts, *alif qaṣīra* is not visible, although it is pronounced as the long vowel ā. The following words are considered the most common examples of *alif qaṣīra*:

this	*hā'ulā'*	هَؤُلاءِ	God	*'ilāhun*	إله
this way	*hākadhā*	هَكَذا	Allah	*'allāhu*	الله
but	*lākin*	لَكِن	this (m.)	*hādhā*	هَذا
			this (f.)	*hādhihi*	هَذِه

1 In this exercise you will hear the sound of the letter *alif* twice in succession, followed by several examples from the lesson. Repeat the sound during the pause, and then repeat the words. Keep in mind that in examples 3 to 6, *alif* carries the *hamza*. Only *hamza* is pronounced; *alif* is silent. 7

1 ا	3 أَبٌ	5 أَهلاً
2 مِصباحٌ	4 إمرَأة	6 إلَيهِ

2 Write the appropriate letter in the blank provided.

1. An isolated *alif ṭawīla* in its basic form. ______
2. A joined *alif ṭawīla*. ______
3. *alif ṭawīla* as a carrier for *hamza* (with *hamza* above and *hamza* below the letter). ______ ______
4. *lām alif*. ______

3 The following words contain either the long vowel *alif* or *alif* as a carrier of the diacritic *hamza*. Write the words in the appropriate column.

صباح	أكل	مساء	بارد	إمرأة	يدها	أم	أخ	رجليها	إبن
morning	to eat	afternoon	cold	woman	her hand	mother	brother	her legs	son

1. Words with the long vowel *alif*	2. Words with *alif* carrying *hamza*

4 Four of the following words contain the letter *lām alif*. Mark them.

	Word with *lām alif*	
1 بلاد	☐	countries
2 ملعب	☐	stadium
3 كلب	☐	dog
4 كلاب	☐	dogs
5 ذهب	☐	to go
6 ملاعب	☐	stadium
7 مصباح	☐	lamp
8 لا تذهب!	☐	Don't go!

Vowels: *alif* ا (2)

alif maqṣūra ى أَلِف مَقْصُورَة

alif maqṣūra is a shortened *alif* that can appear at the end of nouns, verbs, or particles. It represents the long vowel *ā*. It is written, however, like the letter *yā* ي without dots:

he built	*banā*	بَنَى
he went	*mashā*	مَشَى
the biggest	*kubrā*	كُبرَى
the smallest	*ṣuġrā*	صُغرَى
on	*ʿalā*	عَلَى
to	*ʾilā*	إلَى

G11 If a suffix (such as a pronoun) is attached to words that end in *alif maqṣūra*, then *alif maqṣūra* is written again as *alif ṭawīla* ا (usually with nouns and verbs) or as normal *yā* ي (usually with particles).

he built it	*banāhā*	بَنَاهَا
we went	*mashaynā*	مَشَينَا
biggest of the two	*kubrāhumā*	كُبرَاهُمَا
the smallest of the two	*ṣuġrāhumā*	صُغرَاهُمَا
with her	*ladayhā*	لَدَيهَا
to him	*ʾilayhi*	إلَيهِ

madda آ مَدَّة

madda is a sign of lengthening or prolongation of sound; it is written as a horizontal stroke above *alif*: آ.

A8 *madda* lengthens *hamza* ء, so that the short vowel *a* is pronounced as the long vowel *ā*. The mark for

A9 *hamza* ء is replaced by *madda*:

traces	*āthārun*	آثَارٌ	trace	*ʾatharun*	أَثَرٌ
hopes (pl.)	*āmālun*	آمَالٌ	hope (sing.)	*ʾamalun*	أَمَلٌ
horizons	*āfāqun*	آفَاقٌ	horizon	*ʾufuqun*	أُفُقٌ

Silent *alif* ا

In Arabic, the 3rd person masculine plural of verbs conjugated in the past tense ends in *alif* ا. This *alif* ا is only written, not spoken, however. If a pronoun is attached to the verb, the written *alif* ا vanishes again:

G11

They wrote it..	*katabūhu.*	كَتَبُوهُ.	they wrote	*katabū*	كَتَبُوا
They hit him.	*ḍarabūhu.*	ضَرَبُوهُ.	they hit	*ḍarabū*	ضَرَبُوا
They visited him.	*zārūhu.*	زَارُوهُ.	they visited	*zārū*	زَارُوا
They thanked him.	*shakarūhu.*	شَكَرُوهُ.	they thanked	*shakarū*	شَكَرُوا

1 Listen to the words from the lesson and repeat them during the pause. Pay attention to the differences: The first word in each row is spelled with *madda*, the second without *madda*.

8

1	أَثَّر	آثَار
2	أَمَل	آمَال
3	أُفُق	آفَاق

2 Which word is written with *alif maqṣūra* and which with *alif* in its basic form? Enter the words in the appropriate column.

مساء	صغرى	حبلى	سيارة	شعرها	ليلى
afternoon	smallest	pregnant	car	her hair	Leila
نَبَات	مقهى	رماه	كبرى	مشينا	على
plant	café	he threw it	biggest	we went	on

1. Words with *alif* in its basic form	2. Words with *alif maqṣūra*

3 Listen to the words and supply *madda* wherever you hear the long vowel *ā*.
You will hear each word twice.

9

1	اهَات	4	أَثَّر
2	أَخ	5	افَاق
3	الاَم	6	امَال

4 Which words are written with a silent *alif*? Mark them.

		Word with silent *alif*	
1	كتبوه	☐	they wrote it
2	ضحكوا	☐	they laughed
3	ضربوه	☐	they hit him
4	مدحوه	☐	they praised him
5	ناموا	☐	they slept
6	حمدوا	☐	they thanked
7	سَمِعوهُ	☐	they heard it
8	أطاعوه	☐	they obeyed him

Consonants: *hamza* ء هَمزَة (1)

hamza ء is a diacritic, linguistically treated as a consonant, that begins a syllable. It looks like a smaller *ʿain* ع.
A3 It represents a glottal stop (voiceless glottal plosive), as in English "uh-uh" or "uh-oh." In Arabic, every word
A6 and every syllable must begin with a consonant. Therefore *hamza* ء is placed above or below the long vowels
A7 *alif* ا, *yā* ي, or *wāw* و at the beginning of a word or syllable. The placement of the *hamza* ء is governed by various rules.

> In connection with *hamza* ء, the long vowels serve only a carrier function; that is, they are written, but not pronounced!

hamza ء in Initial Position

When *hamza* ء occurs at the beginning of a word, *alif* ا is always the carrier of the *hamza* ء. If *hamza* ء is accompanied by *fatḥa* ـَ or *ḍamma* ـُ, it is placed above *alif*: أَ أُ.
A3
However, if *hamza* ء is accompanied by *kasra* ـِ it is placed below *alif*: إِ

I	*'ana*	أَنَا
your mother	*'umuka*	أُمُكَ
Italy	*'īṭāliyā*	إِيطَالِيَا

hamza ء in Medial Position

Which vowel carries *hamza* ء in the middle of a word depends on whether it is accompanied by *fatḥa* ـَ, *kasra* ـِ or *ḍamma* ـُ and/or on which of the three short vowels precedes *hamza* ء.

- The short vowel *kasra* ـِ (*i*) and the long vowel *yā* ي (*ī*) have first priority as carriers of the *hamza* ء in medial position. That means that *yā* carries the *hamza* ء when it is accompanied by *kasra* ـِ or is preceded by *kasra* ـِ:

one hundred	*mi'atun*	مِئَةٌ
representative	*nā'ibun*	نَائِبٌ
climate	*bay'atun*	بِيئَةٌ

  Note that *yā* ي as carrier of the *hamza* ء is written without dots!

- Second priority as carrier of the *hamza* ء in medial position belongs to the short vowel *ḍamma* ـُ (*u*) and the long vowel *wāw* و (*ū*). That means that *wāw* و carries the *hamza* ء when it is accompanied by *ḍamma* ـُ or is preceded by *ḍamma* ـُ و:

feminine	*mu'annath*	مُؤَنَّث
educator	*mu'addib*	مُؤَدِّب
writer	*mu'allif*	مُؤَلِّف

- Third priority as carrier of the *hamza* ء in medial position belongs to the short vowel *fatḥa* ـَ (*a*)) and the long vowel *alif* ا (*ā*). That means that *alif* ا carries the *hamza* ء when it is accompanied by *fatḥa* ـَ or is preceded by *fatḥa* ـَ:

to ask	*sa'ala*	سَأَلَ
he is late	*ta'akhara*	تَأَخَّرَ
thinking about, deliberating	*muta'ammilun*	مُتَأَمِّلٌ

1 In the following words, the *hamza* is carried by *alif*, *yā*, or *wāw*. Write the words in the appropriate column.

مَسؤول	أَبو	نَائِب	مُؤَنَّث	أَنَا	مِئَة	لُؤلُؤ
responsible	father	assistant	feminine	I	one hundred	pearl
إِنسَان	إِجَابَة	بُؤس	أُكِل	رُؤوس	عَائِد	جَائِع
human being	answer	misery	eaten	heads	coming back	hungry

3. Words with *hamza* above *wāw*	2. Words with *hamza* above *yā*	1. Words with *hamza* above/below *alif*

2 Match the Arabic words with their transcriptions.

A *m'ulimun* — 1 أَبَداً
B *'abadan* — 2 بَائِس
C *mā'ilun* — 3 مُؤَلِف
D *bā'isun* — 4 مَسأَلَة
E *mu'alifun* — 5 مَائِل
F *'akhun* — 6 إِسم
G *mas'alatun* — 7 مُؤلِم
H *'ismun* — 8 أَخ

3 Write the transcribed words in Arabic, and place *hamza* above / below the correct carrier.

Italy	1. *'iṭāliyā*	________
to ask	2. *sa'ala*	________
thinking about, deliberating	3. *muta'amilun*	________
assistant	4. *nā'ibun*	________
believer	5. *m'uminun*	________
coming back	6. *ʿā'idun*	________
son	7. *'ibnun*	________
hundred	8. *mi'atun*	________

Consonants: *hamza* ء هَمزَة (2)

hamza ء Isolated in Medial Position

If *hamza* ء, accompanied by *fatḥa* ـَ, occurs in the middle of a word and follows the long vowel *alif* ا or the long vowel *wāw* و, it stands alone on the line:

we were surprised	*natasā'alu*	نَتَساءَلُ	virtue, sense of honor	*murū'atun*	مُرُوءَةٌ

hamza ء in Final Position

A4 If *hamza* ء at the end of a word follows the long vowels *alif* ا or *wāw* و or a consonant with *sukūn* ـْ, it stands alone on the line:

punishment	*jazā'un*	جَزَاءٌ
asylum	*lujū'un*	لُجُوءٌ
part	*juz'un*	جُزْءٌ

If *hamza* ء at the end of a word follows the short vowel *fatḥa* ـَ, it is placed above *alif* ا. If it occurs at the end of a word and follows *kasra* ـِ, it is placed above *yā* ي. If it occurs at the end of a word and follows *ḍamma* ـُ, it is placed above *wāw* و.

Begin!	*'ibda'*	إبدَأ
(a) reader	*qāri'*	قَارِئ
pearl	*lu'lu'*	لُؤلُؤ

hamzat al-waṣl هَمزَة الوَصل

hamzat al-waṣl serves as an aid to pronunciation. Because an Arabic word cannot begin with a consonant cluster, G21 this cluster must be broken up by *hamzat al-waṣl*, as seen below in the formation of the imperative:

to write	*kataba*	كَتَبَ
Write!	*'uktub*	أُكْتُبْ

hamzat al-waṣl is always placed at the beginning of the word or below *alif* ا. Keep in mind, however, that this *hamzat al-waṣl* normally is not visible but is only pronounced. Only *alif* ا as the *hamza* carrier is written. If the word that is accompanied by *hamzat al-waṣl* is preceded by a particle, for example, then *hamzat al-waṣl* is neither pronounced nor written.

hamzat al-waṣl occurs in particular in the following words:

G4

- The definite article *al* ال:

	unpronounced *hamza*			pronounced *hamza*	
in the house	*fil-bayti*	فِي الْبَيْتِ	the house	*'al-baytu*	الْبَيْتُ

- Some commonly used nouns:

	unpronounced *hamza*			pronounced *hamza*	
Mohammed, son of Farah	*muhamadibn fārah*	مُحمَدابن فَارَح	son	*'ibnun*	ابْنٌ
he and his daughter	*huwa wabnatuhu*	هُوَ وَابْنَتُه	daugh-ter	*'ibnatun*	ابْنَةٌ
What is your name?	*masmuka?*	مَااسْمُكَ؟	name	*'ismun*	اسْمٌ
he and two others	*huwa wathnāni 'ākharāni*	هُوَ وَاثْنَانِ آخَرَانِ	two	*'ithnāni*	اثْنَانِ
he and his wife	*huwa wamra'atuhu*	هُوَ وَامرَأَتُه	wife	*'imra'atun*	امْرَأَةٌ

1 Write the following letters in the blanks provided:

1. *hamza* above *alif* in initial position __________
2. *hamza* on the line in final position __________
3. *hamza* above *wāw* in medial position __________
4. *hamza* below *alif* in initial position __________
5. *hamza* above *yā* in medial position __________
6. *hamza* above *alif* in medial position __________

2 Listen to the following words and place *hamza* above / below the appropriate carrier. Then write the words (with *hamza*) in the appropriate column. You will hear each word twice. 10

never	__________	=	1 ابَداً
to ask	__________	=	2 سَاَلَ
that	__________	=	3 انَّ
question	__________	=	4 سُوالٌ
to eat	__________	=	5 اكَلَ
he eats	__________	=	6 يَاكُلُ

3 Some of the following words are written with *hamzat al-waṣl*, some with normal *hamza*. Write the words in the appropriate column.

اسم	أن	اشترى	أب	البيت	ابن	أمك
name	that	he bought	father	house	son	your mother
قارئ	ابنة	نائب	اكتب	أخ	اثنان	تأخر
reader	daughter	representative	Write!	brother	two	he is late

2. Words with normal *hamza*	1. Words with *hamzat al-waṣl*

Consonants: *bā* ب / *tā* ت / *thā* ث

The consonants *bā* ب, *tā* ت, and *thā* ث have the same basic shape. The difference between the individual letters lies in the number and positioning of the diacritical dots above or below the letter.

bā ب

The consonant *bā* ب is pronounced like the *b* in English **b**oy. It is distinguished by a dot below the letter.
A2 Depending on the position of the letter in a word, *bā* ب (like most other letters of the alphabet) changes its shape:

Final	Medial	Initial	Isolated
ـب	ـبـ	بـ	ب

In the context of a word, this looks as follows:

		Final			Medial			Initial
to write	*kataba*	كَتَبَ	big	*kabīrun*	كَبِيْرٌ	(a) house	*baytun*	بَيْتٌ

tā ت

tā ت is pronounced like the *t* in English **t**oy. It is distinguished by two dots above the letters, and it changes its shape according to its position in a word:

Final	Medial	Initial	Isolated
ـت	ـتـ	تـ	ت

In the context of a word, this looks as follows:

		Final			Medial			Initial
silence	*ṣamtun*	صَمْتٌ	reproach	*ʿitābun*	عِتَابٌ	to follow	*tabiʿa*	تَبِعَ

thā ث

thā ث is pronounced like the unvoiced *th* in English **th**ing. It is distinguished by three dots above the letter. *thā* ث also changes its shape depending on its position in a word:

Final	Medial	Initial	Isolated
ـث	ـثـ	ثـ	ث

In the context of a word, this looks as follows:

		Final			Medial			Initial
to remain, stay	*makatha*	مَكَثَ	dense, thick	*kathīfun*	كَثِيْفٌ	dress	*thawbun*	ثَوْبٌ

bā ب, *tā* ت, and *thā* ث and the Short Vowels

A3 As with all the other letters of the alphabet, the short vowels *fatḥa* ـَ, *kasra* ـِ, and *ḍamma* ـُ can be placed above or below the consonants *bā* ب, *tā* ت, and *thā* ث:

bu	بُ	*bi*	بِ	*ba*	بَ
tu	تُ	*ti*	تِ	*ta*	تَ
thu	ثُ	*thi*	ثِ	*tha*	ثَ

1 In this exercise, you will hear the sound of each letter twice in succession, followed by a sample word from the lesson. Repeat the sound during the pause, and then repeat the word.  11

1 ب بَيْتٌ

2 ت عِتَاْبٌ

3 ث ثَوْبٌ

2 Write each of the letters three times in the table.

ث	ت	ب

3 Join the letters below as in the example provided. The connected letters represent sound sequences.

1 ا + ب + ت + ث = ابتث

2 ب + ا + ث + ث = ____________

3 ث + ت + ب + ا = ____________

4 ت + ا + ث + ب = ____________

5 ا + ث + ا + ت + ب = ____________

6 ب + ت + ب + ث + ا = ____________

7 ث + ت + ث + ب + ا = ____________

8 ت + ا + ت + ث + ب = ____________

4 Separate the letters so that each letter is presented in its isolated form.

1 مـثـب = م + ث + ب

2 ثـمـت = ____________

3 تـبـث = ____________

4 بـكـت = ____________

5 أثاث = ____________

Consonants: *nūn* ن / *yā* ي

nūn ن

The consonant *nūn* ن is pronounced like the *n* in English **n**ot. When isolated, *nūn* ن resembles *bā* ب, *tā* ت, and
A10 *thā* ث. The difference is that the curve is tighter. In initial or medial position, the forms of the four letters are identical. Only the positioning and number of dots is different: *nūn* ن carries a dot above the letter:

Final	Medial	Initial	Isolated
ـن	ـنـ	نـ	ن

In the context of a word, *nūn* ن looks as follows:

		Final			Medial			Initial
to live	*sakana*	سَكَنَ	London	*landan*	لَنْدَنْ	to sleep	*nāma*	نَامَ

If the short vowels *fatḥa* ـَ, *kasra* ـِ, and *ḍamma* ـُ appear above or below the consonant *nūn* ن, its phonetic value changes correspondingly:

nu	نُ	*ni*	نِ	*na*	نَ

yā ي

As a consonant (or semiconsonant), *yā* ي corresponds to the *y* in English **y**et. But if *yā* ي represents a long vowel in a word, it becomes a long *ī* (as in T*i*na).

A3 In its basic form (isolated), *yā* ي has the shape of *nūn* ن but begins at top right with a curved flourish. In initial and medial position, *yā* ي, *bā* ب, *tā* ت, and *thā* ث again are similar. *yā* ي is distinguished by two dots below the letter:

Final	Medial	Initial	Isolated
ـي	ـيـ	يـ	ي

In the context of a word, *yā* ي looks as follows:

		Final			Medial			Initial
to /onto me	*ʿalayya*	عَلَيَّ	Mr.	*sayyid*	سَيِّد	day	*yawmun*	يَوْمٌ

The consonant *yā* ي can also carry the short vowels *fatḥa* ـَ, *kasra* ـِ, and *ḍamma* ـُ:

yu	يُ	*yi*	يِ	*ya*	يَ

1 In this exercise, you will hear the sound of each letter twice in succession, followed by a sample word from the lesson. Repeat the sound during the pause, and then repeat the word.

1	ن	سَكَـنَ
2	ي	سَـيِّـد

2 Write each letter three times in the table.

ي	ن

3 Join the letters as in the example provided.

1	ن + ب + ت	= نَبَتَ	to grow up
2	ب + ن + ت	= ______	girl
3	ن + ا + ب	= ______	eyeteeth
4	أ + ن + ب + ت	= ______	to grow
5	ب + ن + ا + ت	= ______	girls
6	ن + ب + ي	= ______	prophet
7	إ + ث + ن + ا + ن	= ______	two
8	إ + ن + ا + ث	= ______	feminine

4 Match the words with the corresponding row of individual letters.

A	أ + ب + ي + ت	بيت	1	house
B	ب + ي + ب + ة	أنت	2	you
C	ب + ي + ت	باب	3	door
D	ث + ب + ا + ت	أبيت	4	I declined
E	أ + ن + ت	ثياب	5	clothing
F	ب + ا + ب	أثَاب	6	to reward
G	ث + ي + ا + ب	بِيبَةٌ	7	pipe
H	أ + ث + ا + ب	ثبات	8	constancy, reliability

Consonants: *jīm* ج / *ḥā* ح / *khā* خ

jīm ج, *ḥā* ح, and *khā* خ have the same basic shape. The individual letters differ in the positioning and number of the diacritical dots.

jīm ج

The consonant *jīm* ج has the sound of *j* in English **j**am. It is distinguished by a dot in the curve. Depending on its position in a word, *jīm* ج changes its shape:

Final	Medial	Initial	Isolated
ـج	ـجـ	جـ	ج

In the context of a word, this looks as follows:

		Final			Medial			Initial
snow	*thaljun*	ثَلْجٌ	to emigrate	*hajara*	هَجَرَ	neighbors	*jīrānun*	جِيْرَانٌ

ḥā ح

The pronunciation of the consonant *ḥā* ح has no English equivalent; it is a guttural aspirate, stronger and deeper than the *h* in **h**e. *ḥā* ح is written with no dot at all

Final	Medial	Initial	Isolated
ـح	ـحـ	حـ	ح

In the context of a word, *ḥā* ح looks as follows:

		Final			Medial			Initial
to be suitable	*ṣaluha*	صَلُحَ	dryness, aridity	*qaḥṭun*	قَحْطٌ	envy	*hasadun*	حَسَدٌ

khā خ

The phonetic value of the consonant *khā* خ corresponds to a rough Scottish *ch*, as in lo**ch**. *khā* خ is characterized by a dot above the letter:

Final	Medial	Initial	Isolated
ـخ	ـخـ	خـ	خ

In the context of a word, this looks as follows:

		Final			Medial			Initial
to annul	*fasakha*	فَسَخَ	date palm	*nakhlun*	نَخْلٌ	bread	*khubzun*	خُبْزٌ

jīm ج, *ḥā* ح, and *khā* خ and the Short Vowels

If the short vowels *fatḥa* ـَ, *kasra* ـِ, and *ḍamma* ـُ are placed above or below the consonants just mentioned, their phonetic value changes as follows:

ju	جُ	*ji*	جِ	*ja*	جَ
hu	حُ	*hi*	حِ	*ha*	حَ
khu	خُ	*khi*	خِ	*kha*	خَ

1 In this exercise, you will hear the sound of each letter twice in succession, followed by a sample word from the lesson. Repeat the sound during the pause, and then repeat the word.

1 ج ثَلْجٌ
2 ح قَحْطٌ
3 خ خُبْزٌ

2 Write the letters and sound sequences three times each in the table.

ختج	جبح	حجخ	خ	ح	ج

3 Join the letters.

1 ح + ب + ي + ب = ____________ darling
2 ج + ب + ن = ____________ cowardice
3 ح + ج + ب = ____________ to cover
4 ب + ح + ث = ____________ to seek
5 ت + ح + ب = ____________ she loves
6 أ + ج + ا + ب = ____________ to answer
7 إ + ن + ت + خ + ب = ____________ to choose
8 ج + ا + ء = ____________ to come

4 Separate the letters, so that each letter is presented in its isolated form.

1 خَيْبَةٌ = ____________ failure
2 حَبَّةٌ = ____________ grain
3 جَنَّةٌ = ____________ garden
4 حَجَّ = ____________ to make a pilgrimage
5 جَوَابٌ = ____________ answer
6 حِينٌ = ____________ time
7 خَابَ = ____________ to fail
8 جَابَ = ____________ to bring

Consonants: *dāl* د / *dhāl* ذ / *rā* ر / *zāy* ز

A2 *dāl* د, *dhāl* ذ, *rā* ر, and *zāy* ز belong to the group of six letters that can be joined only to a preceding letter but not to a following one. Note that this changes the shape of each in various word positions only slightly or not at all. *dāl* د and *dhāl* ذ and *rā* ر and *zāy* ز each have the same basic form, which is differentiated by the number and positioning of the diacritical dots.

dāl د

The consonant *dāl* د sounds like the *d* in English **d**og. It carries no diacritical dot.

Final	Medial	Initial	Isolated
ـد	ـد	د	د

		Final			Medial			Initial
good	*jayyidun*	جَـيِّـدٌ	principal	*mudīnn*	مُدِيرٌ	store	*dukkānun*	دُكَّانٌ

dhāl ذ

dhāl ذ represents the sound *dh*, like the voiced *th* in English **th**is. *dhāl* ذ is differentiated from *dāl* د by the diacritical dot above the letter.

Final	Medial	Initial	Isolated
ـذ	ـذ	ذ	ذ

		Final			Medial			Initial
to take	*'akhadha*	أَخَـذَ	to put on	*jadhaba*	جَذَبَ	to go	*dhahaba*	ذَهَبَ

rā ر

rā ر is pronounced like a slightly trilled Spanish *r*. It carries no diacritical dot.

Final	Medial	Initial	Isolated
ـر	ـر	ر	ر

		Final			Medial			Initial
to be patient	*ṣabara*	صَبَـرَ	to flee	*haraba*	هَـرَبَ	to profit	*rabiḥa*	رَبِحَ

zāy ز

zāy ز represents a soft, voiced *z* as in English **z**ebra. *zāy* ز is differentiated from *rā* ر by a diacritical dot above the letter.

Final	Medial	Initial	Isolated
ـز	ـز	ز	ز

		Final			Medial			Initial
center	*markazun*	مَركَـزٌ	to marry	*tazzawaja*	تَزَوَّجَ	to visit	*zāra*	زَارَ

dāl د, *dhāl* ذ, *rā* ر, and *zāy* ز and the Short Vowels

du	دُ	*di*	دِ	*da*	دَ
dhu	ذُ	*dhi*	ذِ	*dha*	ذَ
ru	رُ	*ri*	رِ	*ra*	رَ
zu	زُ	*zi*	زِ	*za*	زَ

1 In this exercise, you will hear the sound of each letter twice in succession, followed by a sample word from the lesson. Repeat the sound during the pause, and then repeat the word.

1 د مُدِيْرٌ
2 ذ أَخَذَ
3 ر رَبِحَ
4 ز تَزَوَّجَ

2 Write each letter three times in the table.

ز	ر	ذ	د

3 Join the letters.

1	أ + ب + د + ا	=	____________	never
2	ذ + ا + ب	=	____________	to melt
3	ذ + ب + ا + ب	=	____________	fly
4	ج + د + ي + د	=	____________	new
5	أ + خ + ذ + ا	=	____________	the two of them took it
6	ز + ي + د	=	____________	Zaid
7	د + ر + ا + ج + ة	=	____________	bicycle
8	أ + ر + ز	=	____________	rice
9	د + ي + ا + ر + ه	=	____________	his houses
10	ز+ ي + ا + د + ة	=	____________	more

4 Match the words with the appropriate row of separate letters.

A	ذ + ب + ا + ب	أزرَق	1	blue
B	أ + ر + ا + د	زِيَارَة	2	visit
C	أ + ز + ر + ق	ذُبَابٌ	3	fly
D	ذ + ب + ذ + ب	أَرَادَ	4	to want to
E	ز + ي + ا + ر + ة	ذَبذَبَ	5	to dangle

Consonants: *sīn* س / *shīn* ش / *ṣād* ص / *ḍād* ض

The consonants *sīn* س and *shīn* ش as well as *ṣād* ص and *ḍād* ض, are similar in their isolated form. The difference between the two groups lies in the first part of each letter. *sīn* س and *shīn* ش begin with an open curve, *ṣād* ص and *ḍād* ض with a closed one. Note that all four letters change shape, depending on their position in a word.

sīn س

The consonant *sīn* س is pronounced like the unvoiced *s* in English **s**ee. It carries no diacritical dot.

Final	Medial	Initial	Isolated
ـس	ـسـ	سـ	س

		Final			Medial			Initial
to sit	*jalasa*	جَلَسَ	mosque	*masjidun*	مَسْجِدٌ	six	*sittatun*	سِتَّةٌ

shīn ش

shīn ش sounds like the *sh* in English **sh**ine. It is differentiated from *sīn* س by three diacritical dots above the letter.

Final	Medial	Initial	Isolated
ـش	ـشـ	شـ	ش

		Final			Medial			Initial
army	*jayshun*	جَيْشٌ	wood	*khashabun*	خَشَبٌ	sun	*shamsun*	شَمْسٌ

ṣād ص

English has no equivalent for the sound of the consonant *ṣād* ص. *ṣād* ص is an emphatically velarized *s*, produced by pressing the tongue to the roof of the mouth. The letter carries no diacritical dots.

Final	Medial	Initial	Isolated
ـص	ـصـ	صـ	ص

		Final			Medial			Initial
person	*shakhṣun*	شَخْصٌ	lamp	*miṣbāḥun*	مِصْبَاحٌ	picture	*ṣūratun*	صُورَةٌ

ḍād ض

English also has no equivalent for the sound of the consonant *ḍād* ض. It is an emphatically velarized *d*, produced
A13 by pressing the tongue to the front of the roof of the mouth. In written Arabic, the letter is differentiated from *ṣād* ض by a diacritical dot, which is placed above the closed curve.

Final	Medial	Initial	Isolated
ـض	ـضـ	ضـ	ض

		Final			Medial			Initial
to hold fast	*qabaḍa*	قَبَضَ	annoyance	*ġaḍabun*	غَضَبٌ	to laugh	*ḍaḥika*	ضَحِكَ

sīn س, *shīn* ش, *ṣād* ص, and *ḍād* ض and the Short Vowels

su	سُ	*si*	سِ	*sa*	سَ
shu	شُ	*shi*	شِ	*sha*	شَ
ṣu	صُ	*ṣi*	صِ	*ṣa*	صَ
ḍu	ضُ	*ḍi*	ضِ	*ḍa*	ضَ

1 In this exercise, you will hear the sound of each letter twice in succession, followed by a sample word from the lesson. Repeat the sound during the pause, and then repeat the word.

1 س	سِتَّة	3 ص	مِصْبَاح
2 ش	خَشَب	4 ض	ضَحِك

2 Write each letter and word three times in the table.

come	soap	towels	fat, thick				
حَضَرَ	صَابُون	شَرَاشِف	سَمِين	ض	ص	ش	س

3 Join the letters.

1 ش + م + س = ____________ sun

2 ش + ج + ر = ____________ tree

3 م + ص + ب + ا + ح = ____________ lamp

4 ض + ع + ي + ف = ____________ weak

5 ش + ا + ر + ع = ____________ street

6 ا + ل + ص + ب + ح = ____________ morning

7 س + م + ي + ن = ____________ fat, thick

8 ض + ح + ك = ____________ to laugh

9 ش + ف + ي = ____________ to become healthy

10 ر + س + و + م = ____________ fees

4 Match the words with the corresponding row of separate letters.

A ص + د + ا + ع	1 ضِفْدَع	frog
B س + ل + ا + م	2 شَمْس	sun
C ض + ف + د + ع	3 نَشَاطَات	activities
D ا + س + ت + ر + ا + ح	4 صُفْرَة	yellow
E ف + ض + ة	5 اِسْتَرَاح	to rest
F ص + ف + ر + ة	6 فِضَّة	silver
G ش + م + س	7 صُدَاع	headache
H ن + ش + ا + ط + ا + ت	8 سَلَام	peace

Consonants: *tā* ط/*ẓā* ظ/*ʿain* ع/*ġain* غ

tā ط

A10

English has no equivalent for the sound of the consonant *tā* ط. *tā* ط is an emphatically velarized *t*, produced by pressing the tongue to the roof of the mouth. The letter carries no diacritical dots, and it changes its shape only slightly in different word positions, but it is joined on all sides:

Final	Medial	Initial	Isolated
ـط	ـطـ	طـ	ط

		Final			Medial			Initial
cream	*qishtatun*	قِشْطَةٌ	rain	*maṭarun*	مَطَرٌ	way	*ṭarīqun*	طَرِيْقٌ

ẓā ظ

A13

The sound of the consonant *ẓā* ظ corresponds to an emphatically velarized *dh*; it is produced by pressing the tongue to the front of the roof of the mouth. The shape of the letter *ẓā* ظ is differentiated from *tā* ط in all word positions only by a diacritical dot.

Final	Medial	Initial	Isolated
ـظ	ـظـ	ظـ	ظ

		Final			Medial			Initial
pronunciation	*lafẓun*	لَفْظٌ	umbrella	*miẓallatun*	مِظَلَّةٌ	reverse (side)	*ẓahrun*	ظَهْرٌ

ʿain ع

A12

ʿain ع is the voiced equivalent of the consonant *ha*; it is pronounced as an *a* squeezed out of the back of the throat. The letter carries no diacritical dots and changes its appearance on the basis of word position:

Final	Medial	Initial	Isolated
ـع	ـعـ	عـ	ع

		Final			Medial			Initial
he sells	*yabīʿu*	يَبِيْعُ	teacher (m.)	*muʿallimun*	مُعَلِّمٌ	evening	*ʿishāun*	عِشَاْءٌ

ġain غ

The phonetic value of the consonant *ġain* غ corresponds to an untrilled uvular *r*. *ġain* غ is differentiated from *ʿain* ع in all word positions only by a diacritical dot.

Final	Medial	Initial	Isolated
ـغ	ـغـ	غـ	غ

		Final			Medial			Initial
to reach	*balaġa*	بَلَغَ	Baghdad	*baġdād*	بَغْدَاْد	food, nourishment	*ġidhā'un*	غِذَاْءٌ

tā ط, *ẓā* ظ, *ʿain* ع, and *ġain* غ and the Short Vowels

ṭu	طُ	*ṭi*	طِ	*ṭa*	طَ
ẓu	ظُ	*ẓi*	ظِ	*ẓa*	ظَ
ʿu	عُ	*ʿi*	عِ	*ʿa*	عَ
ġu	غُ	*ġi*	غِ	*ġa*	غَ

1 In this exercise, you will hear the sound of each letter twice in succession, followed by a sample word from the lesson. Repeat the sound during the pause, and then repeat the word.

1 ط مَطَرٌ   2 ظ لَفْظ   3 ع عِشَاءٌ   4 غ بَغْدَاد

2 Write each letter and word once in the table.

tomatoes	rain	tailor	student				
طَمَاطِم	مَطَر	خَيَاط	طَالِب	ـط	ـطـ	طـ	ط
to think	fingernails	umbrella	noon				
ظَنّ	أَظَافِر	مِظَلَّة	ظُهراً	ـظ	ـظـ	ظـ	ظ
greed	hungry	teacher	uncle				
طَمَع	جَائِع	مُعَلِّم	عَمّ	ـع	ـعـ	عـ	ع
branch	tanner	room	to wash				
غُصن	دِبَاغ	الغُرفَة	غَسَل	ـغ	ـغـ	غـ	غ

3 Join the letters.

1 غ + ا + ل = ____________ expensive

2 م + ظ + ل + و + م = ____________ disadvantaged

3 ع + ق + ا + ب = ____________ punishment

4 ا + ل + غ + ل + ا + م = ____________ boy

5 ش + و + ا + ر + ع = ____________ streets

6 ط + ا + ئ + ر + ة = ____________ airplane

4 Separate the letters, so that each letter is presented in its isolated form.

1 إضطَجَع = ____________ to lie, rest

2 مَطَر = ____________ rain

3 ظَلَام = ____________ darkness

4 صُدَاع = ____________ headache

5 غِيَاب = ____________ absence

6 سَقَط = ____________ to fall down

7 عَبَر = ____________ to cross, traverse

8 ظُهراً = ____________ noon, midday

Consonants: *fā* ف / *qāf* ق / *wāw* و

fā ف, *qāf* ق, and *wāw* و are similar in their basic form. The difference lies in the shape and length of the rear curve of the letter and in the number of diacritical dots. Although *fā* ف and *qāf* ق can be joined on all sides, *wāw* و is one of the six letters that can be joined only to the right.

A2

fā ف

The consonant *fā* ف sounds like the *f* in English **f**all. It is characterized by a dot above the letter:

Final	Medial	Initial	Isolated
ـف	ـفـ	فـ	ف

		Final			Medial			Initial
summer	*ṣayfun*	صَيْفٌ	celebration	*ḥaflatun*	حَفْلَةٌ	verb	*fi'lun*	فِعْلٌ

qāf ق

qāf ق represents an unvoiced uvular plosive, produced deeper in the throat than the English *k*. In its basic form (isolated) and in final position, the rear curve, in comparison with *fā* ف, is shorter and deeper. *qāf* ق carries two diacritical dots above the letter:

Final	Medial	Initial	Isolated
ـق	ـقـ	قـ	ق

		Final			Medial			Initial
plate	*ṭabaqun*	طَبَقٌ	sterile	*'aqīmun*	عَقِيْمٌ	(a) little	*qalīlun*	قَلِيْلٌ

wāw و

As a consonant (or semiconsonant), *wāw* و corresponds to the *w* in English **w**ater. However, if *wāw* و represents a long vowel in a word, it becomes a long *ū* (as in J**u**ne). *wāw* و carries no diacritical dot and is joined only with a preceding letter:

A3

Final	Medial	Initial	Isolated
ـو	ـو	و	و

		Final			Medial			Initial
when, if	*law*	لَوْ	coffee	*qahwatun*	قَهْوَةٌ	country, land	*waṭanun*	وَطَنٌ

fā ف, *qāf* ق, and *wāw* و and the Short Vowels

fu	فُ	*fi*	فِ	*fa*	فَ
qu	قُ	*qi*	قِ	*qa*	قَ
wu	وُ	*wi*	وِ	*wa*	وَ

1 In this exercise, you will hear the sound of each letter twice in succession, followed by a sample word from the lesson. Repeat the sound during the pause, and then repeat the word.

1 ف صَيْـف
2 ق قَـلِيْل
3 و قَهْـوَة

2 Write each letter and word three times in the table.

they said	minister	happy			
قـالـوا	وَزِير	فـَرْحـَانٌ	و	ق	ف

3 Join the letters.

1 ف + ق + ي + ر = ____________ poor
2 و + ا + ح + د = ____________ one (f.)
3 ف + ل + م = ____________ film
4 أ + ق + ل + ا + م = ____________ pens
5 و + ق + ف = ____________ to stop, halt
6 أ + ب + و + ه = ____________ her father
7 ش + و + ا + ر + ع = ____________ streets
8 ف + و + ق + ه = ____________ above him

4 Match the words with the corresponding row of separate letters.

A ق + د+ م — 1 فِعل verb
B م+ ل+ ع + ق + ة — 2 قَدَم foot
C و+ ج+ ب + ة — 3 فَرَح luck, happiness
D م + ط + ب + و + خ — 4 كـُوب cup
E ف+ ر+ ح — 5 مِلعَقَة spoon
F ك+ و+ ب — 6 وَجبَة dish (food)
G ف+ع+ ل — 7 مَطبُوخ cooked

Consonants: *kāf* ك / *lām* ل / *mīm* م / *hā* ه

kāf ك

kāf ك is pronounced like the *q* in English **q**ueen. In its basic form (isolated) and in final word position, the letter carries in its curve a mark that resembles a smaller *kāf* in initial position.

Final	Medial	Initial	Isolated
ـك	ـكـ	كـ	ك

		Final			Medial			Initial
bank	*bank*	بَنْك	sugar	*sukkar*	سُكَّر	church	*kanīsatun*	كَنِيْسَةٌ

lām ل

lām ل represents the sound of *l* in English **l**ook. In its basic form (isolated) and in final position, *lām* ل and *kāf* ك are similar in the first part of the letter.
lām ل is also one of the letters that can be joined on all sides. It changes its shape only slightly in the process, however:

Final	Medial	Initial	Isolated
ـل	ـلـ	لـ	ل

		Final			Medial			Initial
pretty	*jamīlun*	جَمِيْلٌ	pen	*qalamun*	قَلَمٌ	meat	*laḥmun*	لَحْمٌ

mīm م

The phonetic value of the consonant *mīm* م is the equivalent of *l* in English **l**ook. In initial position and medial position, *mīm* م loses the vertical, downward-pointing stroke.

Final	Medial	Initial	Isolated
ـم	ـمـ	مـ	م

		Final			Medial			Initial
mouth	*famun*	فَمٌّ	work	*ʿamalun*	عَمَلٌ	(bus, streetcar) stop	*maḥaṭṭatun*	مَحَطَّةٌ

hā ه

The consonant *hā* ه sounds like the *h* in English **h**it. *hā* ه changes greatly in shape, especially in initial position and in medial position.

Final	Medial	Initial	Isolated
ـه	ـهـ	هـ	ه

		Final			Medial			Initial
his house	*baytuhu*	بَيْتُهُ	engineer	*muhandisun*	مُهَنْدِسٌ	this (one) (m.)	*hādhā*	هَذَا

kāf ك, *lām* ل, *mīm* م, and *hā* ه and the Short Vowels

ku	كُ	*ki*	كِ	*ka*	كَ
lu	لُ	*li*	لِ	*la*	لَ
mu	مُ	*mi*	مِ	*ma*	مَ
hu	هُ	*hi*	هِ	*ha*	هَ

1 In this exercise, you will hear the sound of each letter twice in succession, followed by a sample word from the lesson. Repeat the sound during the pause, and then repeat the word.

1 ك كَنِيسَة

2 ل قَلَم

3 م فَم

4 ه مُهَندِس

2 Write each letter and word three times in the table.

hobby	teacher	meat	how				
هِوَايَة	مُعَلِّم	لَحْم	كَيف	ه	م	ل	ك

3 Join the letters.

1 ك + ر + ة = ________________ ball

2 ك + ت + ا + ب = ________________ book

3 ه + و + ا + ي + ة = ________________ hobby

4 م + س + ج + د = ________________ mosque

5 ل + و + ن = ________________ color

6 م + ك + ت + ب + ة = ________________ library

7 ق + ل + م = ________________ pen

8 م + ه + ذ + ب + ة = ________________ polite (f.)

4 Match the words with the corresponding separate letters.

speaking	1	كَلام	م + ل + ع + ب	A
school	2	مَدرَسة	م + ك + ت + ب + ة	B
stadium	3	مَلعَب	ا + ل + ه + ن + د	C
India	4	الهِند	ك + ل + ا + م	D
library	5	مكتَبَة	ا + ل + ه + ن + د + س + ة	E
church	6	كَنيسة	ك + ت + م	F
to keep (a) secret	7	كَتَم	م + د + ر + س + ة	G
engineering	8	الهَندسة	ك + ن + ي + س + ة	H

Personal Information

V2 C2 C3

Personal Details بَيَانٌ شَخصِيٌّ

name	*'al-'ismu*	الإسْمُ
last name	*'ismul-'usrati*	اِسمُ الأُسرَةِ
date of birth	*tārīḫul-wilādati*	تَارِيخُ الوِلادَةِ
place of birth	*makānul-wilādati*	مَكَانُ الوِلادَةِ
nationality	*al-jinsiyatu*	الجِنسِيَّةُ
marital status	*al-waḍʿul-'ā'ilī*	الوَضعُ العائِلِي
place of residence	*makānus-sakani*	مَكَانُ السَكَنِ
address	*al-ʿinwānu*	العِنوَانُ
telephone number	*raqmul hātifi*	رَقمُ الهَاتِفِ
e-mail address	*ʿal-inwān ʿal-iliktrūni*	العُنْوانُ الإلكتروني
job location	*makānul-ʿamali*	مَكَانُ العَمَلِ
occupation	*al-mihnatu*	المِهنَةُ
educational background	*ḥālatut-taʿlīmi*	حَالَةُ التَعلِيم
photo	*ṣuratun*	صُورَةٌ
height	*ṭūlul-qāmati*	طُول القَامَةِ
weight	*'al-wazn*	الوَزْنُ

Documents الوَثَائِق

passport	*jawāzus-safarin*	جَوَاز سَفَر
ID card	*biṭāqatul-hawiyati*	بِطَاقَةُ الهَوِيَةِ
driver's license	*rukhṣatul-qiyādati*	رُخصَةُ القِيادةِ
credit card	*biṭāqatu-'iʾitimānin*	بِطَاقَةُ إئتِمَانٍ

Character Attributes أوصَافٌ تَتَعَلَّقُ بالشَخصِيَةِ

G16

The following adjectives are given in the masculine and feminine forms. Feminine adjectives usually end in *~atun*.

sociable	*ʾijtimāʿiyyu-ṭabʿi / ʾijtimāʿiyatu-ṭabʿi*	إجتِمَاعِيُّ الطَبعِ / إجتِمَاعِيَةُ الطَبع
interesting	*mushawwiqun / ~atun*	مُشَوِّقٌ / مُشَوِّقَةٌ
boring	*mumillun / ~atun*	مُمِلٌّ / مُمِلَّةٌ
arrogant	*mutakabbirun / ~atun*	مُتَكَبِّرٌ / مُتَكَبِّرَةٌ
friendly	*wuddiyun / ~atun*	وُدِّيٌ / وُدِّيَةٌ
quiet, calm	*razīnun / ~atun*	رَزِينٌ / رَزِينَةٌ
talkative	*tharthārun / ~atun*	ثَرثَارٌ / ثَرثَارَةٌ
polite	*muhadh-dhabun / ~atun*	مُهَذَّبٌ / مُهَذَّبَةٌ

Appearance المَظهَر

eye color	*lawnul-ʿuyūni*	لَونُ العُيُونِ
hair color	*lawnush-shaʿri*	لَونُ الشَّعرِ
skin color	*lawnul-bashrati*	لَونُ البَشرَةِ
with a mustache	*dhū shāribin*	ذُو شَارِبٍ
with a beard	*dhū liḥyatin*	ذُولِحيَةٍ
with glasses	*dhū naẓārātin*	ذُو نَظَارَاتٍ
bald	*'aṣlaʿun / ṣalʿā'u*	أَصلَعٌ / صَلعَاءُ
with long hair	*dhū shaʿrin ṭawīlin / dhātu shaʿrin ṭawīlin*	ذُو شَعرٍ طَوِيلٍ / ذَاتُ شَعرٍ طَوِيل
with short hair	*dhū schaʿrin qaṣīrin / dhātu schaʿrin qaṣīrin*	ذُو شَعرٍقَصِيرٍ / ذَاتُ شَعرٍ قَصِيرٍ
pretty	*jamīlun / ~atun*	جَمِيلٌ / جَمِيلَةٌ
ugly	*qabīḥun / ~atun*	قَبِيحٌ / قَبِيحَةٌ
attractive	*jadh-dhābun / ~atun*	جَذَّابٌ / جَذَّابَةٌ
tall	*ṭawīlun / ~atun*	طَوِيلٌ / طَوِيلَةٌ
short	*qaṣīrun / ~atun*	قَصِيرٌ / قَصِيرَةٌ
slim	*naḥīfun / ~atun*	نَحِيفٌ / نَحِيفَةٌ
corpulent	*badīnun / ~atun*	بَدِينٌ / بَدِينَةٌ
fat	*samīnun / ~atun*	سَمِينٌ / سَمِينَةٌ
athletic	*riyāḍiyun / ~atun*	رِيَاضِيٌّ / رِيَاضِيَةٌ

1 These two-part words have gotten mixed up. Put the parts together correctly again.

الوِلادَةِ	مَكَانُ	الإيمَيل	القَامَةِ	اِسمُ	الوَضع	الهَاتِف	حَالَةُ

1 رَقمُ ______________

2 ______________ الأُسرَة

3 العنْوانُ ______________

4 ______________ العَائِلي

5 تَاريخُ ______________

6 ______________ السَكَن

7 طُولُ ______________

8 ______________ التَعلِيم

2 Which adjectives belong to which group? Put them in the appropriate column.

قَصيرٌ	وُدّيٌ	مُمِلٌّ	ذُو شَعرٍقَصيرٍ	طَويلٌ	مُتَكَبِّرٌ	ذُو شَارِبٍ	ثرثارٌ

Character Attributes	Appearance

3 Which documents and/or personal details can you be asked for, and where? Mark the correct answers.

1. Border Control Point
   - A ☐ رَقمُ الهَاتِف
   - B ☐ لَونُ العُيُون
   - C ☐ جَوَاز سَفَر
   - D ☐ بِطَاقَةُ إئتِمَان

2. Bank
   - A ☐ المِهنَة
   - B ☐ بِطَاقَةُ إئتِمَانٍ
   - C ☐ طُولُ القَامَةِ
   - D ☐ لَونُ البَشرَةِ

3. Vehicle Spot Check
   - A ☐ الثِقلُ
   - B ☐ مَكَانُ الوِلادَةِ
   - C ☐ حَالَةُ التَعلِيم
   - D ☐ رُخصَةُ القِيَادَةِ

4 Fill out this form, giving your own personal information.

الإسمُ: ______________

اِسمُ الأُسرَة: ______________

تَاريخُ الوِلادَةِ: ______________

مَكَانُ الوِلادَةِ: ______________

العِنوَانُ: ______________

Vocabulary

Occupations / Job Locations

G2
C3

Occupation مِهنَة

director	*mudīrun / ~atun*	مُدِيرٌ / مُدِيرَةٌ
general manager	*mudīrun ʿāmun / mudīratun ʿāmatun*	مُدِيرٌ عَامٌ / مُدِيرَةٌ عَامَةٌ
representative	*nā'ibun / ~atun*	نَائِبٌ / نَائِبَةٌ
secretary	*sikritirun / sikritiratun*	سِكْرِتِيرٌ / سِكْرِتِيرَةٌ
engineer	*muhandisun / ~atun*	مُهَندِسٌ / مُهَندِسَةٌ
worker	*ʿāmilun / ~atun*	عَامِلٌ / عَامِلَةٌ
businessman / -woman	*tājirun / ~atun*	تَاجِرٌ / تَاجِرَةٌ
bank employee	*muwaẓafun fī bankin / muwaẓafatun fī bankin*	مُوَظَّفٌ فِي بَنكٍ / مُوَظَّفَةٌ فِي بَنكٍ
physician	*ṭabībun / ~atun*	طَبِيبٌ / طَبِيبَةٌ
pharmacist	*ṣaydaliyyun / ~atun*	صَيدَلِيٌّ / صَيدَلِيَّةٌ
painter	*rassāmun / ~atun*	رَسَّامٌ / رَسَّامَةٌ
singer	*muġannin / muġanniyatun*	مُغَنٍّ / مُغَنِّيَةٌ
writer	*kātibun / ~atun*	كَاتِبٌ / كَاتِبَةٌ
firefighter	*'iṭfā'iyun / ~atun*	إِطفَائِيٌّ / إِطفَائِيَةٌ
police officer	*shurṭiyyun / ~atun*	شُرطِيٌّ / شُرطِيَّةٌ
politician	*siyāsiyyun / ~atun*	سِيَاسِيٌّ / سِيَاسِيَّةٌ
teacher	*muʿallimun / ~atun*	مُعَلِّمٌ / مُعَلِّمَةٌ
scientist	*ʿālimun / ~atun*	عَالِمٌ / عَالِمَةٌ
baker	*khabbazun / ~atun*	خَبَّازٌ / خَبَّازَةٌ
hairdresser	*ḥallāqun / ~atun*	حَلَّاقٌ / حَلَّاقَةٌ
waiter	*nādilun / ~atun*	نَادِلٌ / نَادِلَةٌ
salesperson	*bā'iʿun / ~atun*	بَائِعٌ / بَائِعَةٌ
tailor / seamstress	*khayyāṭun / ~atun*	خَيَّاطٌ / خَيَّاطَةٌ
driver	*sā'iqun / ~atun*	سَائِقٌ / سَائِقَةٌ
cook	*ṭabbāhun / ~atun*	طَبَّاخٌ / طَبَّاخَةٌ

Job Location مَكَانُ العَمَلِ

firm, company	*sharikatun*	شَرِكَةٌ
enterprise, concern	*mu'as-sasatun tijāriyatun*	مُؤَسَسَةٌ تِجَارِيَةٌ
office	*maktabun*	مَكتَبٌ
factory	*maṣnaʿun*	مَصنَعٌ
international concern	*mu'as-sasatun ʿālamiyatun*	مُؤَسَّسَةٌ عَالَمِيَةٌ
bank	*bankun*	بَنكٌ
hospital	*mustashfā*	مُستَشفَى
pharmacy	*ṣaydaliyyatun*	صَيدَلِيَّةٌ
studio	*'istūdiyū*	إِستُودِيُو
stage	*masraḥun*	مَسرَحٌ
publishing house	*dārun-nashri*	دَارُ النَّشرِ
fire department	*'iṭfā'iyatun*	إِطفَائِيَةٌ
police	*shurṭatun*	شُرطَةٌ
parliament	*barlamānun*	بَرلَمَانٌ
school	*madrasatun*	مَدرَسَةٌ
institute	*maʿhadun*	مَعهَدٌ
bakery	*makhbazun*	مَخبَزٌ
hairdresser's	*ṣālūnul-ḥallāqati*	صَالُونُ الحِلَاقَةِ
restaurant	*maṭʿamun*	مَطعَمٌ
store	*dukānun*	دُكَانٌ
tailor shop	*maḥalul-khayyāṭati*	مَحَلُّ الخِيَاطَةِ
taxi	*sayāratu 'ujratin*	سَيَارَةُ أُجرَةٍ
staff restaurant / canteen kitchen	*'al-kāntīn / maṭbahun kabīrun*	الكَانتِين / مَطبَخٌ كَبِيرٌ

Vocabulary

1 Who works where? Match the items in the columns.

1	مُعَلِّم	A	مَطبَخ كَبير
2	طَبيب	B	مَعهَد
3	طَبّاخ	C	مَدرَسة
4	عالِم	D	مُستَشفى

2 Either the masculine or the feminine job designation is given in each item. Fill in the missing counterpart, as here: سِكرتيرة - سِكرتير.

1 مُدير ______________________

2 تاجِر ______________________

3 ______________________ مُهَندِسة

4 ______________________ سِياسيّة

5 خَبّاز ______________________

6 بائِع ______________________

7 ______________________ مُعَلِّمة

8 ______________________ طَبيبة

3 Read the paraphrases. What occupation is being described? In your answer, give both the masculine and the feminine forms.

1. Person who cuts hair: ______________________

2. Person who keeps order in the street: ______________________

3. Person who works in a store: ______________________

4. Person who teaches: ______________________

4 What are or were these persons by occupation? Mark the correct answers.

1. John F. Kennedy
   - A ☐ شُرطيّ
   - B ☐ سِياسيّ
   - C ☐ مُهَندِس

2. William Shakespeare
   - A ☐ كاتِب
   - B ☐ حَلّاق
   - C ☐ سَكرتير

3. John Lennon
   - A ☐ طَبّاخ
   - B ☐ بائِع
   - C ☐ مُغَنٍّ

4. Bill Gates
   - A ☐ خَبّاز
   - B ☐ تاجِر
   - C ☐ عالِم

Vocabulary

Countries / Nationalities / Languages

C4
C7

Country الوَطَن			Nationality الجِنسِيَةُ		Language اللُغَة	
Egypt	*miṣr*	مِصر	*miṣriyun / ~atun*	مِصرِيٌّ / مِصرِيَة	*al-ʿarabiyatu*	العَرَبِيَّةُ
Brazil	*barāzīl*	بَرَازِيل	*barāzīliyun / ~atun*	بَرَازِيلِيٌّ / بَرَازِيلِيَّةٌ	*al-burtuġāliyatu*	البُرتُغَالِيَّةُ
China	*'as-ṣīn*	الصِّين	*ṣīniyun / ~atun*	صِينِيٌّ / صِينِيَة	*aṣ-ṣīniyatu*	الصِينِيَّةُ
Germany	*'almāniyā*	أَلمَانِيَا	*'almāniyun / ~atun*	أَلمَانِيٌّ / أَلمَانِيَّةٌ	*al-'almāniyatu*	الأَلمَانِيَّةُ
England	*'injiltara*	إِنجِلْتِرة	*'injilīziyun / ~atun*	إِنجِلِيزِيٌّ / إِنجِلِيزِيَّةٌ	*al-'injilīziyatu*	الإِنجِلِيزِيَّةُ
France	*faransā*	فَرَنسَا	*faransiyun / ~atun*	فَرَنسِيٌّ / فَرَنسِيَّةٌ	*al-faransiyatu*	الفَرَنسِيَّةُ
Holland	*hūlanda*	هُولَندَة	*hūlandiyun / ~atun*	هُولَندِيٌّ / هُولَندِيَّةٌ	*al-hūlandiyatu*	الهُولَندِيَّةُ
India	*al-hind*	الهِند	*hindiyun / ~atun*	هِندِيٌّ / هِندِيَة	*al-hindiyatu*	الهِندِيَّةُ
Italy	*'īṭāliyā*	إِيطَالِيَا	*'īṭāliyun / ~atun*	إِيطَالِيٌّ / إِيطَالِيَّةٌ	*al-'īṭāliyatu*	الإِيطَالِيَّةُ
Japan	*al-yābān*	اليَابَان	*yābāniyun / ~atun*	يَابَانِيٌّ / يَابَانِيَّةٌ	*al-yābāniyatu*	اليَابَانِيَّةُ
Jordan	*al-'urdun*	الأُردُن	*'urduniyun / ~atun*	أُردُنِيٌّ / أُردُنِيَة	*al-ʿarabiyatu*	العَرَبِيَّةُ
Kenya	*kīnyā*	كِينيَا	*kīniyun / ~atun*	كِينِيٌّ / كِينِيَة	*'as-sawāḥiliyatu*	السَّوَاحِلِيَّةُ
Kuwait	*'al-kuwayt*	الكُوَيت	*kuwaytiyun / ~atun*	كُوَيتِيٌّ / كُوَيتِيَة	*al-ʿarabiyatu*	العَرَبِيَّةُ
Libya	*lībiyā*	لِيبيَا	*lībiyun / ~atun*	لِيبِيٌّ / لِيبِيَة	*al-ʿarabiyatu*	العَرَبِيَّةُ
Malaysia	*mālīziyā*	مَالِيزيَا	*mālayziyun / ~atun*	مَالِيزِيٌّ / مَالِيزِيَة	*al-mālayziyatu*	المَالِيزِيَّةُ
Morocco	*'al-maġrib*	المَغرِب	*maġribiyun / ~atun*	مَغرِبِيٌّ / مَغرِبِيَة	*al-ʿarabiyatu*	العَرَبِيَّةُ
Austria	*'an-nimsā*	النِّمسَا	*nimsāwiyun / ~atun*	نِمسَاوِيٌّ / نِمسَاوِيَّةٌ	*al-'almāniyatu*	الأَلمَانِيَّةُ
Pakistan	*bākistān*	بَاكِستَان	*bākistāniyun / ~atun*	بَاكِستَانِيٌّ / بَاكِستَانِيَة	*al-'urdiyatu*	الأُردِيَّةُ
Russia	*rūsiyā*	رُوسِيَا	*rūsiyun / ~atun*	رُوسِيٌّ / رُوسِيَّةٌ	*ar-rūsiya*	الرُوسِيَّةُ
Saudi-Arabia	*as-suʿūdiya*	السُّعُودِية	*suʿūdiyun / ~atun*	سُعُودِيٌّ / سُعُودِيَة	*al-ʿarabiyatu*	العَرَبِيَّةُ
Switzerland	*suwīsrā*	سُوِيسرَا	*suwīsariyun / ~atun*	سُوِيسَرِيٌّ / سُوِيسَرِيَّةٌ	*al-'almāniyatu-suwīsrā*	الأَلمَانِيَّةُ- السُّوِيسرَا
Somalia	*as-sūmāl*	الصُّومَال	*sūmāliyun / ~atun*	صُومَالِيٌّ / صُومَالِيَّةٌ	*aṣ-ṣūmāliyatu*	الصُّومَالِيَّةُ
Spain	*'asbāniyā*	إِسبَّانيا	*'asbāniyun / ~atun*	إِسبَّانِيٌّ / إِسبَانِيَّةٌ	*al-'asbāniyatu*	الأَسبَانِيَّةُ
USA	*'amrīkā*	أَمرِيكَا	*'amrīkiyun / ~atun*	أَمرِيكِيٌّ / أَمرِيكِيَّةٌ	*al-'injilīziyatu*	الإِنجِلِيزِيَّةُ

Verbs أَفعَالٌ

to go to …	*sāqa 'ilā*	سَاقَ إِلى...
to come from …	*ḥaḍara min*	حَضَرَ مِن...
to come (hail) from …	*'atā min*	أَتى مِن...
to live in …	*sakana fī*	سَكَنَ فِي...
to vacation in …	*qaḍal-ʿuṭlata fī*	قَضَى العُطلَةَ فِي...

Vocabulary

1 Which of these countries are direct neighbors? Mark the correct answers.

1 أَلْمَانِيَا
A ☐ إِنْجِلْتَرَة
B ☐ كِينِيَا
C ☐ هُولَنْدَة

2 الكُوَيت
A ☐ إِيطَالِيَا
B ☐ السُّعُودِية
C ☐ اليَابَان

3 الهِند
A ☐ رُوسِيَا
B ☐ بَاكِستَان
C ☐ المَغرِب

2 Which capital goes with which country? Match the columns.

1	القَاهِرَة (Cairo)	A	مِصر
2	بَرلِين (Berlin)	B	إِنْجِلْتَرَة
3	مدريد (Madrid)	C	السُّعُودِية
4	لَندَن (London)	D	أَسبَانِيَا
5	رِيَاض (Riyadh)	E	أَلْمَانِيَا

3 Which language is spoken by the people of which nationality? Fill in the blanks, using this pattern: أَلْمَانِيٌّ يَتَكَلَّمُ الأَلْمَانِيَةَ *('almāniyun yatakalamu al-almāniyata).*

هِندِيٌّ	أَمرِيكِيٌّ	الصُومَالِيَة	الإِيطَالِيَةَ	العَرَبِيَة	صِينِيَّةٌ	إِنْجِلِيزِيَّةٌ	البُرتُغَالِيَةَ

1 سَعُودِيٌّ يَتَكَلَّمُ ________________.

2 ________________ تَتَكَلَّمُ الإِنْجِلِيزِيَةَ.

3 إِيطَالِيٌّ يَتَكَلَّمُ ________________.

4 ________________ يَتَكَلَّمُ الهِندِيَةَ.

5 صُومَالِيَةٌ تَتَكَلَّمُ ________________.

6 ________________ يَتَكَلَّمُ الأمرِيكِيَةَ.

7 بَرَازِيلِيٌّ يَتَكَلَّمُ ________________.

8 ________________ تَتَكَلَّمُ الصِينِيَةَ.

4 Where did these famous personalities live? Note: The country names are preceded by the preposition *min* مِنْ (from), as here: أَلْمَانِيَا - مِنْ أَلْمَانِيَا.

مِصر	مِنْ إِسبَّانِيَا	مِنْ إِنْجِلترة	مِنْ رُوسِيَا	مِنْ إِيطَالِيَا	مِنْ أَمرِيكَا	مِنَ الهِند

1 Elvis Presley ________________.

2 Charles Dickens ________________.

3 Leonardo da Vinci ________________.

4 Omar Sharif ________________.

5 Lenin ________________.

6 Salvador Dali ________________.

7 Mahatma Gandhi ________________.

Family

C5

Family Members أَفْرَاد العَائِلَة

grandfather	*jaddun*	جَدٌّ	grandparents	*'ajdādun*	أَجدادٌ
grandmother	*jaddatun*	جَدَّةٌ			
grandson	*ḥafīdun*	حَفِيدٌ	grandchildren	*aḥfādun*	أَحفَادٌ
granddaughter	*ḥafīdatun*	حَفِيدَةٌ			
father	*'abun*	أَبٌ	parents	*wālidāni*	وَالِدانِ
mother	*'ummun*	أُمٌّ			
husband	*zawjun*	زَوجٌ	married couple	*zawjāni*	زَوجَانِ
wife	*zawjatun*	زَوجَةٌ			
son	*ibnun*	اِبنٌ	children	*'aṭfālun*	أَطفَالٌ
daughter	*ibnatun*	اِبنَةٌ			
brother	*'akh-khun*	أَخٌ	brothers and sisters	*'ikhwatun*	إخوَةٌ
sister	*'ukhtun*	أُختٌ			
uncle (on the father's side)	*'ammun*	عَمٌّ	cousin (m.)	*ibnu 'ammin*	اِبنُ عَمٍّ
			cousin (f.)	*bintu 'ammin*	بِنتُ عَمٍّ
aunt (on the father's side)	*'ammatun*	عَمَّةٌ	cousin (m.)	*ibnu 'ammatin*	اِبنُ عَمَّةٍ
			cousin (f.)	*bintu 'ammatin*	بِنتُ عَمَّةٍ
uncle (on the mother's side)	*khālun*	خَالٌ	cousin (m.)	*ibnu khālin*	اِبنُ خَالٍ
			cousin (f.)	*bintu khālin*	بِنتُ خَالٍ
aunt (on the mother's side)	*khālatun*	خَالَةٌ	cousin (m.)	*ibnu khālatin*	اِبنُ خَالَةٍ
			cousin (f.)	*bintu khālatin*	بِنتُ خَالَةٍ
father-in-law	*ḥamun*	حَمٌ	parents-in-law (parents of the husband / of the wife)	*wālidā az-zawji / az-zawjati*	وَالِدا الزَّوجِ / الزَوجَةِ
mother-in-law	*ḥamātun*	حَمَاةٌ			
son-in-law	*zawjul-ibnati*	زَوجُ الاِبنَةِ			
daughter-in-law	*zawjatul-ibni*	زَوجَةُ الاِبنِ	relatives	*qarābatun*	قَرَابَةٌ

Marital Status الوَضعُ العَائِلِي

married (m.)	*mutazawijun*	مُتَزَوجٌ	divorced (m.)	*muṭallaqun*	مُطَلَّقٌ
married (f.)	*mutazawijatun*	مُتَزَوجَةٌ	divorced (f.)	*muṭallaqatun*	مُطَلَّقَةٌ
unmarried (m.)	*ġajru mutazawijin*	غَيرُ مُتَزَوجٍ	widowed (m.)	*'armalun*	أَرمَلٌ
unmarried (f.)	*ġajru mutazawijatin*	غَيرُ مُتَزَوجَةٍ	widowed (f.)	*'armalatun*	أَرمَلَةٌ

Family Celebrations and Events أحداثٌ هَامَة وحَفلات عَائلِيَة

wedding	*'ursun*	عُرسٌ	divorce	*ṭalāqun*	طَلَاقٌ
engagement	*khiṭbatun*	خِطْبَةٌ	birthday	*yawmul-mīlādi*	يَومُ المِيلَادِ
name-giving ceremony	*'aqīqatun*	عَقِيقَةٌ	burial, funeral	*dafnun*	دَفنٌ

1 Find the appropriate "counterpart," for example, جَدَّةٌ - جَدٌّ.

عَمٌّ	حَفِيدَةٌ	اِبْنٌ	أَخٌ	زَوجُ الابْنَةِ	زَوجَةٌ	أُمٌّ	حَماةٌ

1 أُخْتٌ - ______________________
5 عَمَّةٌ - ______________________

2 زَوجٌ - ______________________
6 أَبٌ - ______________________

3 زَوجَةُ الابْنِ - ______________________
7 حَفِيدٌ - ______________________

4 حَمٌ - ______________________
8 اِبنَةٌ - ______________________

2 Who is it? Solve the riddle.

1. The son of your father, but not you, is your ______________________.
2. The father of your mother is your ______________________.
3. The son of your mother's brother is your ______________________.
4. The daughter of your father's sister is your ______________________.
5. The mother of your husband / your wife is your ______________________.

3 What is the marital status of these people? Write the missing word in the blank, for example, مُتَزَوِّجٌ.

1. Akhmed has a wife. ______________________ هُوَ
2. Zakariya's wife is dead. ______________________ هُوَ
3. Kadija has divorced her husband. ______________________ هِيَ
4. Jamila lives alone. ______________________ هِيَ

And what is your marital status? ______________________ أَنَا

4 What invitation (دَعوَة) is sent on what occasion? Match the two columns.

Invitation to ... دَعوَة إلَى ...

1. Tariq and Zahra plan to get married.
2. Halima is celebrating her birthday.
3. Warda and Salim have had a baby.

A دَعوَة إلَى حَفلَة مِيلادٍ!

B دَعوَة إلَى عَقِيقَةٍ!

C دَعوَة إلَى حَفلَةِ عُرسٍ!

Vocabulary

Recreation / Hobbies

C8

Hobby هِوَايَة

traveling	*siyāḥatun*	سِيَاحَةٌ
reading	*qira'atun*	قِرَاءَةٌ
learning languages	*taʿalumul-luġāti*	تَعَلُّمُ اللُّغَاتِ
cooking	*ṭabkhun*	طَبْخٌ
meeting friends	*muqābalatul-'aṣdiqā'i*	مُقَابَلَةُ الأَصدِقَاءِ
watching TV	*mushāhadatut-tilfizyūni*	مُشَاهَدَةُ التِلفِزيُونِ
photography	*taṣwīrun*	تَصْوِيرٌ
singing	*ġināun*	غِنَاءٌ
dancing	*ar-raqṣu*	الرَّقْص
going to parties / celebrations	*'iḥtifālun (bil 'aʿyādi)*	اِحتِفَالٌ (بِالأَعيَادِ)
going shopping	*ash-shirā'u*	الشِّرَاء
playing computer games	*laʿib ʿalā jihāzil-kūmbuyūtar*	لَعِب عَلَى جِهَازِ الكُومبِيُوتَر
hiking	*tajawwulun*	تَجَوُّلٌ
walking	*tanazzaha*	تَنَزُّهٌ

Art and Culture فَن وثَقَافَة

painting (art form)	*fannur-rasmi*	فَنُّ الرَّسمِ
painting (activity)	*rasama*	رَسَمَ
music	*mūsīqā*	مُوسِيقَى
playing an instrument	*ʿazafa*	عَزَفَ
going to the theater	*'adh-dhahābu 'ilal-masraḥi*	الذَّهَابُ إِلَى المَسرَح
going to a movie	*'adh-dahahābu 'ilās-sīnimā*	الذَّهَابُ إِلَى سِينِمَا
going to a concert	*'adh-dhahābu 'ilā ḥaflati mūsīqā*	الذَّهَابُ إِلَى حَفلَةِ مُوسِيقَى
theater	*masraḥun*	مَسرَحٌ
movie theater	*sīnimā*	سِينِمَا
exhibition	*maʿriḍun*	مَعْرِضٌ
concert	*ḥaflatu mūsīqā*	حَفلَةُ مُوسِيقَى
attending an exhibition	*ziyāratu maʿriḍin*	زِيَارَةُ مَعْرِضٍ
seeing a film	*mushāhadatu filmin*	مُشَاهَدَةُ فِلمٍ
seeing a play	*mushāhadatu masraḥiyatin*	مُشَاهَدَةُ مَسرَحِيَةٍ

Sports رِيَاضَة

soccer	*kuratul-qadami*	كُرَةُ القَدَمِ
basketball	*kuratus-sallati*	كُرَةُ السَّلَّةِ
volleyball	*al kuratuṭ-ṭā'iratu*	الطَّائِرَةُ الكُرَةُ
swimming	*sabaḥa*	سَبَحَ
playing soccer	*laʿiba kuratal-qadami*	لَعِبَ كُرَةَ القَدَمِ
playing basketball	*laʿiba kuratas-sallati*	لَعِبَ كُرَةَ السَلَةِ
tennis	*kuratul-miḍrabi*	كُرَةُ المِضرَب
swimming	*sabāḥatun*	سِبَاحَةٌ
track and field	*riyāḍiyyun*	رِيَاضِيٌّ
jogging	*rakaḍa*	رَكَضَ
watching soccer	*mushāhadatu kuratal-qadami*	مُشَاهَدَةُ كُرَةِ القَدَم
watching basketball	*mushāhadatu kuratas-sallati*	مُشَاهَدَةُ كُرَةِ السَلَةِ

1 What does Salim enjoy, and what does Warda enjoy? Match the hobbies with the appropriate person. Caution! The hobbies are in the accusative case. G5 G6

القِراءَةُ	الرَّسم	الغِنَى	لَعب كُرَةَ القَدَم	الرَّكض
الرَّقص	السِّيَاحَة	السِّبَاحَة	الذِهَابَ إِلَى المَسرَح	التَجَوُّل

Salim: سَالِم يُحِبُّ

1. Singing: ______________________
2. Traveling: ______________________
3. Swimming: ______________________
4. Hiking: ______________________
5. Playing soccer: ______________________

Warda: وَردَة تُحِبُّ

6. Reading: ______________________
7. Dancing: ______________________
8. Painting: ______________________
9. Jogging: ______________________
10. Going to the theater: ______________________

And what are your hobbies? ______________________

2 What goes together? Make the correct matches.

1 الذَّهابُ إِلَى
2 (ال) لَعِبُ
3 مُشَاهَدَةُ

A كُرَةَ المِضْرَب
B التِلفِزيُون
C عَلَى جِهَازِ الكُومبِيُتَر
D السِينَمَا
E كُرَةَ القَدَم
F المَسرَح
G فِلم
H حَفْلَةِ مُوسِيقَى
I مَسرَحِيَةٍ

3 What other people describe as hobbies became occupations for these individuals. What field were they active in? Mark the correct box.

1. Robert de Niro
A ☐ السِّبَاحَةُ
B ☐ الكُرَةُ الطَّائِرَةُ
C ☐ التَّمثِيلُ

2. Michael Schumacher
A ☐ الفَن
B ☐ رِيَاضَة
C ☐ مُوسِيقَى

3. Vincent van Gogh
A ☐ مُوسِيقَى
B ☐ مَسرَح
C ☐ فَنُّ الرَّسم

Vocabulary

Numbers

A1

0 – 10 ١٠ - ٠

G29

zero	*ṣifrun*	صِفْرٌ			
one	*wāḥidun / ~atun*	واحِدٌ / واحِدَةٌ	first	*'awwalun / 'ūlā*	أَوَّلٌ / أُولَى
two	*'ithnāni / 'ithnatāni*	إِثْنَانِ / إِثْنَتَانِ	second	*thānin / thāniyatun*	ثانٍ / ثانِيَةٌ
three	*thalāthun / thalāthatun*	ثَلاثٌ / ثَلاثَةٌ	third	*thālithun / ~atun*	ثالِثٌ / ثالِثَةٌ
four	*'arba'un / 'arba'atun*	أَرْبَعٌ / أَرْبَعَةٌ	fourth	*rābi'un / ~atun*	رابِعٌ / رابِعَةٌ
five	*khamsun / khamsatun*	خَمْسٌ / خَمْسَةٌ	fifth	*khāmisun / ~atun*	خامِسٌ / خامِسَةٌ
six	*sittun / sittatun*	سِتٌّ / سِتَّةٌ	sixth	*sādisun / ~atun*	سادِسٌ / سادِسَةٌ
seven	*sab'un / sab'atun*	سَبْعٌ / سَبْعَةٌ	seventh	*sābi'un / ~atun*	سابِعٌ / سابِعَةٌ
eight	*thamānin / thamāniyatun*	ثَمانٍ / ثَمانِيَةٌ	eighth	*thāminun / ~atun*	ثامِنٌ / ثامِنَةٌ
nine	*tis'un / tis'atun*	تِسْعٌ / تِسْعَةٌ	ninth	*tāsi'un / ~atun*	تاسِعٌ / تاسِعَةٌ
ten	*'ashrun / 'asharatun*	عَشْرٌ / عَشَرَةٌ	tenth	*'āshirun / ~atun*	عاشِرٌ / عاشِرَةٌ

11 – 19 ١١ - ١٩

eleven	*'aḥada 'ashara /* *'iḥdā 'asharta*	أَحَدَ عَشَرَ / إِحْدَى عَشْرَةَ	eleventh	*ḥādī 'ashara /* *ḥādiyata 'asharta*	حادِيَ عَشَرَ / حادِيَةَ عَشْرَةَ
twelve	*'ithnā 'ashara /* *'ithnatā 'asharta*	إِثْنا عَشَرَ / إِثْنَتا عَشْرَةَ	twelfth	*thānīya 'ashara /* *thāniyata 'asharta*	ثانِيَ عَشَرَ / ثانِيَةَ عَشْرَةَ
thirteen	*thalātha 'asharta /* *thalāthata 'ashara*	ثَلاثَ عَشْرَةَ / ثَلاثَةَ عَشَرَ	thirteenth	*thālitha 'ashara /* *thālithata 'asharta*	ثالِثَ عَشَرَ / ثالِثَةَ عَشْرَةَ
fourteen	*'arba'a 'asharta /* *'arba'ata 'ashara*	أَرْبَعَ عَشْرَةَ / أَرْبَعَةَ عَشَرَ	fourteenth	*rābi'a ashara /* *rābi'ata 'asharta*	رابِعَ عَشَرَ / رابِعَةَ عَشْرَةَ
fifteen	*khamsa 'asharta /* *khamsata 'ashara*	خَمْسَ عَشْرَةَ / خَمْسَةَ عَشَرَ	fifteenth	*khāmisa 'ashara /* *khāmisata 'asharta*	خامِسَ عَشَرَ / خامِسَةَ عَشْرَةَ
sixteen	*sitta 'asharta /* *sittata 'ashara*	سِتَّ عَشْرَةَ / سِتَّةَ عَشَرَ	sixteenth	*sādisa 'ashara /* *sādisata 'asharta*	سادِسَ عَشَرَ / سادِسَةَ عَشْرَةَ
seventeen	*sab'a 'asharta /* *sab'ata 'ashara*	سَبْعَ عَشْرَةَ / سَبْعَةَ عَشَرَ	seventeenth	*sābi'a 'ashara /* *sābi'ata 'asharta*	سابِعَ عَشَرَ / سابِعَةَ عَشْرَةَ
eighteen	*thamāniya 'asharta /* *thamāniyata 'ashara*	ثَمانِيَ عَشْرَةَ / ثَمانِيَةَ عَشَرَ	eighteenth	*thāmina 'ashara /* *thāminata 'asharta*	ثامِنَ عَشَرَ / ثامِنَةَ عَشْرَةَ
nineteen	*tis'a 'asharta /* *tis'ata 'ashara*	تِسْعَ عَشْرَةَ / تِسْعَةَ عَشَرَ	nineteenth	*tāsi'a 'ashara /* *tāsi'ata 'asharta*	تاسِعَ عَشَرَ / تاسِعَةَ عَشْرَةَ

20 – 90 ٢٠ - ٩٠

twenty	*'ishrūna*	عِشْرُونَ	sixty	*sittūna*	سِتُّونَ
thirty	*thalāthūna*	ثَلاثُونَ	seventy	*sab'ūna*	سَبْعُونَ
forty	*'arba'ūna*	أَرْبَعُونَ	eighty	*thamānūna*	ثَمانُونَ
fifty	*khamsūna*	خَمْسُونَ	ninety	*tis'ūna*	تِسْعُونَ

100 – … … - ١٠٠

one hundred	*mi'atun*	مِئَةٌ	one thousand	*'alfun*	أَلْفٌ
two hundred	*mi'atāni*	مِئَتانِ	one million	*malyūnun*	مَلْيُونٌ

1 Put the numbers in the correct order. Then add the corresponding ordinal numbers.

أَربع	ثَلاث	سِتّ	إثنان	تِسع	سَبع	ثَمانٍ	خمس

1 واحِدُ 1. أَوَّلُ ______ 4 ______ 4. ______ 7 ______ 7.

2 ______ 2. ______ 5 ______ 5. ______ 8 ______ 8.

3 ______ 3. ______ 6 ______ 6. ______ 9 ______ 9.

2 Write out these telephone numbers in words.

1 51043 خَمسَةٌ ______

2 89267 ______

3 Use numerals (11, 12 …) to express the numbers spelled out here.

A أَحَدَ عَشَرَ ______ D ثَمانِيَةَ عَشَرَ ______ G سِتَّةَ عَشَرَ ______

B أَرْبَعَةَ عَشَرَ ______ E خَمسَةَ عَشَرَ ______ H ثَلاثَةَ عَشَرَ ______

C تِسعَةَ عَشَرَ ______ F سَبعَةَ عَشَرَ ______ I إثنَا عَشَرَ ______

4 The first part of each two-digit number is missing. Fill in the blanks.

أَربعُ	سَبعُ	سِتُّ	ثَلاثُ	ثَمانُ	خمسُ	تِسعُ

A 20 عِشرُونَ E 60 ______ ونَ

B 30 ______ ونَ F 70 ______ ونَ

C 40 ______ ون G 80 ______ ونَ

D 50 ______ ونَ H 90 ______ ونَ

5 Numbers from 20 on are formed by placing the number in the ones' place before the number in the tens' place. The two (or more) numbers are joined with the letter *wāw* و , which stands for "and":

132 مِئَةٌ وإثنانِ وثلاثِينَ 21 وَاحِدٌ وعِشرُونَ

Write out the numbers given in numerals.

A 31 ______ C 142 ______

B 67 ______ D 250 ______

Time Designations

Seasons فُصُولُ السَّنة

winter	*shitā'*	شِتاءٌ	summer	*ṣayf*	صَيف
spring	*rabīʿ*	رَبيع	fall, autumn	*kharīf*	خَريف

Months الشُّهُور

January	*kānūnath-thānī*	كَانُون الثَّانِي	July	*tammūz*	تَمُّوز
February	*shabāṭ*	شَبَاط	August	*'āb*	آب
March	*'ādhār*	آذار	September	*'aylūl*	أَيلُول
April	*nīsān*	نِيسَان	October	*tashrīnal-'awal*	تَشرِينَ الأَوَّل
May	*'ayyār*	أَيَّار	November	*tashrīnath-thānī*	تَشرِينَ الثَّانِي
June	*ḥuzayrān*	حُزَيرَان	December	*kānūnal-'awal*	كَانُون الأَوَّل

The date in the Arabic calendar follows the Islamic lunar calendar. Newspapers generally give both the Islamic date and the Christian date in addition. You will find the months of the Islamic calendar in the mini-dictionary.

Days of the Week أَيَّامُ الأَسبُوع

week	*'usbūʿ*	أُسبُوع	Thursday	*yawmul-khamīsi*	يَومُ الخَمِيس
Monday	*yawmul 'ithnayni*	يَومُ الإِثنَين	Friday	*yawmul yumʿati*	يَومُ الجُمعَةِ
Tuesday	*yawmul-thulāthā'i*	يَومُ الثُّلاثَاء	Saturday	*yawmul-sabti*	يَومُ السَّبتِ
Wednesday	*yawmul-'arbiʿā'i*	يَومُ الأَربِعَاءِ	Sunday	*yawmul-'aḥad*	يَومُ الأَحَد

A1

Date التَّاريخ (Arabic notation: year / month / day)

1998 (= year one thousand nine hundred and ninety-eight)	*sanata 'alfin wa tisʿumi'atin wa thamānī wa tisʿīna*	سَنَة أَلفٍ وَتِسعُمِئَة وَثَمَانِي وتسعِين	1998
2006	*sanata 'alfayni wa sitta*	سَنَة أَلفَين وسِتَّة	2006
01.12.2006 (= the first of the twelfth month of the year two thousand and six)	*'al-'awalu min 'ash-shahri 'ath-thanīʿashara sanata 'alfayni wa sitta*	الأَوَّل مِن الشَّهرِ الثَّانِي عَشَرَ سَنَةَ أَلفَينِ وسِتَّة	2006/12/1

Time of Day السَّاعَة

hour	*sāʿatun*	سَاعَةٌ	on the dot, exactly	*biḍabṭi / tamāman*	بِالضَبطِ / تَمَاماً
minute	*daqīqatun*	دَقِيقَةٌ	before, until, to	*qabla*	قَبلَ
second	*thāniyatun*	ثَانِيَةٌ	after	*baʿda*	بَعدَ
clock	*sāʿatun*	سَاعَةٌ	half	*niṣfun*	نِصفٌ

To make it clear that it is morning, midday, or evening, attach the corresponding time of day to the time:

9:00 (= hour ninth morning)	*as-sāʿatu at-tāsiʿatu ṣabāḥan*	السَّاعَةُ التَّاسِعَةُ صَباحاً
12:25 (= hour twelfth and 25 minutes midday)	*as-sāʿatuth-thāniyata ʿasharata wa khamsun wa ʿishrūna daqā'iqa ẓuhran*	السَّاعَةُ الثَّانِيَةَ عَشْرَةَ وَخَمسٌ وَعِشرُونَ دَقِيقَة ظُهراً
19:30 (= hour nineteenth and 30 minutes evening)	*as-sāʿatu at-tāsiʿata ʿasharata wa niṣf masā'an*	السَّاعَةُ التَّاسِعَةَ عَشْرَةَ وَنِصف مَسَاءً

1 What season do these months belong to? Put the names in the appropriate columns.

آذار　تَشرينَ الثّاني　أيّار　تمّوز　أيلول　آب
حُزَيران　نيسان　شُباط　كانون الأوّل　كانون الثّاني　تَشرينَ الأوّل

رَبيع	صَيف	خَريف	شِتاء

2 Match the spelled-out dates with their numeric equivalents.

V6

1 الخامِسُ عَشَر مِن الشَهرِ الأوّل سَنَةَ ألفَين وَ سِتّة
2 الثالِث عَشَرَ مِن الشَهرِ الخامِس سَنَةَ ألفَين وَ سِتّة
3 العاشِرُ مِن الشَهرِ التاسِع سَنَةَ ألفَين وَ سِتّة
4 الثالِث مِن الشَهرِ الحادي عَشَرَ سَنَةَ ألفَين وَ سِتّة

A 03.11.2006
B 13.05.2006
C 15.01.2006
D 10.09.2006

3 What time is it? – كَم السّاعَةُ الآنَ؟ Fill in the appropriate words.

السّاعَةُ الثّانِيَةَ عَشْرَةَ　وَخَمْس عَشْرَة دَقيقَة صَباحاً　بَعدَ الظُهرِ
السّاعَةُ الثامِنَةُ　السّاعَةُ الثامِنَةُ

14:00

1 السّاعَةُ الثّانِيَةُ ______
______

20:30

2 ______
وَنِصف مَساءً

12:50

3 ______
وَخَمسُونَ دَقيقَة بَعدَ الظُهرِ

11:15

4 السّاعَةُ الحادِيَةَ عَشْرَةَ ______
______

08:20

5 ______ وَعِشرُونَ دَقيقَة صَباحاً

In Town

C11

General عَام

town, city	*madīnatun*	مَدِينَةٌ	large street	*shāriʿun raʾīsī*	شَارِعٌ رَئِيسِيٌّ
village / country	*qaryatun / rīfun*	قَرْيَةٌ / رِيفٌ	avenue	*ṭarīqun*	طَرِيقٌ
quarter, (city) district	*ḥayyun*	حَيٌّ	center	*markazun*	مَرْكَزٌ
street	*shāriʿun*	شَارِعٌ	old town	*al-madīnatu al-qadīmatu*	المَدِينَةُ القَدِيمَةُ
capital	*ʿāṣimatun*	عَاصِمَةٌ	province	*ʾiqlīmun / muqāṭaʿatun*	إِقْلِيمٌ / مُقَاطَعَةٌ

Facilities and Buildings مُنْشَآةٌ وَأَبْنِيَة

square	*maydānun*	مَيْدَانٌ	monument	*tidhkāriyyun*	تِذْكَارِيٌّ
bank	*bankun*	بَنْكٌ	store	*dukānun*	دُكَانٌ
swimming pool	*masbaḥun*	مَسْبَحٌ	park	*ḥadīqatun ʿāmatun*	حَدِيقَةٌ عَامَةٌ
mosque	*masjidun*	مَسْجِدٌ	post office	*barīdun*	بَرِيدٌ
church	*kanīsatun*	كَنِيسَةٌ	police station	*shurṭatun*	شُرْطَةٌ
library	*maktabatun*	مَكْتَبَةٌ	town hall	*dārul-baladiyati*	دَارُ البَلَدِيَةِ
fire department	*firqartul-maṭāfʾi*	فِرْقَةُ المَطَافِئ	sports field	*malʿabun lir-riyāḍati*	مَلْعَبٌ لِلرِّيَاضَةِ
gallery	*riwāqun / maʿriḍun*	رِوَاقٌ / مَعْرِضٌ	train station	*maḥaṭatul-qiṭāri*	مَحَطَةُ القِطَارِ
movie theater	*sīnimā*	سِينِمَا	university	*jāmiʿatun*	جَامِعَةٌ
hospital	*mustashfā*	مُسْتَشْفَى	kindergarten	*ḥaḍānatul-ʾaṭfāli*	حَضَانَةُ الأَطْفَالِ
school	*madrasatun*	مَدْرَسَةٌ	pharmacy	*ṣaydaliyatun*	صَيْدَلِيَةٌ
museum	*mathafun*	مَتْحَفٌ			

C13

Stores / Shops دَكَاكِين

store	*dukkānun*	دُكَّانٌ	bakery	*makhbazun*	مَخْبَزٌ
grocery store	*dukkānul-mawād al-ġidhāʾiyati*	دُكَّانُ المَوَادِ الغِذَائِيَةِ	bookstore	*maktabatun*	مَكْتَبَةٌ
			market / bazaar	*sūqun*	سُوقٌ
flower shop	*dukkānun libayʿil-ʾazhāri*	دُكَّانٌ لِبَيْعِ الأَزْهَارِ	butcher's shop	*majzaratun*	مَجْزَرَةٌ
			greengrocer	*baqqālun*	بَقَّالٌ
sporting goods store	*dukkānu ʾadawātir-riyāḍati*	دُكَّانُ أَدَوَاتِ الرِيَاضَةِ	newspaper stand / kiosk	*kushkun li bayʿis-ṣuḥufi*	كُشْكٌ لِبَيْعِ الصُحُفِ
shoe store	*dukkānul-ʾaḥdhiyati*	دُكَّانُ الأَحْذِيَةِ	toy store	*dukkānun li bayʿil-luʿabi*	دُكَّانٌ لِبَيْعِ اللُعَبِ
department store	*matjarun ʿāmun*	مَتْجَرٌ عَامٌّ			
clothing store	*dukkānul-malābisi*	دُكَّانُ المَلَابِسِ			

1 Mark the correct box. Where do you go when you …

1. … need to see a doctor?
A ☐ مَسجِدٌ
B ☐ مَسبَحٌ
C ☐ مُستَشفَى
D ☐ بَنكٌ

2. … want to buy something?
A ☐ بَنكٌ
B ☐ مَتجَر عَام
C ☐ فِرقَةُ المَطَافِئ
D ☐ مَحطَةُ القِطَار

3. … need medicine?
A ☐ صَيدَلِيَّةٌ
B ☐ مَدرَسَةٌ
C ☐ حَدِيقَةٌ عَامَةٌ
D ☐ بَرِيدٌ

4. … want to take a walk?
A ☐ دُكَانُ الأَحذِيَة
B ☐ مَجزَرَةٌ
C ☐ مَكتَبَةٌ
D ☐ حَدِيقَةٌ عَامَةٌ

2 What store do you go to when you want to buy the following items? Fill in the blanks.

المَوَاد الغِذَائِيَة	اللُعَب	المَلابِس	مَكتَبَة	أحذِيَة	مَخبَزٌ	الرِيَاضَة

1. groceries: دُكَّانُ ____________
2. shoes: دُكَّانُ ____________
3. bread: ____________
4. toys: دُكَّانٌ لِبَيع ____________
5. books: ____________
6. clothing: دُكَّانُ ____________
7. tennis raquets: دُكَّانُ ____________

3 There are many places of interest in Cairo. Translate these sights into Arabic. Keep in mind that the missing nouns are part of an *idafa* structure and must be in the nominative case. G9

1. Al-Azhar Mosque ____________ الأَزهَر
2. Al-Tahrir Square (Freedom Square) ____________ التَحرِير
3. Al-Goma'a Market (Friday Market) ____________ الجُمعَة
4. Egyptian Museum ____________ المِصري
5. Al-Azhar University ____________ الأَزهَر

Vocabulary

Restaurant / Foods and Beverages

C12

Food Service مَجالُ المَطاعِم

bar	bārun / mashrabun	بَارٌ / مَشْرَبٌ
café	maqhā	مَقهَى
restaurant	maṭʿamun	مَطعَمٌ
canteen / staff cafeteria	'al-kāntīn	الكَانتِين

At a Restaurant فِي دَاخِلِ المَطعَم

waiter / waitress	nādilun / ~atun	نَادِلٌ / نَادِلَةٌ
table	ṭāwilatun	طَاوِلَةٌ
to order, to reserve	ṭalabun / ḥajzun	طَلَبٌ / حَجزٌ
menu	qā'imatuṭ-ṭaʿāmi	قَائِمَةُ الطَعَام
menu / meal	wajbatun	وَجبَةٌ
table d'hôte, prix fixe	wajbatul-yawmi	وَجبَةُ اليَوم

On the Table عَلَى المَائِدَة

plate	ṭabaqun / ṣaḥnun	طَبَقٌ / صَحنٌ
knife	sikkīnun	سِكِّينٌ
cup	finjānun	فِنجَانٌ
(wine) glass	k'asu (nabīdhin)	كَأسُ (نَبيذٍ)
napkin	manādīlul-mā'idati	مَنَادِيلُ المَائِدَة
glass	k'asun	كَأْسٌ
fork	shawkatun	شَوكَةٌ
spoon	milʿaqatun	مِلعَقَةٌ

Food مَأكُولاتٌ

to eat	'akala	أَكَلَ
to eat a snack	'aklun khafīfun	أَكلٌ خَفِيفٌ
food, dish	ṭaʿāmun	طَعَامٌ
appetizer, snack	muqabbilātun	مُقَبِّلاتٌ
soup	ḥasā'un	حَسَاءٌ
dish, food	wajbatun	وَجبَةٌ
meat dish	wajbatu laḥmin	وَجبَةُ لَحمٍ
fish dish	wajbatu samakin	وَجبَةُ سَمَكٍ
vegetable dish	wajbatu khuḍrawātin	وَجبَةُ خُضرَوَاتٍ
dessert	taḥliyatun	تَحلِيَةٌ
ice cream	jīlātī	جيلاتي
cake	kaʿkun	كعكٌ
tart, torte	tūratun	تورتَةٌ
fruit	fākihatun	فَاكِهَةٌ

Beverages مَشرُوبات

to drink	shariba	شَرِبَ
alcoholic	'al-kuḥūl	الكُحُول
beer	jiʿatun / bīratun	جِعَةٌ / بِيرَةٌ
wine	nabīdhun	نَبِيذٌ
champagne, sparkling wine	shambāniyā	شَمبَانِيَا
beverage, drink	sharābun	شَرَابٌ
nonalcoholic, alcohol-free	khālin minal-kuḥūli	خَالٍ مِنَ الكُحولِ
tea	shāyun	شَايٌ
coffee	qahwatun	قَهوَةٌ
juice	ʿaṣīrun	عَصِيرٌ
water	mā'un	مَاءٌ
mineral water	mā'un maʿdaniyyun	مَاءٌ مَعدَنِيٌّ

1 Mark the word that doesn't belong in each row.

1 الكَانتِين - كَاسٌ - مَقهَى - مَطعَمٌ
2 قَهوَةٌ - شَايٌ - عَصِيرٌ - جِعَةٌ
3 طَبَقٌ - سِكِّينٌ - حَسَاءٌ - شَوكَةٌ
4 نَادِلٌ - وَجبَةُ سَمَكٍ - تَحلِيَةٌ - شَرَابٌ

2 Put the words in the correct menu categories.

كَعكٌ	قَهوَةٌ	جِيلاتِي	مَاءٌ مَعدَنِيٌّ	بِيرَةٌ	عَصِيرٌ	نَبِيذٌ	شَايٌ

مَشرُوبَاتٌ خَالِيَة مِنَ الكُحولِ	مَشْروبَاتٌ كُحُولِيَةٌ	تَحلِيَةٌ

3 Do the crossword puzzle. Make sure the individual letters of the words are written in their basic form (isolated).

Down:

1 You can get coffee and cake there.
3 Mineral water
6 You use this to eat
7 Restaurant
8 ... المَائدَةِ
10 You use this to cut

Across (from right to left):

2 Menu
4 Alcoholic beverage
5 Something sweet at the end of a meal, cold
9 He brings you the menu.

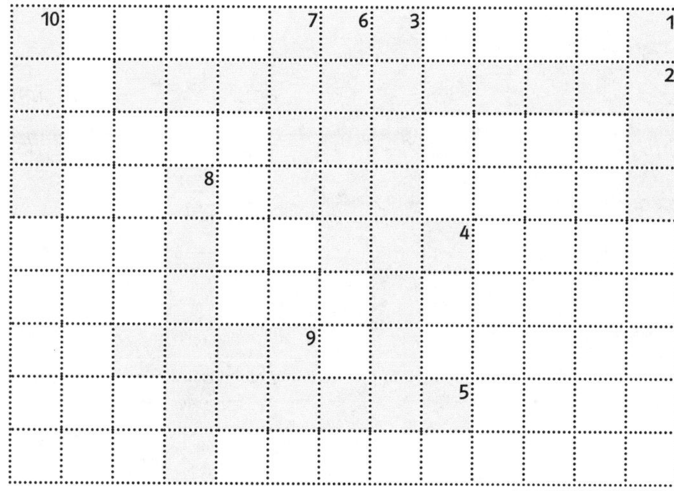

Groceries / Quantities

V8
C13

Vegetables خُضرَوَاتٌ

cucumber	*khayārun*	خِيَارٌ	tomato	*ṭamāṭimun*	طَمَاطِمٌ
potato	*baṭāṭisun*	بَطَاطِسٌ	pepper	*filfilun 'akhḍarun*	فِلفِلٌ أَخضَرٌ
cabbage	*kurunbun*	كُرُنبٌ	lettuce	*salaṭatun*	سَلطَةٌ
carrot	*jazarun*	جَزَرٌ	onion	*baṣalun*	بَصَلٌ

Dairy Products مُنتجَاتُ الحَلِيبِ

sour cream	*qishṭatun rā'ibatun*	قِشطَةٌ رَائِبَةٌ	milk	*ḥalībun*	حَلِيبٌ
(whipping) cream	*qishṭātun makhfūqatun*	قِشطَةٌ مَخفُوقَةٌ	cheese	*jubnun*	جُبنٌ
yogurt	*labanun*	لَبَنٌ	butter	*zubdatun*	زُبدَةٌ

Meat لَحمٌ

beef	*laḥmu baqarin*	لَحمُ بَقَرٍ	poultry	*dawajinun*	دَوَاجِنٌ
lamb	*laḥmu khārūfin*	لَحمُ خَرُوفٍ	chicken	*dajājun*	دَجَاجٌ
goat	*laḥmu maʿizin*	لَحمُ مَعِزٍ	dried meat	*laḥmun mujaffafun*	لَحمٌ مُجَفَّفٌ
mutton	*laḥmu ḍanin*	لَحمُ ضَأنٍ	pork	*laḥmu khinzīrin*	لَحمُ خِنزِيرٍ

Baked Goods خُبزٌ وكَعكٌ

bread	*khubzun*	خُبزٌ	cake	*kaʿkun*	كَعكٌ
roll	*raġīfun ṣaġīrun*	رَغِيفٌ صَغِيرٌ	cookie	*baskuwayt*	بَسكُوِيت
white bread	*khubzun 'abyaḍun*	خُبزٌ أَبيَض	tart, torte	*tūratun (kaʿkun)*	تُورتَةٌ (كَعكٌ)

Seasonings / Spices تَوَابِلٌ

salt	*milḥun*	مِلحٌ	paprika	*filfilun 'aḥmarun*	فِلفِلٌ أَحمَرٌ
sugar	*sukkarun*	سُكَّرٌ	vinegar	*khallun*	خَلٌّ
pepper	*filfilun*	فِلفِلٌ	oil (edible)	*zaytun*	زَيتٌ

Grains, etc. حُبُوبٌ وَغيرهَا

rice	*ruzz*	رُزٌّ	flour	*ṭaḥīnun / daqīqun*	طَحِينٌ / دَقِيقٌ
cracked wheat	*qamḥ nāʿim*	قَمح نَاعِم	egg	*bayḍatun*	بَيضَةٌ
noodles, pasta	*maʿkarūnatun*	مَعكَرُونَةٌ			

Quantities عَرضُ الكَمِيَةِ

bottle	*zujajatun*	زُجَاجَةٌ	liter	*litr*	لِتر
gram	*ġrāmun*	غْرَامٌ	package	*ṭardun ṣaġīrun*	طَردٌ صَغِيرٌ
kilo	*kīlū*	كِيلُو	slice	*qurṣun*	قُرصٌ

1 In each row, mark the word that does not belong.

1 لَحمُ بَقَرٍ - دَجاجٌ - طَمَاطِمٌ - لَحمُ مَعِزٍ - لَحمُ خَرُوفٍ

2 خَيَارٌ - زُبدَةٌ - فِلفِلٌ أخضَرٌ - كُرُنبٌ - جَزَرٌ

3 قِشطَةٌ رَائِبَةٌ - حَلِيبٌ - زُبدَةٌ - سُكَّرٌ - لَبَنٌ

2 Translate the shopping list into Arabic.

1. Rice ______________________
2. Bread ______________________
3. Meat ______________________
4. Lettuce ______________________
5. Cheese ______________________
6. Flour ______________________
7. Oil ______________________

3 This is a recipe for tabbouleh (parsley and cracked wheat salad), a typical Arab appetizer. Fill in the missing words in the recipe.

فِلفل أسود	ملح	قَمح نَاعِم	زَيت زَيتُون	طَمَاطم	بَصل

for 3–4 people

½ cup cracked wheat (or bulgur) (1)
4 large tomatoes (2)
3–4 bunches parsley
1 bunch green onions (3)
½ cup lemon juice
1 bunch fresh mint
½ cup olive oil (4)
salt (5)
pepper (6)

½ فنجان ______________________ (1)
4 ______________________ (2) كَبيرة
3 - 4 حَزَم بقدُونس
1 حَزمَة ______________________ (3)
½ فنجان عَصير الليمُون
1 حَزمَة نَعنَع أخضَر
½ فنجان ______________________ (4)
______________________ (5)
______________________ (6)

How does the recipe go from there? Wash the cracked wheat and squeeze it dry. Add the lemon juice and let the mixture stand for about a half hour.
Wash the parsley, green onions, mint leaves, and tomatoes, and chop them into small pieces. Add them to the wheat mixture. Stir in the olive oil, and season to taste with lemon juice, salt, and pepper. Mix well and serve on fresh lettuce leaves. Bon appétit!

Vocabulary

V11

Clothing / Colors

V8 C13

Clothing مَلابِس

women's clothing, ladies' wear	*malābisun nisā'iyatun*	مَلابِسٌ نِسَائِيَّةٌ	men's clothing, menswear	*malābisun lir-rijāli*	مَلابِسٌ لِلرِّجَالِ

Articles of Clothing ملابس مُتَنَوِّعَة

underwear	*malābisun dākhiliyatun*	مَلابِسٌ دَاخِلِيَّةٌ	shirt	*qamīṣun*	قَمِيصٌ
shoes	*'aḥdhiyatun*	أَحذِيَةٌ	sweater, pullover	*kanzatun*	كَنزَةٌ
blouse	*bulūzatun*	بُلُوزَةٌ	coat	*mi'ṭafun*	مِعطَفٌ
trousers, pants	*sirwālun*	سِروَالٌ	skirt	*tannūratun*	تَنُّورَةٌ
cap	*ṭāqiyatun*	طَاقِيَةٌ	rain jacket	*mimṭarun*	مِمطَرٌ
socks	*jawāribun*	جَوارِبٌ	dress	*fustānun / thawbun*	فُستَانٌ / ثَوبٌ
suit	*badhlatun*	بَذلَةٌ	jacket	*sutratun*	سُترَةٌ
T-shirt	*tīshīrt*	تِيشِيرت			
to put on (shoes)	*tana''ala / labisa (ḥidhā'an)*	تَنَعَّلَ / لَبِسَ (حِذَاءً)	to take off	*khala'a*	خَلَعَ
to dress / get dressed	*labisa*	لَبِسَ	to undress (oneself)	*khala'a*	خَلَعَ
to wear	*labisa*	لَبِسَ	to try on	*qāsa*	قَاسَ
(it) fits	*munāsibun*	مُنَاسِبٌ	(it) doesn't fit	*ġayru munāsibin*	غَيرُ مُنَاسِبٍ

Size مَقَاس

big	*kabīrun / ~atun*	كَبِيرٌ / كَبِيرَةٌ	small	*ṣaġīrun / ~atun*	صَغِيرٌ / صَغِيرَةٌ
long	*ṭawīlun / ~atun*	طَوِيلٌ / طَوِيلَةٌ	short	*qaṣirun / ~atun*	قَصِيرٌ / قَصِيرَةٌ
wide (large)	*wāsi'un / ~atun*	وَاسِعٌ / وَاسِعَةٌ	tight	*ḍayyiqun / ~atun*	ضَيِّقٌ / ضَيِّقَةٌ

Style طِرَاز

elegant	*'anīqun / ~atun*	أَنِيقٌ / أَنِيقَةٌ	chic	*rā'i'un / ~atun*	رَائِعٌ / رَائِعَةٌ
fashionable	*zayyun sha'i'un*	زَيٌّ شَائِعٌ	sporty	*riyāḍiyun / ~atun*	رِيَاضِيٌّ / رِيَاضِيَة

Colors أَلوَان

white	*'abyaḍun / bayḍāun*	أَبيَضٌ / بَيضَاءُ	gray	*ramādīyun / ~atun*	رَمَادِي / رَمَادِيَةٌ
yellow	*'aṣfarun / ṣafra'un*	أَصفَرٌ / صَفرَاءُ	red	*'aḥmarun / ḥamra'un*	أَحمَرٌ / حَمرَاءُ
black	*'aswadun / sawda'un*	أَسوَدٌ / سَودَاءُ	brown	*bunniyun / bunniyatun*	بُنِّيٌّ / بُنِّيَةٌ
blue	*'azraqun / zarqā'un*	أَزرَقٌ / زَرقَاءُ	green	*'akhḍar'un / khaḍra'un*	أَخضَرٌ / خَضرَاءُ

1 Which words belong to which category? Write the words supplied below in the appropriate column.

كَبير	واسِع	رياضِي	أبيَض	زِيّ شائع	أحمَر
أزرَق	رائِع	قَصير	رَمادِي	أنيق	طَويل

أَلوان	طِراز	مِقياس

2 What are these colors called in Arabic? Match the items in the two columns.

1	black	أحمَر	A
2	red	أصفَر	B
3	blue	أخضَر	C
4	yellow	أسوَد	D
5	green	أبيَض	E
6	white	أزرَق	F

3 Fill in the opposites of the verbs and adjectives, for example, واسِع - ضَيِّق.

1 مُناسِب - ____________________

2 لَبِس - ____________________

3 كَبير - ____________________

4 طَويل - ____________________

4 Read the paraphrases. Which articles of clothing are being referred to?

1. "Articles of clothing" for the feet.
2. Women wear this; it can be short or long.
3. A long time ago, only men could wear this item of clothing.

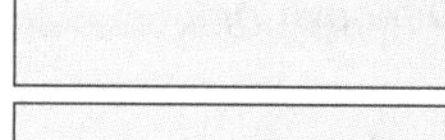

4. This is worn over clothing when it's cold outside.
5. Many men wear this in the office.
6. This is worn on the head.
7. It has short sleeves.

Housing and Furniture

C14

Place of Residence مَكَانُ السَّكَنِ

hotel	*funduqun*	فُنْدُقٌ	single-story, one-story	*dhū ṭābiqin wāḥidin*	ذُو طَابِقٍ واحِدٍ
house / building	*baytun*	بَيْتٌ	two-story	*dhū ṭābiqayni*	ذُوطَابِقَيْنِ
privately owned home	*baytun shakhṣi*	بَيْتٌ شَخْصِي	multistory / high-rise	*ʿimāratun ʿāliyatun*	عِمَارَةٌ عَالِيَةٌ

In a Building فِي عِمَارَةٍ

apartment	*shuqatun sakani-yyjatun*	شُقَّةٌ سَكَنِيَّةٌ	room	*ġurfatun*	غُرْفَةٌ
floor, story	*ṭābiqun*	طَابِقٌ	stairs	*baytus-sulam*	بَيْتُ السُّلَّمِ
1st / 2nd floor	*at-ṭābiqul 'awwal / 'ath-thānī*	الطَّابِقُ 1/2	elevator	*maṣʿadun*	مَصْعَدٌ
garage	*mir'ābun*	مِرْآبٌ	basement, cellar	*qabuwun*	قَبْوٌ

Rooms غُرَفٌ

balcony	*shurfatun*	شُرْفَةٌ	toilet, WC	*mirḥāḍun*	مِرْحَاضٌ
study, workroom	*ġurfatul-ʿamali*	غُرْفَةُ العَمَلِ	children's room	*ġurfatul-'aṭfāli*	غُرْفَةُ الأَطْفَالِ
bedroom	*ġurfatunnawmi*	غُرْفَةُ النَّومِ	kitchen	*maṭbakhun*	مَطْبَخٌ
living room	*ġurfatul-julūsi*	غُرْفَةُ الجُلُوسِ	bathroom	*ḥammamun*	حَمَّامٌ

In a Room فِي غُرْفَةٍ

door	*bābun*	بَابٌ	window	*nāfidhatun*	نَافِذَةٌ
floor	*'arḍiyyatun*	أَرْضِيَّةٌ	ceiling	*saqfun*	سَقْفٌ
corner	*zāwiyatun / ruknun*	زَاوِيَةٌ / رُكْنٌ	wall	*ḥā'iṭun*	حَائِطٌ

Furnishings أَثَاثُ السَّكَنِ

shower	*dūshun*	دُوشٌ	living room cabinet	*dūlābu ġufaril julūsi*	دولابُ غُرْفَةِ الجُلُوسِ
armchair	*kanabatun*	كَنَبَةٌ			
chair	*kursiyyun*	كُرْسِيٌّ	sofa, couch	*'arīkatun*	أَرِيكَةٌ
computer	*kūmbuyūtar*	كُومْبِيُوتَرْ	armoire, cupboard, cabinet	*dūlābun / khazānatun*	دولابٌ / خِزَانَةٌ
lamp	*miṣbāḥun*	مِصْبَاحٌ	kitchen cupboard	*dūlābul-maṭbakhi*	دولابُ المَطْبَخِ
bookshelf, shelving	*raffun*	رَفٌّ	table	*ṭāwilatun*	طَاوِلَةٌ
bed	*sarīrun*	سَرِيرٌ	refrigerator	*thalājatun*	ثَلاجَةٌ
bed linen	*mulāātun*	مُلاآتٌ	television set, TV	*tilfizyūnun*	تِلِفِزْيُونٌ
picture	*ṣūratun*	صُورَةٌ	curtain	*sitārun*	سِتَارٌ
sink	*ḥawḍul-ġasli*	حَوضُ الغَسلِ	mirror	*mir'ātun*	مِرْآةٌ
			bathtub	*ḥawḍul-'istiḥmāmi*	حَوضُ الإستِحمَامِ

Vocabulary

1 Mark the word in each row that doesn't belong.

1 غُرفَةُ النوم - مَطبَخٌ - غُرفَةُ الجُلُوس - بَابٌ

2 دُوشٌ - حَوضُ الإستِحمَام - تِلفِزيُونٌ - حَوضُ الغَسلِ

3 سَرِيرٌ - فُندُقٌ - بَيتٌ - شَقَّةٌ سَكَنِيَّةٌ

4 ذُو طَابِقٍ واحِدٍ - ذُوطَابِقَين - عِمَارَةٌ عَالِيَةٌ - نَافِذَةٌ

2 What are the names of these rooms or places?

1. The room you sleep in is the ______________________________.
2. The room you cook in is the ______________________________.
3. The place where you keep your car is the ______________________________.
4. The room you bathe in is the ______________________________.

3 Fill in the blanks in this description of an apartment. Watch out! The words supplied here are not declined, so pay attention to the word endings.

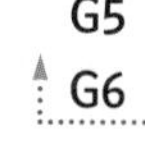

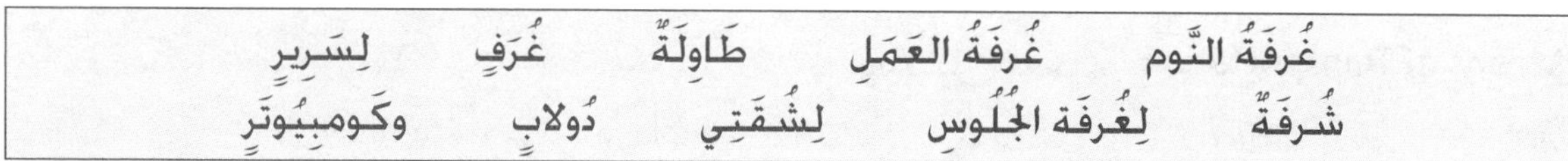

1. My apartment has three rooms. — ______ ثَلاثَةُ ______.
2. The bedroom is small. — ______ صَغِيرَةٌ.
3. Only the bed and the armoire fit into it. — تَتَّسِعُ ______ و ______ فَقَط.
4. In the study, there's a big table with a computer. — فِي ______ ______ كَبِيرَةٌ ______.
5. The living room has a big balcony. — ______ ______ كَبِيرَةٌ.

4 What furnishings can you normally find in a hotel room? Fill in the words below.

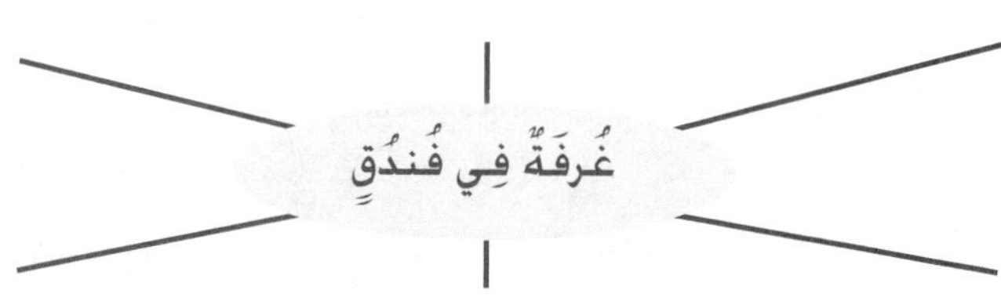

Transportation

C11

General عَامٌ

English	Transliteration	Arabic
traffic, transportation	*muwāṣalātun*	مُوَاصَلاتٌ
fine	*ġarāmatun*	غَرَامَةٌ
ticket (for transportation)	*tadhkaratun / tadhkaratur-rukūbi*	تَذكَرَةٌ / تَذكَرَةُ الرُّكُوبِ
traffic jam	*'izdiḥāmun*	ازدِحَامٌ
crosswalk	*mamarrul-mushāti*	مَمَرُّ المُشَاةِ
fork	*nuqṭatu tafaruʿin*	نُقطَةُ تَفَرُّعٍ
intersection	*taqāṭuʿun*	تَقَاطُعٌ
parking place / lot	*mawqifus-sayyārati*	مَوقِفُ السَّيَارَاتِ
stop (bus, etc.)	*mawqifun*	مَوقِفٌ
traffic light	*'ishāratul-murūri*	إشَارَةُ المُرُورِ

Streets and Roads شَوَارِعٌ

English	Transliteration	Arabic
freeway, superhighway	*at-tariqu as-sayyāru*	الطَّرِيقُ السَّيَّارُ
street, road	*shāriʿun*	شَارِعٌ
expressway	*shāriʿun sarīʿun*	شَارِعٌ سَرِيعٌ
detour	*taḥwīlatun*	تَحوِيلَةٌ

Stations / Terminals مَحَطَات

English	Transliteration	Arabic
bus station	*maḥaṭatul-bāṣāti*	مَحَطَّةُ البَاصَاتِ
train station	*maḥaṭatul-qiṭāri*	مَحَطَّةُ القِطَارِ
port	*mīnā'un*	مِينَاءٌ
airport	*maṭārun*	مَطَارٌ

Means of Transportation وَسَائِلُ النَّقلِ

English	Transliteration	Arabic
bus	*bāṣun*	بَاصٌ
car	*sayyāratun*	سَيَارَةٌ
bicycle	*darrajatun hawā'iyatun*	دَرَّاجَةٌ هَوَائِيَةٌ
ship	*safīnatun*	سَفِينَةٌ
airplane	*ṭa'iratun*	طَائِرَةٌ
subway	*mitrū*	مِترُو
taxi	*sayyāratu 'ujratin*	سَيَارَةُ أُجرَةٍ
streetcar	*bāṣ kahriba'ī*	بَاص كَهرَبَائِي
train	*qiṭārun*	قِطَارٌ

Road Users المُشتَرِكُونَ فِي المُرُورِ

English	Transliteration	Arabic
driver	*sā'iqun*	سَائِقٌ
passenger	*rākibun*	رَاكِبٌ
traffic policeman	*shurṭiyyul-murūri*	شُرطِيُّ المُرُورِ
pedestrian	*māshin / rājilun*	مَاشٍ / رَاجِلٌ

Verbs أَفعَالٌ

English	Transliteration	Arabic
to drive / go / ride	*sāqa*	سَاقَ
to arrive	*waṣala*	وَصَلَ
to leave, drive away	*ġādara / raḥala*	غَادَرَ / رَحَلَ
to enter	*sāqa 'ilad-dakhili*	سَاقَ إِلَى الدَّاخِلِ
to turn	*'inʿaṭafa*	إنعَطَفَ
to stand / be stationary	*waqafa*	وَقَفَ
to stop	*'awqafa*	أَوقَفَ
to cross	*ʿabara*	عَبَرَ
to call a taxi	*'istadʿā sayyarata 'ujratin*	إستَدعَى سَيَّارَةَ أُجرَةٍ
to park a car	*'awqafa sayyāratan fī mir'ābin*	أَوقَفَ سَيَّارَةً فِي مِرْآبٍ
to board, get on	*saʿida 'ilā*	صَعِدَ (إِلَى)
to get off /out	*nazala*	نَزَلَ

1 Mark the box next to each correct answer.

1. Where does an airplane trip begin?
   - A ☐ مَحَطَّةُ البَاصَاتِ
   - B ☐ مَطَارٌ
   - C ☐ مَحَطَّةُ القِطَارِ

2. Where do you park a car?
   - A ☐ مَمَرُّ المُشَاةِ
   - B ☐ تَقَاطُعٌ
   - C ☐ مَوقِفُ السَّيَّارَاتِ

3. By whom is a bus driven?
   - A ☐ رَاكِبٌ
   - B ☐ شُرطِيُّ المُرُورِ
   - C ☐ سَائِقٌ

4. What do you do at a red light?
   - A ☐ سَاقَ
   - B ☐ أَوقَفَ
   - C ☐ إنعَطَفَ

2 Which is the slowest means of transportation, and the fastest? Number the boxes in the correct order.

☐ بَاص ☐ قِطَارٌ ☐ طَائِرَةٌ ☐ دَرَّاجَةٌ هَوَائِيَّةٌ ☐ سَيَّارَةٌ

3 Which nouns can be combined with which verb? Match the items in the two columns.

1	سَيَّارَةُ أُجرَةٍ	A	أوقَفَ سَيَّارَةً فِي مِرْآبٍ
2	نُقطَةُ تَفَرُّعٍ	B	إستَدعَى
3	مَوقِفُ السَّيَّارَاتِ	C	إنعَطَفَ
4	مَمَرُّ المُشَاةِ	D	عَبَرَ

4 Riding the bus. Which Arabic word would you use for each English word in parentheses? Fill in the blanks.

غَرَامَةٌ	مَوقِفٌ	رَكِبَ	سَائِقٌ	نَزَلَ	صَعَدَ	تَذكَرَةٌ	وَقَفَ

1. Before you go anywhere, you buy a (ticket) ____________________, otherwise you have to pay a (fine) __________ .
2. Then you wait at a (stop) ____________________.
3. When the bus comes, you can (board, get on) ____________________.
4. Often you have to show the ticket (to the driver) ________________ .
5. When the bus (stops) at the stop you want, you can (get off) ________________ .

Vocabulary

Body / Personal Care / Health

Body جِسْمٌ

eyes	*ʿuyūnun*	عُيُونٌ	nose	*'anfun*	أَنفٌ
eyebrows	*ḥājibāni*	حَاجِبانِ	skin	*jildun / basharatun*	جِلدٌ / بَشَرَةٌ
ears	*'ādhānun*	آذانٌ	shoulders	*katifāni*	كَتِفَانِ
mouth	*famun*	فَمٌ	feet	*'aqdāmun*	أَقدَامٌ
teeth	*'asnānun*	أَسنَانٌ	abdomen	*baṭnun*	بَطنٌ
palms	*'akufun*	أَكُفٌ	fingers	*'aṣābiʿun*	أَصَابِعٌ
head	*r'asun*	رَأسٌ	hands	*'aydī*	أيدي
neck	*ʿunuqun*	عُنُقٌ	hair	*shaʿrun*	شَعرٌ
throat	*ḥalqun*	حَلْقٌ	arms	*dhirāʿāni*	ذِرَاعَانِ
legs	*'arjulun*	أَرجُلٌ	bottom	*ʿajzun / duburun*	عَجزٌ / دُبُرٌ
breast, chest	*ṣadrun*	صَدرٌ	face	*wajhun*	وَجهٌ
lips	*shafatāni*	شَفَتَانِ			

Body Care عِنَايَة بِالجِسمِ

showering	*ḥmmāmun*	حَمَّامٌ	shower gel	*jallu-lulġusli*	جَلُّ الغُسلِ
bathing	*'istiḥmāmun*	إستِحمَامٌ	shampoo	*shāmbū*	شَامبُو
washing	*ġuslun*	غُسلٌ	soap	*ṣābūnun*	صَابُونٌ
to bathe, wash (oneself)	*'iġtasala*	إغتَسَلَ	razor, shaver	*'ālatul-ḥalāqati*	آلَةُ الحِلاقَةِ
to shave (oneself)	*ḥalaqa*	حَلَقَ	towel	*minshafatun*	مِنشَفَةٌ
to comb one's hair	*tanashshafa*	تَنَشَّفَ	comb	*mishṭun*	مِشطٌ
to put on	*mashaṭa*	مَشَطَ	lotion, cream	*muraṭabun lil-bishrati*	مُرَطِّبٌ لِلبَشَرَةِ
lotion	*dahana*	دَهَنَ	toothpaste	*maʿjunul-'asnāni*	مَعجُونُ الأسنَانِ
to brush one's teeth	*naẓafa 'asnānahu*	نَظَّفَ أَسْنَانَهُ	toothbrush	*furshatul-'asnāni*	فُرشَةُ الأَسنَانِ

Health صِحَةٌ

sick, ill	*marīḍun / ~atun*	مَرِيضٌ / مَرِيضَةٌ	to run a fever	*maḥmūm*	مَحمُومٌ
healthy	*ṣaḥīḥun / ~atun*	صَحِيحٌ / صَحِيحَةٌ	to have diarrhea	*'ishālun*	إسهَالٌ
to hurt	*m'ulimun*	مُؤلِمٌ	medicine	*dawā'un*	دَوَاءٌ
pain	*'alamun*	أَلَمٌ	to take	*tanāwala*	تَنَاوَلَ
to sweat	*ʿariqa*	عَرِقَ	tablet, pill	*qurṣun*	قُرصٌ
to burn oneself	*ḥaraqa*	حَرَقَ	to break something	*kasara*	كَسَرَ

Tip: Draw a human body and label it with Arabic words. Then you can memorize the terms more easily!

Vocabulary

1 Which of these body parts belong to the face (وَجه) and which to the rest of the body (جِسم)?

حَاجبانِ كَتِفانِ ذِرَاعانِ عُيُونٌ أَنفٌ فَمٌ أَصَابعٌ أَسنَانٌ شَفَتانِ أَرجُلٌ

جِسمٌ	وَجهٌ

2 What is the order of these body parts, when you look at the human body from top to bottom? Put the words in the correct blanks.

بَطنٌ كَتِفانِ رَأسٌ عُنُقٌ أَقدَامٌ صَدرٌ شَعرٌ أَرجُلٌ

1 ______ 5 ______

2 ______ 6 ______

3 ______ 7 ______

4 ______ 8 ______

3 Which personal care items are used for which purposes? Make the correct matches.

1 صَابُونٌ A أَصَابعٌ

2 آلَةُ الحِلاقَةِ B إغتَسَلَ

3 مِشطٌ C تَنَشَّفَ

4 مِنشَفَةٌ D حَلَقَ

5 فُرشَةُ الأسنَانِ E مَشَطَ

4 When something hurts, you say ... عِندِي أَلَمٌ فِي (*'indī 'alamun fī ...*). Complete the sentences.
Note: The preposition *fī* فِي must always be followed by the genitive. In some cases, the answers are already declined. G5 G6

G27

الحَلقِ الأَسنَانِ مَحمُومٌ البَطنِ الصَدرِ صَحِيحٌ

1 عِندِي أَلَمٌ فِي ______. 4 عِندِي أَلَمٌ فِي ______.

2 عِندِي أَلَمٌ فِي ______. 5 عِندِي أَلَمٌ فِي ______.

3 أَنَا ______. (I'm running a fever.) 6 أَنَا ______! (I'm healthy!)

V15

Verbs

Feelings شُعُور

to love	*ʼaḥabba*	أَحَبَّ	to like	*raġiba*	رَغِبَ فِي
to hate	*kariha*	كَرِهَ	to feel	*shaʿara*	شَعَرَ

Senses حَوَاسّ

to hear	*samiʿa*	سَمِعَ	to see	*raʼā / shāhada*	رَأَى / شَاهَدَ
to listen	*ʼistamaʿa*	إِستَمَعَ	to look	*naẓara (ʼilā)*	نَظَرَ (إِلَى)
to touch	*masaka / lamasa*	مَسَكَ / لَمَسَ	to smell	*shamma*	شَمَّ

Everyday Activities نَشَاطَاتٌ يَومِيَة

to work	*ʿamila*	عَمِلَ	to get up	*qāma*	قَامَ
to rest	*ʼistarāḥa*	إِستَرَاحَ	to sleep	*nāma*	نَامَ

Movement حَرَكَةٌ

to come here	*jāʼa*	جَاءَ	to carry	*ḥamala*	حَمَلَ
to run	*mashā*	مَشَى	to sit	*jalasa*	جَلَسَ
to walk, go	*dhahaba*	ذَهَبَ	to sit down	*jalasa*	جَلَسَ
to lie	*ʼiḍṭajaʿa*	إِضطَجَعَ	to stand up	*qāma*	قَامَ

Language لُغَةٌ

to answer	*ʼajāba*	أَجَابَ	to say something	*qāla*	قَالَ
to speak	*takallama*	تَكَلَّمَ	to tell	*taḥaddatha*	تَحَدَّثَ
to ask	*sʼala*	سَأَلَ	to be silent	*sakata*	سَكَتَ

Mental Activities نَشَاطَات ذِهنِيَّة

to think	*fakkara*	فَكَّرَ	to write	*kataba*	كَتَبَ
to mean	*ʿanā*	عَنَى	to read	*qaraʼa*	قَرَأَ
to learn	*taʿallama*	تَعَلَّمَ	to understand	*fahima*	فَهِمَ
to forget	*nasiya*	نَسِيَ	to know	*ʿalima*	عَلِمَ

Miscellaneous مُتَفَرِقَات

to be	*kāna*	كَانَ	to want (to)	*ʼarāda*	أَرَادَ
to have	*malaka*	مَلَكَ	to have to (must)	*ʼuḍṭurra*	أُضطُرَّ
to do, to make	*faʿala*	فَعَلَ	to help	*sāʿada*	سَاعَدَ
to be able (can)	*ʼistaṭāʿa*	إِستَطَاعَ	to stop	*kaffa (ʿan)*	كَفَّ (عَنْ)
to live / reside	*ʿāsha / sakana*	عَاشَ / سَكَنَ	to begin, to start	*badaʼa*	بَدَأَ
to seek	*baḥatha*	بَحَثَ			

1 Fill in the blanks with verbs that mean the opposite.

إسْتَرَاحَ   تَكَلَّمَ   أَحَبَّ   كَفَّ   أَجَابَ   جَلَسَ

1 سَكَتَ - ______________________

2 سَأَلَ - ______________________

3 بَدَأَ - ______________________

4 كَرِهَ - ______________________

5 قَامَ - ______________________

6 عَمِلَ - ______________________

2 If you had to express these sentences in Arabic, what verb would you use? Fill in the blanks.

فَهِمَ   عَمِلَ   أَحَبَّ   اِسْتَطَاعَ   فَعَلَ   رَأَى   أَرَادَ   ذَهَبَ

1. Hassan *loves* his wife. ______________________
2. Zarina *can* help. ______________________
3. Bishara *wants* a new toy. ______________________
4. Zayd *works* all day long. ______________________
5. I *see* you. ______________________
6. Where *are* you *going*? ______________________
7. I *understand* you well. ______________________
8. What *are* you *doing*? ______________________

3 In the grid below, find the following verbs: love, hate, stand up, be able (can), stop, seek, make, sit, be silent, say something. Diagonally and vertically, you can search from left to right and/or from top to bottom. Horizontally, search from right to left. Remember that the individual letters are presented in their basic form: that is, isolated.

A1
A2

ك	ك	ج	س	ن	ب	ح	أ	و	ض
س	ر	ع	ل	ح	ث	ث	ا	س	ي
ك	غ	ه	ل	س	ث	ا	ب	ك	ش
ج	ا	م	ا	ش	ض	ك	ق	ت	ي
ل	ع	ف	ك	س	م	ا	ق	ع	غ
ز	ف	ف	ك	ع	ت	س	ط	ا	ق
ط	ب	ض	فّ	و	ك	ط	ظ	و	ا
ن	ح	ص	ط	غ	ك	م	ا	و	ل
ا	ث	ي	ع	ك	س	ج	ش	ع	م

Nominal Sentence الجملة الإسمية

G18 Arabic has two different kinds of sentences: nominal sentences and verbal sentences. The difference is that a nominal sentence (*al-jumla al-'ismiya*)—unlike a verbal sentence—can be formed without a verb.

Simple Nominal Sentence

G2 G12 In Arabic, you can form simple sentences (nominal sentences) that consist of a subject and a predicate. The subject is the reference point or topic of the sentence. In a nominal sentence, the subject can be a noun, a personal pronoun, or a demonstrative pronoun. The predicate is the information that describes the subject more precisely. In a nominal sentence, the predicate can be an adjective, a noun, or an adverb and/or a prepositional phrase. Consequently a nominal sentence requires no verb at all:

G16 G25 G27

"The room big." (= The room is big.)	*al-ġurfatu wāsiʿatun.* (noun / adj.)	الغرفةُ واسعةٌ.
I (am) happy.	*'ana farḥānun.* (pers. pron. / adj.)	أنَا فَرْحَانٌ.
This one (is) healthy.	*hādhā salīmun.* (dem. pron. / adj.)	هَذَا سَلِيمٌ.
This woman (is) a doctor.	*hādhihil-mar'atu ṭabībatun.* (noun / noun)	هَذِهِ المَرأةُ طَبِيبَةٌ.
The doctor (is) here.	*'aṭṭabību hunā.* (noun / adv.)	الطّبِيبُ هُنَا.
He (comes) from Cairo.	*huwa minal-qāhirati.* (pers. pron. / prep. phrase)	هُوَ مِن القَاهِرَةِ.

Simple Interrogative Sentence

G15 In simple interrogative sentences, the nominal sentence is preceded by a question word (such as *hal* هَلْ). The subject – predicate sentence structure is retained in questions:

The room big?	*hal hādhil-ġurfatu wāsiʿatun?*	هَلْ هَذِهِ الغُرفَةُ وَاسِعَةٌ؟
(Am) I happy?	*hal 'ana farḥānun?*	هَلْ أنَا فَرحَانٌ؟
This one healthy?	*hal hādhā salīmun?*	هَلْ هَذَا سَلِيمٌ؟
This woman a doctor?	*hal hādhil-mar'atu ṭabībatun?*	هَلْ هَذِهِ المَرأةُ طَبِيبَةٌ؟
The doctor here?	*halit-ṭabību hunā?*	هَل الطّبِيبُ هُنَا؟
(Does) He (come) from Cairo?	*hal huwa minal-qāhirati ?*	هَلْ هُوَ مِن القَاهِرَةِ؟

Nominal sentences use the subject – predicate structure. Nominal sentences require no verb and are always in the present tense. In questions, a question word is placed before the simple nominal sentence (subject – predicate).

1 Underline the predicate in the following sentences.

1 أنَا فَرْحَانٌ.

2 الطّبيبُ هُنَا.

3 الغرفةُ واسعةٌ.

4 هَذَا سَلِيمٌ.

5 هَذِهِ المَرأَةُ طَبِيبَةٌ.

2 Use the words supplied below to form simple sentences: two with a demonstrative pronoun and an adjective, and four with a personal pronoun and an adjective.

هُوَ he	طَبِيبَةٌ doctor (f.)	أَنَا I	سَلِيمٌ healthy	هَذِهِ this one (f.)	طَوِيلٌ big
هَذَا this one (m.)	قَصِيرٌ small	أَنتَ you (m.)	سَمِينٌ fat	هِيَ she	جَمِيلَةٌ pretty

1. Personal pronoun + adjective:

____

____

____

____

2. Demonstrative pronoun + adjective:

____

____

3 Change these statements to questions.

1 هَذَا سَلِيمٌ. ______________________؟

2 هُوَ مِن القَاهِرَةِ. ______________________؟

3 هَذِهِ طَبِيبَةٌ. ______________________؟

4 الغُرْفَةُ وَاسِعَةٌ. ______________________؟

5 الطّبيبُ هُنَا. ______________________؟

4 Write four simple sentences about yourself. For example, tell where you come from, what your occupation is, how you look, and how you feel.

V1

V2

1 ______________________.

2 ______________________.

3 ______________________.

4 ______________________.

Grammar

Nouns الأسماء: Gender

G3 Arabic nouns (*al-'asmā'*) are characterized by four elements: gender, number, state (definite / indefinite), and
G8 case. These pieces of grammatical information are expressed in the noun endings. The basic form of nouns is the indefinite (indeterminate) form. Indefinite nouns are not accompanied by an article.

G4 Gender

Arabic has two genders: masculine and feminine. In addition, a distinction is made between nouns that refer to animate beings and those that refer to inanimate objects.

- Persons, personal identifiers (such as occupations), and animals belong to the *haqiqi* حقيقي category (real masculine / feminine):

(a) man	*radjul**un*** (m. Sing.)	رَجُلٌ
(a) bull	*thawr**un*** (m. Sing.)	ثورٌ
(a) woman	*imra'**atun*** (f. Sing.)	اِمرأةٌ
(a) dove	*hamām**atun*** (f. Sing.)	حَمامةٌ

Indefinite masculine nouns end in *tanwin* ـٌ (double *ḍamma*). The noun ends in *-un*. Indefinite feminine nouns can be recognized by the so-called feminine marker *ta marbuṭa* ة at the end of the word, which carries the *tanwin* ـٌ (double *ḍamma*). The consonant that precedes *ta marbuṭa* ة also carries the *tanwin* ـً (double *fatḥa*),
A4 whereas the feminine noun ends in *-a-tun*.

G8 Nouns that can be both masculine and feminine (such as occupations) are always made to agree in gender, by replacing the masculine ending *-un* with *-a-tun*:

(a) doctor (m.) / (a) doctor (f.)	*ṭabīb**un**/ṭabīb**atun***	طَبيبٌ / طَبيبَةٌ
(a) friend (m.) / (a) friend (f.)	*ṣadīq**un**/ṣadīq**atun***	صَدِيقٌ / صَدِيقَةٌ

- Nouns that denote masculine or feminine things are known as *majazi* مَجازي (metaphorical masculine / feminine):

(a) chair	*kursiy**un*** (m. sing.)	كرسيٌّ
(a) bottle	*qārūr**atun*** (f. sing.)	قارورة

- There are, however, a number of masculine nouns that end in *ta marbuṭa* ة. These *lafthi* لفظي (literal feminine nouns) are exclusively men's names:

man's name	*ḥamz**atun***	حمزَةٌ

- Conversely, some feminine nouns do not end in *ta marbuṭa* ة. These *al-mu'anath al-m'anawi* المؤنث المعنوي include women's names, as well as some feminine nouns that denote things (especially paired body parts such as hands or legs).

woman's name	*zayna**bun***	زينبٌ
(a) hand	*ya**dun*** (f. sing.)	يدٌ
(a) leg	*rijl**un*** (f. sing.)	رِجلٌ

Grammar

1 Listen to the sentences, paying attention to the different endings of the nouns. Underline the masculine and feminine nouns and names. Then write the words in the appropriate column of the table. Even if words appear several times, enter them only once in the list. 19

This is Zaid and Hala's family.	هَذِهِ أُسْرَةُ زَيْدٍ وَ هَالَة.	1
They have a daughter and a son.	لَهُمَا اِبنَةٌ وَابْنٌ.	2
The daughter's name is Halima.	اِسْمُ الابْنَةِ حَلِيْمَة.	3
The son's name is Omar.	اِسْمُ الابْنِ عُمَر.	4
The family comes from Cairo.	الأَسْرَةُ مِن القَاهِرَة.	5
The family has a house in Cairo.	لِلأَسْرَةِ بَيْتٌ فِي القَاهِرَة.	6

2. feminine	1. masculine

2 The following designations of occupation are all given in the feminine form.
Add the masculine equivalent.

soldier ________	جُنْدِيّة	5	judge ________	قَاضِيَة	1
driver ________	سَائِقَة	6	lawyer ________	مُحَامِيَة	2
teacher ________	مُعلمَة	7	newswoman ________	مُذِيعَة	3
doctor ________	طَبِيبَة	8	policewoman ________	شُرطِيّة	4

3 To tell what occupation a person has, you say:

Halima (is) teacher. *halīmatun mu'alimatun.* حَلِيْمَةٌ مُعلمَة.

Look at the sentences, paying close attention to the endings. Decide which are correct and which are incorrect. Then make the necessary corrections.

	correct	incorrect		
________	☐	☒	حَلِيْمَةٌ مُعَلمةٌ.	1
________	☐	☐	هالةٌ طبيبٌ.	2
________	☐	☐	عليٌ طَالِبَةٌ.	3
________	☐	☐	مُحَمدٌ مُهَنْدِسَةٌ.	4
________	☐	☐	حسنٌ سائقٌ.	5
________	☐	☐	خديجةٌ مهندسٌ.	6
________	☐	☐	رملةٌ محاميةٌ.	7
________	☐	☐	مُخْتَارٌ تاجِرٌ.	8

Nouns: Number

In addition to the singular and the plural, Arabic has a third grammatical number: the dual. In the plural, a distinction is also drawn between the sound (external) plural and the broken (internal) plural.

Singular مُفْرَدٌ

G2 A singular noun is referred to as *mufradun*.

(a) wise man	*ʿāqi**lun*** (m. sing.)	عَاقِلٌ
(a) car	*sayyā**ratun*** (f. sing.)	سَيَارَةٌ

Dual مُثَنَى

A noun is in the dual (*muthana*) when it refers to precisely two persons, animals, or things. In the dual, the (indefinite) singular ending *-un* (m.) or *-a-tun* (f.) disappears and is replaced by *alif* ا and *nūn* ن at the end of the word. Below *nūn* ن is *kasra* ـِ, and the noun ends in *-āni* or *-a-tāni*.

two wise men	*ʿāqi**lāni*** (m. dual)	عَاقِلانِ
two cars	*sayyā**ratāni*** (f. dual)	سَيَارَتَانِ

Sound Plural of Masculine Nouns جَمعُ المُذَكَر السَّالِم

The sound plural of masculine nouns (*jamʿul-mudhakar as-salim*) always refers to persons. The singular ending *-un* (m.) is replaced by *wāw* و (long vowel) and *nūn* ن at the end of the word. Above *nūn* ن is *fatḥa* ـَ, and the noun ends in *-ūna*.

wise men	*ʿāqi**lūna*** (m. pl.)	عَاقِلُونَ
writers	*kāti**būna*** (m. pl.)	كَاتِبُونَ

Sound Plural of Feminine Nouns جَمعُ المُؤنَث السَّالِم

In the sound plural of feminine nouns (*jamʿul-muʾanath as-salim*), the singular ending *-a-tun* (f.) is replaced by *alif* ا and *tā* ت. *tā* ت carries *tanwin* ـٌ (double *ḍamma*), and the noun ends in *-ātun*.

cars	*sayyā**rātun*** (f. pl.)	سَيَارَاتٌ
wise women	*ʿaqi**lātun*** (f. pl.)	عَاقِلاتٌ

G8 The (nominative) endings in the singular, dual, and sound plural:

feminine	masculine	
-a-tun	*-un*	singular
-a-tāni	*-āni*	dual
-ātun	*-ūna*	plural

Broken Plural جمع التكسير

In the broken plural (*jamut-taksīr*), internal changes are made in the word. Because there are no universally valid rules for this, although most nouns have a broken plural form, you will need to memorize the plural every time you learn a new word.

(a) man	***raju**lun* (m. sing.)	رَجُلٌ
men	***rijā**lun* (m. pl.)	رِجَالٌ
(a) newspaper	*ja**rīdatun*** (f. sing.)	جَرِيدَةٌ
newspapers	*ja**rāʾidun*** (f. pl.)	جَرَائِدٌ

Grammar

1 The following nouns are in either the singular or the dual. Write the words in the appropriate column of the table below.

رَجُل man	إمرَأتَانِ woman	عَاقِل wise man	عَاقِلانِ wise man	سَيَارَة car	رَجُلانِ man
سَيَارَتَانِ car	إمْرَأة woman	جَرِيدَتَانِ newspaper	حَمَامَة dove	جَرِيدَة newspaper	حَمَامَتَانِ dove

2. Dual	1. Singular

2 Form the masculine or feminine plural.

	2. f. plural	f. sing.			1. m. plural	m. sing.
language	________	لُغَة A		observer	________	مُرَاقِب A
government	________	حُكُومَة B		representative	________	مَندُوب B
firm, company	________	شَركَة C		writer	________	كَاتِب C
embassy	________	سَفَارَة D		Muslim	________	مُسلِم D
train station	________	مَحَطَة E		engineer	________	مُهَندِس E
continent	________	قَارَة F		player	________	لاعِب F
car	________	سَيَارَة G		floor	________	أرض G
airplane	________	طَائِرَة H		assistant	________	مُسَاعِد H

3 Match the broken plural with the corresponding word in the singular.

		broken plural	singular	
men	1	رِجَال	مَكتَب	A
newspapers	2	جَرَائِد	طَرِيق	B
dresses	3	ثِيَاب	جَرِيدَة	C
offices	4	مَكَاتِب	صُورَة	D
ways	5	طُرُق	رَجُل	E
photos	6	صُوَر	ثَوب	F

Grammar

Nouns: Definite Article *al* ال

G2 G8

The basic form of a noun is always the indefinite (indeterminate) form of the word. In the singular, it ends in *-un* (m.) or *-a-tun* (f.). Arabic has no indefinite article (as in English "a doctor," "an example"). Indefinite nouns are made into definite (determinate) nouns by placing the definite article *al* ال in front of them. In the process, the word endings change as follows:

		definite			indefinite
the teacher	*al-mu'alimu* (m. sing.)	المُعلم	(a) teacher	*mu'alimun* (m. sing.)	مُعلمٌ
the teacher	*al-mu'alimatu* (f. sing.)	المُعَلِمَةُ	(a) teacher	*mu'alimatun* (f. sing.)	مُعَلِمَةٌ
the two teachers	*al-mu'alimāni* (m. dual)	المُعَلِمَانِ	two teachers	*mu'alimāni* (m. dual)	مُعَلِمَانِ
the two teachers	*al-mu'alimatāni* (f. dual)	المُعَلِمَتَانِ	two teachers	*mu'alimatāni* (f. dual)	مُعَلِمَتَانِ
the teachers	*al-mu'alimūna* (m. pl.)	المُعَلِمُونَ	teachers	*mu'alimūna* (m. pl.)	مُعَلِمُونَ
the teachers	*al-mu'alimātu* (f. pl.)	المُعَلِمَاتُ	teachers	*mu'alimātun* (f. pl.)	مَعَلِمَاتٌ

The article *al* ال is used for both masculine and feminine words alike, and it remains unchanged in the dual and the plural. The article *al* ال and the noun that follows it constitute a single word, which is written and spoken as a unit. Keep in mind that proper names are always definite, but they never include the article *al* ال .

The pronunciation of the article *al* ال changes if the (indefinite) noun begins with one of the following consonants:

ت ث د ذ ر ز س ش ص ض ط ظ ل ن

In this case, although the letter *lām* ل in the article *al* ال continues to be written, it is not pronounced. The first consonant of the (indefinite) noun carries *shadda* ـّ, and this means that the sound of the consonant is lengthened (doubled):

		definite			indefinite
the car	*as-sayyāratu*	السَّيَارَةُ	(a) car	*sayyāratun*	سَيَارَةٌ
the cook	*aṭ-ṭabbākhu*	الطَّبَّاخُ	(a) cook	*ṭabbākhun*	طَبّاخٌ

The 14 letters of the alphabet listed above, which require assimilation with the *lām* ل of a preceding article, are known as "sun letters."

		definite			indefinite
the sun	*ash-shamsu*	الشَّمسُ	sun	*shamsun*	شَمسٌ

The remaining 14 letters of the alphabet, which are preceded by *al* ال with no assimilation, are known as "moon letters."

أ ب ج ح خ ع غ ف ق ك م ه و ي

		definite			indefinite
the moon	*al-qamaru*	القَمَرُ	moon	*qamarun*	قَمَرٌ

1 Fill in the definite form of these indefinite nouns.

door ________	بَابٌ	6	book ________	كِتَابٌ	1
lamps ________	مَصَابِيحُ	7	house ________	بَيتٌ	2
store ________	دُكَانٌ	8	refrigerator ________	ثلاّجَةٌ	3
policewomen ________	شُرطِيَاتٌ	9	students (m. dual) ________	طَالِبَانِ	4
city ________	مَدِينَةٌ	10	engineers ________	مُهَنْدِسُونَ	5

2 Which letters of the alphabets are sun letters, and which are moon letters?

ن أ ل ه
ظ ك ط
ح ض ص
ش ب ف
س ج ز
و غ ع
ر ذ د ث
خ ق م
ت ي

2. moon letters		1. sun letters	
________	________	________	________
________	________	________	________
________	________	________	________
________	________	________	________
________	________	________	________
________	________	________	________
________	________	________	________

3 Listen to the words, and decide in which ones the definite article *al* is followed by a sun letter, and in which it is followed by a moon letter.

المَطْبَخُ	السَّمَاءُ	القَهْوَةُ	الفَمُ	الشَّمْسُ	البَابُ
kitchen	sky	coffee	moon	sun	door
التِّجارَةُ	الزَّوجَةُ	الكُرْسِيُ	الظِّلُ	اليَومُ	الرَّبِيعُ
trade, industry	wife	chair	shadow	day	spring

2. by moon letters	1. by sun letters
________	________
________	________
________	________
________	________
________	________
________	________

Grammar

Nouns: Singular Declension

A3 G7 G8

Arabic has three cases: nominative, genitive, and accusative. A distinction is made between the declension of definite (determinate) nouns and the declension of indefinite (indeterminate) nouns. The latter is referred to as nunation. Nouns in general are subdivided in turn into declinable nouns (*al-mu'rab*) and partially declinable nouns. If a noun is declinable, the word ending changes, depending on the case the word is in. The different case endings are expressed by the three short vowels *fatḥa* ـَ, *kasra* ـِ and *ḍamma* ـُ.

Declinable Singular Noun المعرب

- **Nominative**: A noun is in the nominative case if it is the subject of a sentence or is the predicate in a nominal sentence (tells "who" or "what").

G1

The man came.	*jā'ar-rajulu.* (nom. m. sing.)	جَاءَالرَّجُلُ.
The woman came.	*jā'atil-mar'atu.* (nom. f. sing.)	جَاءَت المَرأةُ.

G4

With determinate nouns in the nominative singular, *ḍamma* ـُ appears above the last letter of the word, and the noun ends in *-u* (m.) or *-a-tu* (f.):

the man	*ar-rajulu* (nom. m. sing.)	الرَّجُلُ
the woman	*al-mar'**atu*** (nom. f. sing.)	المَرأةُ

- **Genitive**: A noun is in the genitive case if it is preceded by a preposition. Here the noun represents the object of the preposition.

I walked past the man.	*marartu bir-rajuli.* (gen. m. sing.)	مَرَرتُ بِالرَّجُلِ.

G9

The genitive also indicates that something belongs to someone or is associated with someone (ownership or relationship).

This is the woman's house.	*hādhā baytul mar'ati.* (gen. f. sing.)	هَذَا بَيتُ المَرأةِ.

With determinate nouns in the genitive singular, *kasra* ـِ appears below the last letter of the word, and the noun acquires the final sound *-i* (m.) or *-a-ti* (f.):

the teacher's / of the teacher	*'al-mu'alim**i*** (gen. m. sing.)	المُعَلِمِ
the teacher's / of the teacher	*'al-mu'alim**ati*** (gen. f. sing.)	المُعَلِمَةِ

- **Accusative**: A noun is in the accusative case if it is the direct object of a sentence.

I saw the man.	*ra'aytur-rajula.* (acc. m. sing.)	رَأَيتُ الرَّجُلَ

With determinate nouns in the accusative singular, *fatḥa* ـَ appears above the last letter of the word, and the noun ends in *-a* (m.) or *-a-ta* (f.).

the man	*ar-rajul**a*** (acc. m. sing.)	الرَّجُلَ
the woman	*al-mara'**ata*** (acc. f. sing.)	المَرأةَ

G8

The case endings in the singular:

feminine singular	masculine singular	
-a-tu	*-u*	nominative
-a-ti	*-i*	genitive
-a-ta	*-a*	accusative

1 The following words are in the nominative, genitive, or accusative. Match them correctly.

factory	A nom.	المَصْنَعَ	7	bag	A nom.	الحَقِيْبَةَ	4	pen	A nom.	القَلَمِ	1
hotel	B gen.	الفُنْدُقُ	8	room	B gen.	الغُرْفَةِ	5	shoe	B gen.	الحِذَاءَ	2
waiter	C acc.	النَّادِلِ	9	child	C acc.	الطِّفْلُ	6	teacher (m.)	C acc.	المُعَلِّمُ	3

2 Fill in the appropriate vowel signs above the first word in the nominative, and then decline it in the genitive and accusative.

	acc. sing.	genitive sing.	nom. sing.	
house	__________	__________	البَيت	1
man	__________	__________	الرّجُل	2
principal	__________	__________	المُدير	3
food / meal	__________	__________	الطّعَام	4
spoon	__________	__________	المِلْعَقَة	5
paper	__________	__________	الوَرَقَة	6

3 Match the two columns correctly.

1 Muktar came.	قَالَ مُحَمَّدٌ ... A
2 The bag is in the room.	قَرَأْتُ كِتَاباً. B
3 Mohamed said ...	الحَقِيْبَةُ فِي الغُرْفَةِ. C
4 I wore a shirt.	هَذَا بَيْتُ المَرْأَةِ. D
5 Ali traveled by train.	لَبِسْتُ قَمِيْصاً. E
6 I read a book.	جَاءَ مُخْتَارٌ. F
7 That is the woman's house.	نَامَ الطِفْلُ. G
8 The child slept.	سَافَرَ عَلِيٌّ بِالْقِطَارِ. H

4 Complete the sentences by adding a word of your choosing in the required case.

Muktar bought	(acc.) . __________ اشْتَرَى مُخْتَارٌ	1
The principal is in	(gen.) . __________ المُدِيرُ فِي	2
... was delicious.	(nom.) .لَذِيذاً __________ كَانَ	3
They sat under	(gen.) . __________ جَلَسُوا تَحْتَ	4

Grammar

Nouns: Dual / Plural Declension

G5

Declinable Noun in the Dual

- **Nominative**: In the nominative dual, the (definite) singular endings *-u* (m.) and *-a-tu* (f.) vanish and are replaced by *alif* ا and *nūn* ن at the end of a word. Below *nūn* ن is *kasra* ـِ, and the noun ends in *āni* (m.) or *-a-tāni* (f.).

the (two) teachers	*al-mu'alim**āni*** (nom. m. dual)	الْمُعَلِمَانِ
the (two) teachers	*al-mu'alim**atāni*** (nom. f. dual)	الْمُعَلِمَتَانِ

- **Genitive/Accusative**: In the genitive dual and accusative dual, *-āni* and *-a-tāni* (= nominative dual) are replaced by *yā* ي and *nūn* ن in final position. Below *nūn* ن is *kasra* ـِ, and the noun ends in *-ayni* (m.) or *-a-tayni* (f.).

of the (two) teachers	*al-mu'alim**ayni*** (gen. m. dual)	الْمُعَلِمَيْنِ
the (two) teachers	*al-mu'alim**atayni*** (acc. f. dual)	الْمُعَلِمَتَيْنِ

Declinable Noun in the Plural (Masculine)

- **Nominative masculine**: In the nominative masculine plural, the (definite) singular ending *-u* (m.) is replaced by *wāw* و (long vowel) and *nūn* ن in final position. Above *nūn* ن is *fatha* ـَ, and the noun ends in *-ūna*.

the teachers	*al-mu'alim**ūna*** (nom. m. pl.)	الْمُعَلِمُونَ

- **Genitive/Accusative masculine**: In the genitive and accusative masculine plural, *-ūna* (nominative masculine plural) is replaced by *yā* ي (long vowel) and *nūn* ن in final position. Above *nūn* ن is *fatha* ـَ, and the noun ends in *-īna*.

the teacher	*al-mu'alim**īna*** (gen. m. pl.)	الْمُعَلِمِينَ
the teachers	*al-mu'alim**īna*** (acc. m. pl.)	الْمُعَلِمِينَ

Declinable Noun in the Plural (Feminine)

- **Nominative feminine**: In the nominative feminine plural, the (definite) singular ending *-a-tu* (f.) is replaced by *alif* ا and *tā* ت at the end of the word. Above *tā* ت is *ḍamma* ـُ, and the noun ends in *-ā-tu*.

the teachers	*al-mu'alim**ātu*** (nom. f. pl.)	الْمُعَلِمَاتُ

- **Genitive/Accusative feminine**: In the genitive and accusative feminine plural, *alif* ا and *tā* ت are retained at the end of the word. However, *ḍamma* ـُ above *tā* ت is replaced by *kasra* ـِ under *tā* ت. The ending *-ā-tu* (nominative feminine plural) becomes *-ā-ti*.

of the teachers	*al-mu'alim**āti*** (gen. f. pl.)	الْمُعَلِمَاتِ
the teachers	*al-mu'alim**āti*** (acc. f. pl.)	الْمُعَلِمَاتِ

G8

The case endings in the dual and plural:

plural (f.)	plural (m.)	dual (f.)	dual (m.)	
-ā-tu	*-ūna*	*-a-tāni*	*-āni*	nominative
-ā-ti	*-īna*	*-a-tayni*	*-ayni*	genitive
-ā-ti	*-īna*	*-a-tayni*	*-ayni*	accusative

The broken plural has the same case endings as a sound noun in the singular!

G3

Grammar

1 Find the appropriate plural form of the nouns given in the singular: الحَدِيقَةُ (garden), المُشَاهِد (spectator), الجَامِعَة (university). Pay attention to gender and case.

	3		2		1
	(acc. sing. f.) الجَامِعَةَ		(gen. sing. m.) المُشَاهِدِ		(nom. sing. f.) الحَدِيقَةُ
☐	الجَامِعَاتَ A	☐	المُشَاهِدِينُ A	☐	الحَدَائِقِ A
☐	الجَامِعَاتُ B	☐	المُشَاهِدِينَ B	☐	الحَدَائِقَ B
☐	الجَامِعَاتِ C	☐	المُشَاهِدَاتُ C	☐	الحَدَائِقُ C

2 The following nouns are either in the nominative dual (masculine or feminine) or in the genitive dual (masculine or feminine). Put the words in the appropriate column.

الرَّجُلَيْنِ	القَمِيصَانِ	الوَلَدَيْنِ	الشَرِيطَتَانِ	الطَالِبَيْنِ	الكِتَابَانِ	المُعَلِّمَتَيْنِ	الرِسَالَتَانِ
man	shirt	boy	cassette	student	book	teacher	letter
الشُرْطِيَتَيْنِ	المَتْحَفَانِ	المَدِينَتَانِ	المَقْعَدَانِ	الطَالِبَتَيْنِ	المُعَلِّمَيْنِ	النَافِذَتَانِ	الطَبِيبَتَيْنِ
policeman	museum	city	chair	student	teacher	window	doctor

4. genitive dual f.	3. genitive dual m.	2. nominative dual f.	1. nominativd dual m.

3 Fill in the blanks with the correct case of the nouns given in parentheses.

These are (two) women.	(nom. dual) (اِمرَأَةٌ)	هَاتَانِ ____________	1
I saw the teachers.	(acc. pl.) .(المُعَلِّمُ)	رَأَيتُ ____________	2
Malik is a policeman.	(nom. sing.) .(شُرطِي)	مَالِك ____________	3
I was with the teachers (f.).	(gen. pl.) .(المُعَلِّمَةُ)	كُنتُ عِندَ ____________	4
They were with the principal.	(gen. sing.) .(المُدِيرُ)	كَانُوا مَعَ ____________	5
I ate (two) apples.	(acc. dual) .(تُفَاحَةٌ)	أَكَلتُ ____________	6
The editor came.	(nom. pl.) .(المُحَرِّرُ)	جَاءَ ____________	7
That is the (two) girls' room.	(gen. dual) .(البِنتُ)	هَذِهِ غُرفَةُ ____________	8

Grammar

Nouns: Partially Declinable Nouns الإسمُ المَقصُور

Arabic has nouns that can be only partially declined. They can be divided into the following categories:

- Nouns that are declined only in the dual and plural but not in the singular. These include, among others, nouns that end in *alif maqṣūra*.

A7

(a) young man	*fatā*	فَتَى
(a) hospital	*mustashfā*	مُستَشفَى
(a) gate	*marmā*	مَرمَى

Singular:

The hospital is being remodeled.	*juddidal-mustashf**ā**.* (nom. f. sing.)	جُدِّدَ المُستَشفَى.
I went to the hospital.	*dhahabtu 'ilal-mustashf**ā**.* (gen. f. sing.)	ذَهَبتُ إلَى المُستَشفَى.

Dual und plural:

The (two) hospitals are being remodeled.	*juddidal-mustashfay**āni**.* (nom. f. dual)	جُدِّدَ المُستَشفَيَانِ.
I went to the hospitals.	*dhahabtu 'ilal-mustashfay**āti**.* (gen. f. pl.)	ذَهَبتُ إلَى المُستَشفَيَاتِ.

- Nouns that are declined only in the singular and dual but not in the plural.

	nom. plural		nom. dual		nom. singular	
village / villages	*qurā*	قُرَى	*qaryatāni*	قَريَتَانِ	*qaryatun*	قَريَةٌ
occasion(s)	*qaḍāyā*	قَضَايَا	*qaḍiyatāni*	قَضِيَتَانِ	*qaḍiyatun*	قَضِيَةٌ

I came past a village.	*marartu biqarya**tin**.* (gen. f. sing.)	مَرَرتُ بِقَريَةٍ.
I came past villages.	*marartu biqur**ā**.* (gen. f. pl.)	مَرَرتُ بِقُرَى.

- Nouns that in the indefinite state (usually in the plural) are not declined with *tanwin* and have only two case endings. These so-called *al-mamnūʿ minas-ṣarf* المَمنُوع مِنَ الصَرف (diptotes) are declined in the nominative with *ḍamma* ـُ and in both the accusative and the genitive with *fatḥa* ـَ. The genitive ending *kasra* ـِ disappears completely in the indefinite state. In the definite state, the nouns follow the normal rules of declension.

A4
G8

	genitive definite			genitive indefinite	
in the desert	*fis-ṣaḥrā'**i***	فِي الصَحرَاءِ	in (a) desert	*fī ṣaḥrā'**a***	فِي صَحرَاءَ
in the streets	*fish-shawāriʿ**i***	فِي الشَوَارِعِ	in streets	*fī shawāriʿ**a***	فِي شَوَارِعَ

G5
G6

Some other diptotes are:

presidents	*ru'asā'u*	رُؤَسَاءُ
offices	*makātibu*	مَكَاتِبُ
restaurants	*maṭāʿimu*	مَطَاعِمُ

If an adjective accompanies the diptotes, then it is declined in the regular way:

I know beautiful streets.	*'aʿrifu shawāriʿ**a** jamīla**tan**.*	أعرِفُ شَوَارِعَ جَمِيلَةً.
I came past beautiful streets.	*marartu bishawāriʿ**a** jamīla**tin**.*	مَرَرتُ بِشَوَارِعَ جَمِيلَةٍ.

G16

1 Mark the sentence that correctly renders the English sentence.

1 This building is new.

A هَذَا المَبنَى جَدِيدٌ. ☐
B هَذَا المَبنِي جَدِيدٌ. ☐
C هَذَا المَبنَا جَدِيدٌ. ☐

2 We're going to Café Nayib.

A نَذهَبُ إلَى مَقهِي نَجِيب. ☐
B نَذهَبُ إلَى مَقهَى نَجِيب. ☐
C نَذهَبُ إلَى مَقهِيَةِ نَجِيب. ☐

3 He cleans the hospitals.

A هُوَ يُنَظِفُ المُستَشفَياتُ. ☐
B هُوَ يُنَظِفُ المُستَشفَياتِ. ☐
C هُوَ يُنَظِفُ المُستَشفَى. ☐

2 Decline these nouns: الهَدِيَةُ (the gift), القَرِيَةُ (the village), الزَاوِيَةُ (the corner), البَقِيَةُ (the rest, remainder).

acc. pl.	gen. pl.	nom. pl.	acc. dual	genitive dual	nom. dual	acc. sing.	genitive sing.	nom. sing.	
								الهَدِيَةُ	1
								القَرِيَةُ	2
								الزَاوِيَةُ	3
								البَقِيَةُ	4

3 Decide whether the sentences containing diptotes are correct or incorrect.
Pay attention to the case endings.

		incorrect	correct
1	اشتَرَيتُ تَوابِلَ مِنَ السُوقِ. I bought spices in the market.	☐	☒
2	وُزَراءُ مِن أُورُبَا يَجتَمِعُونَ اليَومَ. Ministers from Europe are meeting today.	☐	☐
3	هَذِهِ العِمَارَةُ تَحتَوِي مَكَاتِباً كَثِيرَةً. This building has many offices.	☐	☐
4	الوَزِيرُ يَعرِفُ رُؤَساءَ كُثُر. The minister knows many presidents.	☐	☐
5	هَذَا الفِلفلُ مِنَ الهِند. These peppers are from India.	☐	☐
6	أَكَلُوا فِي مَطاعِمَ عَدِيدَةٍ. They have eaten in many restaurants.	☐	☐

Grammar

Nouns: Nunation تَنوين

A3 The declension of indefinite (indeterminate) nouns is called nunation (*tanwin*). Literally, *tanwin* means
A4 "making an n." It entails adding the final *n* sound of the letter *nūn* ن to the (definite) case endings *-u*
G5 (nominative), *-i* (genitive), and *-a* (accusative). For indefinite nouns, the short vowels *fatḥa* ـً, *kasra* ـٍ, and *ḍamma* ـٌ are doubled above the last letter of the word.

(*tanwin*) *fatḥa* ـً

(*tanwin*) *kasra* ـٍ

(*tanwin*) *ḍamma* ـٌ

The case endings of indefinite nouns in the singular, therefore, are *-un* ـٌ (nom. m.), *-in* ـٍ (gen. m.), and *-an* ـً (acc. m.) or *-a-tun* (nom. f.), *-a-tin* (gen. f.), and *-a-tan* (acc. f.).

(a) student (nom. f.)	*ṭālibat**un***	طَالِبَةٌ
(a) student (acc. f.)	*ṭālibat**an***	طَالِبَةً
(of a student) (gen. f.)	*ṭālibat**in***	طَالِبَةٍ

G6 In the dual and plural, indefinite nouns are declined like definite nouns (dual / plural); that is, they have the same case endings (the feminine plural is an exception).

The case endings of indefinite and definite nouns are as follows:

definite	indefinite			
-u	*-un*	m.	singular	nominative
-a-tu	*-a-tun*	f.		
-āni	*-āni*	m.	dual	
-a-tāni	*-a-tāni*	f.		
-ūna	*-ūna*	m.	plural	
-ā-tu	*-ā-tun*	f.		
-i	*-in*	m.	singular	genitive
-a-ti	*-a-tin*	f.		
-ayni	*-ayni*	m.	dual	
-a-tayni	*-a-tayni*	f.		
-īna	*-īna*	m.	plural	
-ā-ti	*-ā-tin*	f.		
-a	*-an*	m.	singular	accusative
-a-ta	*-a-tan*	f.		
-ayni	*-ayni*	m.	dual	
-a-tayni	*-a-tayni*	f.		
-īna	*-īna*	m.	plural	
-ā-ti	*-ā-tin*	f.		

G3
G4
- Definite nouns always are preceded by the article *al* ال; indefinite nouns do not use an article!
- The broken plural has the same case endings as a sound noun in the singular!
- Proper names are definite, but they usually have the case endings of indefinite nouns and are not preceded by the article *al* ال!

Grammar

1 Listen to the words and decide which *tanwin* they contain.

ـٌ	ـٍ	ـً	
☐	☐	☐	1
☐	☐	☐	2
☐	☐	☐	3
☐	☐	☐	4
☐	☐	☐	5
☐	☐	☐	6
☐	☐	☐	7
☐	☐	☐	8

2 Match the correct ending on the left with the appropriate word on the right. Keep in mind that some words are definite and some are indefinite.

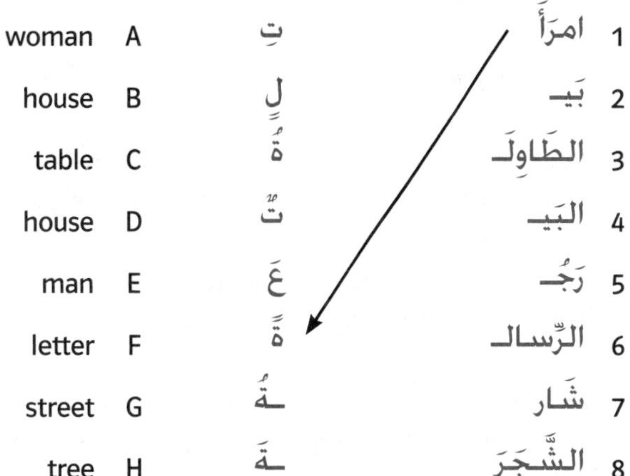

woman	A	تِ	امرَأ	1
house	B	لٍ	بَيـ	2
table	C	ةٍ	الطَاوِلَـ	3
house	D	تٌ	البَيـ	4
man	E	عَ	رَجُـ	5
letter	F	ةً	الرِّسالـ	6
street	G	ـةُ	شَار	7
tree	H	ـةَ	الشَّجَر	8

3 Complete the sentences by putting the nouns given in parentheses in the case required.

Ali ate an apple.	أَكَلَ عَلِيّ __________ (تُفَاحَةٌ). (acc. sing.)	1
They sat under a big tree.	جَلَسْنَ تَحْتَ __________ (شَجَرَةٌ) كَبِيرَةٍ. (gen. sing.)	2
You (two) have read a book.	قَرَأْتُمَا __________ (كِتَابٌ). (acc. sing.)	3
They traveled with friends.	سَافَرُوا مَعَ __________ (أَصدِقَاءُ). (gen. pl.)	4
I saw Ali on a train.	رَأَيتُ عَلِياً فِي __________ (قِطَارٌ). (gen. sing.)	5
We saw lions.	رأَينَا __________ (أُسُودٌ). (acc. pl.)	6

Grammar

Nouns: Genitive Construction الإِضَافَة

Relationships of possession are expressed in Arabic with the genitive construction *idafa*. Literally, *idafa* means "adding." To express ownership or relationship, two or more nouns are placed in succession:

the book of the teacher	*kitābul-muʿalimi*	كِتَابُ الْمُعَلِمِ
the house of the woman	*baytul-mar'ati*	بَيتُ الْمَرأَةِ

Because Arabic, unlike English, has almost no compound nouns (such as wallpaper), such words are also formed by using the genitive construction:

(a) case of books (= bookcase)	*sundoqun lil kutubi* *(= sundoqu kutubin)*	صُندُوقٌ لِلكُتُبِ (= صُندُوقُ كُتُبٍ)
(a) letter of love (= love letter)	*risālatu ḥubbin*	رِسالَةُ حُبٍّ

The following rules apply to the genitive construction:

G5 G8

- The first word of the genitive construction is the control word. It can be in the nominative, genitive, or accusative, depending on whether the genitive expression is the subject or object of the sentence, or on whether it follows a preposition.
- The second word of the genitive construction is the attribute. It is always in the genitive. If the genitive construction consists of more than two words, the other nouns are also in the genitive.

A4 G8

- The control word is always indefinite (that is, it is never preceded by the article *al* ال). However, it is formed without nunation; it does not end in *-n*.
- The attribute can be a definite or indefinite noun. If it is definite, the entire genitive construction is considered to be definite. If it is indefinite, the entire construction is indefinite.

G4 G11

- A definite attribute is a proper name, a noun preceded by the article *al* ال, or a noun to which a pronoun is attached.
- If the definite genitive construction consists of more than two nouns, only the last word uses the article *al* ال. In this case, all the other nouns, including the control word, are considered to be definite, although they do not use the article *al* ال.

a book of a teacher	*kitābu muʿalimin*	كِتَابُ مُعَلِمٍ
the book of a teacher	*kitābul-muʿalimi*	كِتَابُ الْمُعَلِمِ
a book of the teacher	*kitābul-muʿalimi*	كِتَابُ الْمُعَلِمِ
the book of the teacher	*kitābul-muʿalimi*	كِتَابُ الْمُعَلِمِ
a son of the teacher of the language (= language teacher)	*ibnu muʿalimil-luġati*	ابنُ مُعَلِمِ اللُغَةِ
the son of the teacher of the language	*ibnu muʿalimil-luġati*	ابنُ مُعَلِمِ اللُغَةِ
The book of the teacher is new.	*kitābul-muʿalimi jadīdun.*	كِتَابُ الْمُعَلِمِ جَدِيدٌ.
I saw the son of the teacher of the language.	*ra'aytu ibnu muʿalimil-luġati.*	رَأَيتُ ابنَ مُعَلِمِ اللُغَةِ.

1 Form simple *idafa* constructions by writing the correct form of the words in parentheses in the blanks.

1 بَابُ ________ (بَيتٌ)	the door of the house
2 قَلَمُ ________ (طَالِبٌ)	a pen of the student
3 مَحَطَةُ ________ (قِطَارٌ)	a stop of a train
4 غُرفَةُ ________ (نَومٌ)	the room of (the) sleeping
5 مُسَاعِدُ ________ (وَزِيرٌ)	the assistant of a minister
6 ابنُ ________ (سَائِقٌ) السَيَارَةِ	the son of the driver of the car
7 مُوَظَفُ ________ (وَزَارَةٌ) ________ (عَدلٌ)	an employee of the ministry of (the) justice
8 قَرَأتُ ________ (كِتَابٌ) مُدِيرِ ________ (مَعهَدٌ).	I read the book of the principal of the institute.

2 Decide whether the *idafa* constructions are correct or incorrect. Pay attention to the article and the case endings.

	correct	incorrect	
1 البِطَاقَةُ تَهنِئَةٌ	☐	☐	the greeting card
2 فِنجَانُ قَهوَةٍ	☐	☐	a cup of coffee
3 عُلبَةُ سَجَائر	☐	☐	a pack of cigarettes
4 المُعظَم مَقَاعِدٌ	☐	☐	the most seats
5 نَاطِحَاتٌ السَحَابِ	☐	☐	the skyscrapers
6 شَجَرَةً تُفَاحٌ	☐	☐	an apple tree
7 بَائِعُ الأزهَارِ	☐	☐	the flower vendor
8 آخِراً الطَابُورِ	☐	☐	the end of the line

3 What are these words in Arabic? They all form an *idafa* construction.

1 ________________	children's room
2 ________________	white bread
3 ________________	menu / bill of fare

Grammar

G10

Personal Pronouns (Independent) الضمير المُنفَصِل

Arabic distinguishes between two groups of pronouns: independent pronouns (*al-damīr al-munfasil*) and pronouns that are attached as suffixes.
G11

Personal Pronoun as Subject

G1
The independent personal pronouns serve as the subject of the sentence (who? or what?).

"I from Cairo." (= I am from Cairo.)	*'ana minal-qāhirati.*	أنَا مِن القَاهِرَة.
"You (f.) interesting." (= You are interesting.)	*'anti muthīratun lil'ihtimāmi.*	أنتِ مُثِيرَةٌ لِلاِهتِمَام.

			personal pronouns (subject)
I	*'anā*	أنَا	1st person singular
you (m.)	*'anta*	أنتَ	2nd person singular
you (f.)	*'anti*	أنتِ	
he / it	*huwa*	هُوَ	3rd person singular
she / it	*hiya*	هِيَ	
we	*naḥnu*	نَحنُ	1st person plural
you (m./f. dual)	*'antumā*	أنتُمَا	2nd person dual / plural
you (m. pl.)	*'antum*	أنتُم	
you (f. pl.)	*'antunna*	أنتُنَّ	
they (m./.f. dual)	*humā*	هُمَا	3rd person dual / plural
they (m. pl.)	*hum*	هُم	
they (f. pl.)	*hunna*	هُنَّ	

Note that in the 2nd person singular and in the 2nd and 3rd person plural, a distinction is made between masculine and feminine pronouns.

They (m. pl.) are polite.	*hum muhadh-dhabūna.*	هُم مُهَذَّبُونَ.
They (f. pl.) are polite.	*hunna muhadh-dhabātun.*	هُنَّ مُهَذَّبَاتٌ.

When speaking of a mixed group of men and women, you always use the masculine form of the personal pronoun (2nd/3rd person plural). The 3rd person feminine singular is used to speak of animals or things in the plural.

G18–G21
In Arabic, the subject of a sentence usually is indicated in the prefix or suffix of a verb:

(I) Travel to Germany.	***u**sāfiru ilā 'almāniyā.*	أُسافِرُ الى أَلمَانيا.
Why did (you) eat cold food?	*limāthā 'akal**ta** ṭa'āman bāridan?*	لِماذا أَكَلتَ طَعاماً بارداً؟

The independent personal pronouns can be used in addition, in order to emphasize the subject of the action or to contrast it with another subject.

I bought it.	***'ana** ishtaraytuhu.*	أنَا اِشتَرَيتُهُ.

Grammar

1 Which personal pronoun do you use when you …

1. are speaking yourself ________________
2. are talking about an uncle ________________
3. are talking about a girlfriend ________________
4. are talking to two friends (m.) ________________
5. are speaking on behalf of a group ________________
6. are addressing a stranger ________________
7. are talking about friends (m. and f.) ________________
8. are talking about two of your aunts ________________

2 Replace the nouns with the corresponding personal pronouns.

1	(البِنتُ) ____________ جَميلَةٌ.	(The girl) is pretty.
2	(البِنتانِ) ____________ يَدرُسانِ.	(The two girls) are learning.
3	(الرَّجُلُ) ____________ يَسُوقُ سَيّارَةً.	(The man) drives a car.
4	(الرِجالُ) ____________ مُشَوِّقونَ.	(The men) are interesting.
5	(البَقَرَةُ) ____________ سَمينَةٌ.	(The cow) is fat.
6	(الأبقارُ) ____________ كَثيرَةٌ.	(The cows) are numerous (many).
7	(النِّساءُ) ____________ يَحتَفِلنَ.	(The women) are having a party.
8	(البَناتُ وَالبَنينَ) ____________ يلعَبُونَ.	(The boys and girls) are playing.

3 Put these statements in the dual or plural.

1	أَناطَبِيبٌ.	(1st person plural m.) نَحنُ أَطِبّاءُ.	I am a doctor.
2	هِيَ مُعَلِّمَةٌ.	(plural) ________________	She is a teacher.
3	أَنتِ تاجِرَةٌ.	(plural) ________________	You are a businesswoman.
4	هِيَ مُحامِيَّةٌ.	(dual) ________________	She is a lawyer.
5	هُوَ سائِقٌ.	(plural) ________________	He is a driver.
6	أَنتَ شُرطِيٌّ.	(dual) ________________	You are a policeman.
7	أَنا مُهَندِسَةٌ.	(plural) ________________	I am an engineer (f.).
8	هُوَ جُندِيٌّ.	(dual) ________________	He is a soldier.

Personal Pronouns / Possessive Pronouns (Attached) الضَمِير المُتَّصِل

The object forms of the personal pronouns as well as the possessive pronouns (*al-dhamir al-muttaṣil*) are attached as suffixes to elements such as a preposition or a noun.

Personal Pronoun as Object

The personal suffixes represent the object of the sentence (whom or what? to / for whom?):

I'm going to him. *'adhhabu 'ilayhi.* أَذهَبُ إلَيهِ.   I saw him. *ra'aytuhu.* رَأيتُهُ.

						personal pronouns (object suffixes)
he teaches me	*'allamanī*	عَلَّمَنِي	me	*-nī*	نِي	1st pers. sing.
	'allamaka	عَلَّمَكَ	you (m.)	*-ka*	كَ	2nd pers. sing.
	'allamaki	عَلَّمَكِ	you (f.)	*-ki*	كِ	
	'allamahu	عَلَّمَهُ	him / it	*-hu / hi*	ـهُ / هِ	3rd pers. sing.
	'allamahā	عَلَّمَهَا	her / it	*-hā*	هَا	
	'allamanā	عَلَّمَنَا	us	*-nā*	نَا	1st pers. dual / pl.
	*'allama**kumā***	عَلَّمَكُمَا	you (m./f/ dual)	*-kumā*	كُما	2nd pers. dual / pl.
	*'allama**kum***	عَلَّمَكُم	you (m. pl.)	*-kum*	كُم	
	*'allama**kunna***	عَلَّمَكُنَّ	you (f. pl.)	*-kunna*	كُنَّ	
	*'allama**humā***	عَلَّمَهُمَا	them (m./f. dual)	*-humā*	هُمَا	3rd pers. dual / pl.
	*'allama**hum***	عَلَّمَهُم	them (m. pl.)	*-hum*	هُم	
	*'allama**hunna***	عَلَّمَهُنَّ	them (f. pl.)	*-hunna*	هُنَّ	

G5

The 3rd person masculine singular has two different forms for the accusative (*-hu*) and the genitive (*-hi*). All the other suffixes remain the same in the accusative and genitive. For animals or things in the plural, use the personal suffixes for the 3rd person feminine singular.

Possessive Pronouns

The possessive suffixes express possession or ownership (whose?)

I'm reading my book. *'aqra'u kitābī.* أقرَأُ كِتَابِي.

They are attached to the singular, dual, and plural forms of a noun.

						possessive pronouns (suffixes)
my pen	*qalamī*	قَلَمِي	my	*-ī*	ي	1st pers. sing.
	*qalamu**ka***	قَلَمُكَ	your (m. sing.)	*-ka*	كَ	2nd pers. sing.
	*qalamu**ki***	قَلَمُكِ	your (f. sing.)	*-ki*	كِ	
	*qalamu**hu***	قَلَمُهُ	his / its	*-hu / hi*	ـهُ / هِ	3rd pers. sing.
	*qalamu**hā***	قَلَمُهَا	her / its	*-hā*	هَا	
	*qalamu**nā***	قَلَمُنَا	our	*-nā*	نَا	1st pers. dual / pl.
	*qalamu**kumā***	قَلَمُكُمَا	your (m./f. dual)	*-kumā*	كُما	2nd pers. dual / pl.
	*qalamu**kum***	قَلَمُكُم	your (m. pl.)	*-kum*	كُم	
	*qalamu**kunna***	قَلَمُكُنَّ	your (f. pl.)	*-kunna*	كُنَّ	
	*qalamu**humā***	قَلَمُهُمَا	their (m./f. dual)	*-humā*	هُمَا	3rd pers. dual / pl.
	*qalamu**hum***	قَلَمُهُم	their (m. pl.)	*-hum*	هُم	
	*qalamu**hunna***	قَلَمُهُنَّ	their (f. pl.)	*-hunna*	هُنَّ	

Grammar

1 Mark the boxes to indicate which sentences correctly render the English sentence.

3	2	1
I bought them (the books).	He's coming to you (f. pl.).	I see you (m. sing.).
☐ أَنَااشْتَرَيْتُهُنَّ. A	☐ هُوَ يَأْتِيكُم. A	☐ أَنَا أَرَاهُم. A
☐ أَنَااشْتَرَيْتُهُ. B	☐ هُوَ يَأْتِيكُنَّ. B	☐ أَنَا أَرَاكَ. B
☐ أَنَااشْتَرَيْتُهَا. C	☐ هُوَ يَأْتِيكَ. C	☐ أَنَا أَرَاهُ. C

2 Complete the sentences by attaching the personal suffix in the appropriate case. The subject pronouns in the first line tell you which person to use for the object suffix. G10

أَنْتُم	أَنْتُمَا	هُوَ	أَنتِ		
______	______	______	______	أَذْهَبُ إِلَيـ ... I'm going to ...	1
______	______	______	______	لَقِيتُـ ... I met ...	2

3 Rewrite the sentences in the blanks provided, completing them by attaching the appropriate possessive suffix to the second part.

This is my book.	هَذَا كِتَابِي.	هَذَا كِتَابُـ	1
I took your (f. sing.) coat.	______	أَخَذتُ مِعْطَفَـ	2
These are your (m. pl.) rooms.	______	هَذِهِ غُرَفُـ	3
We saw their (dual) children.	______	رَأَيْنَا أَطفالَـ	4
These are our cars.	______	هَذِهِ سَيَارَاتُـ	5
This is his donkey.	______	هَذَا حِمَارُـ	6
They (m. pl.) wrote their letter.	______	كَتَبُوا رِسالَتَـ	7
These are your (dual) shoes.	______	هَذِهِ أَحْذِيَتُـ	8

Grammar

Demonstrative Pronouns أَسْمَاءُ الإِشَارَة

Demonstrative pronouns (*'asmā' al-'ishāra*) are used to indicate persons, animals, or things that are close to or far from the speaker in terms of space and time.

This is Zaid.	*hādhā zaid.*	هَذَا زَيد.
That is Samira.	*tilka samīra.*	تِلْكَ سَمِيرة.

The object can also be abstract:

That is a good idea.	*hādhihi fikratun jayyida.*	هَذِهِ فِكْرَةٌ جَيِّدَة.

hādhā هَذَا and *hādhihi* هَذِهِ

The demonstrative pronouns *hādhā* هَذَا and *hādhihi* هَذِهِ indicate something nearby:

	feminine		masculine		
this, that	*hādhihi*	هَذِهِ	*hādhā*	هَذَا	singular
these (two)	*hātāni*	هَاتَانِ	*hādhāni*	هَذَانِ	dual nominative
(of/to) these (two)	*hātayni*	هَاتَيْنِ	*hādhayni*	هَذَيْنِ	dual genitive/accusative
these	*hā'ulā'i*	هَؤُلاءِ	*hā'ulā'i*	هَؤُلاءِ	plural

G2
G3 In the singular and dual, *hādhā* هَذَا and *hādhihi* هَذِهِ agree with the following noun in gender and number.
G5 In the dual, they also agree with the case of the noun:
G7

This is the language teacher (m.).	*hādhā mudar-risul-luġati.*	هَذا مُدَرِّسُ اللُّغَةِ.
This is the language teacher (f.).	*hādhihi mudar-risatul-luġati.*	هَذِهِ مُدَرِّسَةُ اللُّغَةِ.
I studied with these two women.	*darastu ma'a hātayni al-mar'atayni.*	دَرَسْتُ مَعَ هَاتَيْنِ المَرْأَتَيْنِ.
These men are representatives in Parliament.	*hā'ulā'ir-rijālu 'a'ḍā'un fil-barlamāni.*	هَؤُلاءِ الرِّجَالُ أَعْضَاءٌ فِي البَرْلَمَانِ.
These women are representatives in Parliament.	*hā'ulā'in-nisā'u 'a'ḍā'un fil-barlamāni.*	هَؤُلاءِ النِّسَاءُ أَعْضَاءٌ فِي البَرْلَمَانِ.

dhālika ذَلِكَ and *tilka* تِلْكَ

The demonstrative pronouns *dhālika* ذَلِكَ and *tilka* تِلْكَ indicate something far away. They agree in gender only in the singular:

	feminine		masculine		
that	*tilka*	تِلْكَ	*dhālika*	ذَلِكَ	singular
those	*'ula'ika*	أولَئِكَ	*'ula'ika*	أولَئِكَ	plural

That man is interesting.	*dhālikar-rajulu muthīrun lil'ihtimāmi.*	ذَلِكَ الرَّجُلُ مُثِيرٌ لِلاهتِمَام.
That woman is interesting.	*tilkal-mar'atu muthīratun lil'ihtimāmi.*	تِلْكَ المَرْأَةُ مُثِيرَةٌ لِلاهتِمَام.

With demonstrative pronouns, no distinction is made between genders in the plural. The plural forms refer only to persons. To indicate several animals or things, you must use *hādhihi* هَذِهِ (feminine singular) or *tilka* تِلْكَ (feminine singular):

These are my cows.	*hādhihi 'abqārī.*	هَذِهِ أَبقَارِي.
Those flowers are very pretty.	*tilka 'azhārun jamīlatun jiddan.*	تِلْكَ الأَزهَارُ جَمِيلَةٌ جِداً.

1 Complete the sentences with هَـذَا or هَـذِهِ. The nouns are names.

1 ______ حَلِيْمَةٌ.

2 ______ هالة.

3 ______ عليٌّ.

4 ______ مُحَمدٌ.

5 ______ حسنٌ.

6 ______ خديجةٌ.

7 ______ رملةٌ.

8 ______ مُخْتَارٌ.

2 Underline the demonstrative pronouns in the sentences.

1 هَاتَانِ تَعمَلانِ مَعِي.	These (two) work with me.
2 هَذِهِ البِنتُ ذَكِيَّةٌ.	This girl is smart.
3 لاأَعرِفُ أُولئِكَ الرِجَالِ.	I don't know those men.
4 يَذهَبُ إِلَى المَدْرَسَةِ مَعَ هَذَينِ الوَلَدَينِ.	He goes to school with these (two) boys.
5 هَذا وَالِدِي.	This is my father.
6 سَافَرتُ مَعَ هَاتَينِ المَرأَتَينِ.	I traveled with these (two) women.
7 الكُتُبُ مَعَ تِلكَ الطَالِبَةِ.	The books are with that student (f.).

3 Decide whether the sentences are correct or incorrect, and then make the needed corrections.

	correct	incorrect		
1 هَؤلاءِ أصدِقَائِي.	☐	☐	______	These are my friends.
2 اشتَرَيتُ هَذَانِ المِعطَفَ الجَمِيلَ.	☐	☐	______ ______	I bought this pretty coat.
3 هَذَا مُحَرِرَةٌ.	☐	☐	______	This is an editor (f.).
4 أولئِكَ أَبقَارِي.	☐	☐	______	Those are my cows.
5 اِشتَغَلَتْ مَعَ أولئِكَ الرِّجَالِ.	☐	☐	______ ______	She worked with these men.
6 لايَعرِفُون هَاتَينِ اللُّغَتَينِ.	☐	☐	______ ______	They don't speak these two languages.
7 تِلكَ شَجَرَةٌ.	☐	☐	______	That is a tree.
8 شَرِبتُم بِتِلكَ الأكوَابِ.	☐	☐	______ ______	You drank out of those cups.

Relative Pronouns الأَسـمَاءُ المَوصُولَة

Relative pronouns link a dependent (subordinate) clause to a main clause. They refer to a noun or a nominal group in the main clause. The antecedent can be the subject or object of the main clause.

The woman who wanted to talk to you has come.	*yā'atil-mar'atu al-latī 'arādat 'an tataḥadatha ma'aka.*	جَاءَت المَرأَةُ التِي أرادَتْ أن تَتَحدث مَعَكَ.
I saw the woman who tried to call you.	*ra'aytul-mar'ata al-latī ḥāwalat 'an tat-taṣila bika.*	رَأيتُ المَرأَةَ التِي حَاوَلَتْ أن تَتَّصِلَ بِكَ.

al-ladhī الَّذِي and *al-latī* الَّتِي

G4 *al-ladhī* الَّذِي (who, that, which m.) and *al-latī* الَّتِي (who, that, which f.) always refer to definite (determinate) nouns.

		feminine		masculine	
who / that / which (nom.) whose / of that / of which (gen.) whom / that / which (acc.)	*al-latī*	الَّتِي	*al-ladhī*	الَّذِي	singular
who / that / which	*al-latāni*	اللَّتَانِ	*al-ladhāni*	اللَّذَانِ	dual (nom.)
whose / of those / of which (gen.) whom / those / which (acc.)	*al-latayni*	اللَّتَينِ	*al-ladhayni*	اللَّذَينِ	dual (gen./ acc.)
who / that / which (nom.) whose / of those / of which (gen.) whom / those / which (acc.)	*al-lātī /* *al-lawātī*	اللاَّتِي / اللَّوَاتِي	*al-ladhīna*	الَّذِينَ	plural

G2 G3 G5 G7

The relative pronouns agree with the antecedent in gender and number, and in the dual they also agree in case:

the student who comes from Syria	*at-ṭālibul-ladhī jā'a min sūriyā*	الطَّالِبُ الذِي جَاءَ مِنْ سُورِيَا
the students who come from Syria	*at-ṭalabatul-ladhīna jā'ū min sūriyā*	الطَّلَبَةُ الذِينَ جَاؤُوا مِنْ سُورِيَا
with the two students who come from Syria	*'indat-ṭālibataynil-latayni jā'atā min sūriyā*	عِندَ الطَّالِبَتَينِ اللَّتَينِ جَاءتَا مِنْ سُورِيَا

G11 If the antecedent is not the subject but rather the object of the main clause, in the dependent clause a personal pronoun (suffix) must be attached to the verb or, as in the following example, to the preposition:

This is the car of the man whom we are seeking.	*hādhihī sayāratur-rajuli al-ladhī nabḥathu 'an**hu**.*	هَذِهِ سَيَارَةُ الرَّجُلِ الذِي نَبحَثُ عَنهُ.

G8 If the relative pronoun refers to an indefinite subject or object, it is omitted altogether. The suffix ending, which indicates the object of the main clause, is retained, however:

A woman, (who) wanted to talk to you, has come.	*yā'at imra'atun 'arādat 'an tataḥadatha ma'aka.*	جَاءَت اِمرأةٌ أرادَتْ أن تَتَحدَّثَ مَعَكَ.
I saw a woman, (who) tried to call you.	*ra'aytu mar'atan ḥāwalat 'an tataṣila bika.*	رَأيتُ اِمرأةً حَاوَلَتْ أن تَتَّصِلَ بِكَ.

In the plural, *al-ladhīna* الَّذِينَ and *al-lātī / al-lawātī* اللاَّتِي / اللَّوَاتِي refer only to persons. If the relative pronoun refers to several animals or things, *al-latī* الَّتِي (feminine singular) is used.

1 Complete the sentences by adding the appropriate relative pronoun.

The student for whom you waited has come.	1 جَاءَ الطَّالِبُ ________ كُنتَ تنتظِرُهُ.
I met the woman about whom you were asking me.	2 لَقِيتُ المَرأَةَ ________ سَأَلتَنِي عَنهَا.
These are the (two) men whom we visited.	3 هَذَانِ هُمَا الرَّجُلَانِ ________ زُرنَاهُمَا.
I was with the (two) students who studied with us.	4 كُنتُ مَعَ الطَّالِبَينِ ________ دَرَسَامَعَنَا.
They took the newspapers that I bought.	5 أَخَذُوا الجَرائِدَ ________ اشتَرَيتُهَا.
These are the (two) books that I borrowed.	6 هَذَانِ هُمَا الكِتَابَانِ ________ استَعَرتُهُمَا.
These are the women who came from Syria.	7 هَؤُلاءِ هُمُ النِّسَاءُ ________ جِئنَ مِن سُورِيَا.

2 Decide whether the sentences are correct or incorrect.

	incorrect	correct	
This is the car that I bought.	☐	☐	1 هَذِهِ هِيَ السَّيَارَةُ الذِي اشتَرَيتُهَا.
A man who wanted to speak with you has come.	☐	☐	2 جَاءَ رَجُلُ الذِي يُرِيدُ أَن يَتَحَدَّثَ مَعَكَ.
The guest who was with us has left.	☐	☐	3 سَافَرَ الضَّيفُ الذِي كَانَ مَعَنَا.
These are the dresses that I bought.	☐	☐	4 هَذِهِ هِيَ المَلَابِس التِي اشتَرَيتُهَا.
I saw a woman who tried to call you.	☐	☐	5 رَأَيتُ اِمرَأَةً التِي حَاوَلَت أَن تَتَّصِلَ بِكَ.
This is the article, which I wrote.	☐	☐	6 هَذَا هُوَ المَقَال اللذَانِ كَتَبتُهُ.

3 Read the sentences carefully, paying attention to the gender, number, and case of the antecedent and the relative pronoun. Change the antecedent and pronoun to the dual, and write both in the blank.

the men whom we met	________________	1 الرِّجَالُ الذِينَ لَقِينَاهُم
with the student who was with you	________________	2 مَعَ الطَّالِبِ الذِي كَانَ مَعَكَ.
the woman who bought the vegetables	________________	3 المَرأَةُ التِي كَانَت تَبِيعُ الخُضرَوَات
the students who came from Syria	________________	4 الطَّلَبَةَ الذِينَ جَاؤُوا مِن سُورِيَا
the friend (m.) who visited me	________________	5 الصَّدِيقُ الذِي زَارَنِي
under the tree, which I planted	________________	6 تَحتَ الشَّجَرَةِ التِي زَرَعتُهَا

Grammar

Interrogative Pronouns أَدواتُ الإِسْتِفهَام

G1 The rules for forming a question in Arabic are simple. In general, interrogative pronouns and question words
G15 (*adawātu 'istifhāmin*) are placed in front of a statement (or a single word). The sentence structure is not
G18 changed. Some pronouns and question words precede only nouns, others only verbs. Then there are others
that can be used in connection with nouns as well as verbs.

man مَنْ, *mādhā* مَاذَا and *mā* مَا

The interrogative pronouns *man* مَنْ (who? whom? to / for whom?) and *mādhā* مَاذَا (what?) can be the subject and object of a question. *man* مَنْ is used with nouns and verbs, whereas *mādhā* مَاذَا is used primarily with verbs. The interrogative pronoun *mā* مَا (what?) is usually the subject of a question and precedes nouns.

Who are you (m.)?	*man 'anta?*	مَنْ أنتَ؟	subject
What has happened?	*madhā ḥadatha?*	مَاذَا حَدَثَ؟	
What (is your (m.)) name?	*masmuka?*	مَا اسمُكَ؟	
Whom did you (pl.) meet?	*manil-taqajtum?*	مَنِ الْتَقَيتُم؟	object
To whom did you (sing.) give the book?	*man 'aʿṭajtal-kitāba?*	مَنْ أعطَيتَ الكِتَابَ؟	
What did they eat?	*mādhā 'akalū?*	مَاذَا أكَلُوا؟	

All the pronouns are invariable; that is, they do not change their gender, number, and case. Only *man* مَنْ
A3 changes its form when it precedes a consonant cluster. Because the pronoun ends in *sukūn* ـْ, *kasra* ـِ is
A4 inserted as an auxiliary vowel:

Who is speaking?	*manil-mutakalim?*	مَنِ المُتَكَلِم؟

man مَنْ is also used to ask about relationships of possession (whose?). In this case, however, it generally follows
the object of the sentence. If *man* مَنْ continues to introduce the question, it is linked with the prepositional
G26 particle *li* لِ (for) to become *liman* لِمَنْ :

Whose car is this?	*liman hādhis-sayyāratu?*	لِمَنْ هَذِهِ السَّيَارَةُ؟
Whose car is this?	*sayyāratu man hādhihi?*	سَيَارَةُ مَنْ هَذِهِ؟

'ayyu أَيُّ and *'ayyatu* أَيَّةُ

G2 *'ayyu* أَيُّ (which?) and the feminine form *'ayyatu* أَيَّةُ (which?) always refer to nouns and can be the subject and
G5 object of a question. The pronoun not only changes its form according to gender but also must agree in case
G6 (for example, it is in the genitive after prepositions):

Which cake did they eat?	*'ayyu kaʿkin 'akalū?*	أيُّ كَعكٍ أكَلُوا؟
Which newspaper did you read?	*'ayyatu majallatin qar'ata?*	أيَّةُ مَجَلَّةٍ قَرَأتَ؟
From which country does he come?	*min 'ayyi baladin huwa?*	مِنْ أيِّ بَلَدٍ هُوَ؟

1 Complete the questions, using the interrogative pronouns مَنْ, مَاذَا or مَا .

... did you give the pen?	أعطَيتَ القَلَمَ؟ ______	1
... color is it?	لَونُهُ؟ ______	2
... did you make?	فَعَلتَ؟ ______	3
... did she say?	قَالَتْ؟ ______	4
... is her name?	اسمُهَا؟ ______	5
... are they?	هُمْ؟ ______	6
... is speaking?	المُتَكَلِم؟ ______	7
... did you see?	رَأَيتُم؟ ______	8
... is the meaning of it?	مَعنَى هَذَا؟ ______	9

2 Put the words in the right order, so that they form complete questions.

1 قَالَ / هَذَا / مَنْ؟

______

2 أَكَلتُم / مَاذَا؟

______

3 هُوَ / مَا / عِنوَانُك؟

______

4 لِمَن / الكِتَاب / هَذَا؟

______

5 تَقصُدُ / طَالِبَةٍ / أَيَّةُ؟

______

6 مِن / دُكَانٍ / أَيِّ / اشتَرَيتَه؟

______

3 Match the English translation with the questions.

1 Which tree?	A لِمَنْ هَذَا البَيت؟
2 Whose bag is that?	B مَا هِيَ جِنسِيَّتُك؟
3 Whose house is that?	C مَاذَا طَلَبتَ؟
4 From which city?	D حَقِيبَةُ مَنْ هَذِهِ؟
5 What did you order?	E أَيَّةُ شَجَرَةٍ؟
6 What is your nationality?	F مِنْ أَيِّ مَدِينَةٍ؟

Question Words الإِسْتِفْهَام أَدَواتُ

kayfa كَيفَ

A3

The question word *kayfa* كَيفَ (how?) is placed at the beginning of the sentence, and the actual sentence structure remains unchanged. *kayfa* كَيفَ is invariable and always ends in *fatha* ـَ. It precedes nouns or verbs.

How are you?	*kayfa ḥāluka?*	كَيفَ حَالُكَ؟
How was the food?	*kayfa kānat-ṭaʿāmu?*	كَيفَ كَانَ الطَّعَامُ؟
How did you come to the United States?	*kayfa waṣ alta ʾilā ʾalwilāiāti ʾal muttahidati?*	كَيفَ وَصَلتَ إِلَى الوِلايَاتِ المُتَّحِدَةِ؟

kam كَمْ

G3 G6 G8

kam كَمْ (how much?) itself is invariable. Depending on the context, however, the number, state, and case of the following noun change. If *kam* كَمْ is used in the sense of "how much?" it is followed by an indefinite (indeterminate) noun in the accusative singular (masculine or feminine). If the question word means "how much is?" then a definite (determinate) noun in the nominative is placed after it:

How many books do you have?	*kam kitāban ʿindaka?*	كَمْ كِتَاباً عِندَ كَ؟
"How much is your age?" (= How old are you?)	*kam ʿumruka?*	كَمْ عُمرُكَ؟

limādhā لِمَاذا

G14 G26

The question word *limādhā* لِمَاذا (why? for what?) is made up of the prepositional particle *li* لِ (for) and the interrogative pronoun *mādhā* مَاذَا (what?). It is invariable.

Why is the teacher (too) late?	*limādhā ta'akharal-muʿalimu?*	لِمَاذا تَأخَرَ المُعَلِمُ؟
Why are they on strike?	*limādhā yataẓāharūna?*	لِمَاذا يَتَظَاهَرُونَ؟

'ayna أَينَ and *matā* مَتَى

A6

'ayna أَينَ (where?) and *matā* مَتَى (when?) precede nouns or verbs and are invariable, even if they follow a preposition. Note that *matā* مَتَى ends in *alif maqṣūra*.

Where is my blue shirt?	*'ayna qamīṣī 'al-'azraq?*	أَينَ قَمِيصي الأزرق؟
"From where you?" (= Where are you from?)	*min 'ayna 'anta?*	مِنْ أَينَ أنتَ؟
When should we meet?	*matā naltaqī?*	مَتَى نَلتَقِي؟
From when until when?	*min matā 'ilā matā?*	مِنْ مَتَى إلَى مَتَى؟

hal هَلْ and *'a* أ

hal هَلْ and *'a* أ introduce questions that are answered with yes or no. *'a* أ never precedes nouns that carry the definite article *al* ال.

Have you cooked the meal?	*hal ṭabakhtat-ṭaʿāma?*	هَلْ طَبختَ الطَعَامَ؟
Yes, I have cooked it.	*naʿam, ṭabakhtuhu.*	نَعَم، طَبَختُهُ.
Is this Hala?	*'ahādhihi hāla?*	أَهَذِهِ هَالَة؟
No, this is Warda.	*lā, hādhihi warda.*	لا، هَذِهِ وَردة.

1 Complete the questions by using the question words أَينَ , لِمَاذَا , كَمْ , كَيفَ or مَتَى.

... is the weather in the United States?	الجَوُّ فِي الولايَاتِ المُتَّحِدَةِ؟ ________	1
... does this coat cost?	قِيمَةُ هَذَا المِعطَفِ؟ ________	2
... are they late?	تَأَخَّرُوا؟ ________	3
... do you feel this morning?	أَصبَحتَ؟ ________	4
... weren't you in school?	غِبتَ عَنِ المَدرَسَةِ؟ ________	5
... is the ticket window?	مَكتَبُ التَذاكِرِ؟ ________	6
... and ... does the train leave?	يُغَادِرُ القِطَارُ؟ ________ ومِن ________	7
... did you come back?	رَجَعتَ؟ ________	8

2 Write appropriate questions for the answers given below.

I buy many books because reading is my hobby.	أشتَرِي كُتُباً كَثِيرَةً لأنَّ القِرَاءَةَ هِوَايَتِي.	؟ ________	1
We can meet at six o'clock.	يُمكِنُ أن نَلتَقِيَ فِي السّاعَةِ السّادِسَةِ.	؟ ________	2
Maybe we'll meet at the train station.	يُمكِنُ أن نَلتَقِيَ فِي مَحَطَةِ القِطَارِ.	؟ ________	3
Now it is nine o'clock.	السَاعَةُ الآن التَّاسِعَةَ صَبَاحاً.	؟ ________	4
At six, at the entrance.	فِي السَّاعَةِ السّادِسة, أَمَامَ المَدخَلِ.	؟ ________	5
Yes, I come from the United States. And you?	نَعَم, أنا مِن الولايَاتِ المُتَّحِدَةِ. وأَنتَ؟	؟ ________	6
I live in Chicago.	أنا أعِيشُ فِي شِيكَاغُو.	؟ ________	7
Yes, this is my sister.	نَعَم, هَذِهِ أُختِي.	؟ ________	8

3 Match the English translation with the questions.

1 From when until when?	مَتَى يُغَادِرُ القِطَارُ؟ A
2 When did you go away on a trip?	مَتَى نَلتَقِي؟ B
3 When should we meet?	مِنْ مَتَى إِلَى مَتَى؟ C
4 When will the strike be over?	مَتَى سَافَرتَ؟ D
5 When does the train leave?	مَتَى يَصِلُ البَاصُ؟ E
6 When does the bus arrive?	مَتَى تَنتَهِي المُظَاهَرَاتُ؟ F

Grammar

Adjectives صِفَات

Adjectives give additional information about persons or things. An adjective can be an attribute or a predicate.
G1 As an attribute it describes a noun; as a predicate it describes the subject of a nominal sentence. Unlike English, Arabic always places adjectives after the noun they modify.

"Car old" (= old car) (attribute)	*sayāratun qadīmatun*	سَيَارَةٌ قَدِيمَةٌ
The car (is) old. (predicate)	*hādhihis-sayāratu qadīmatun.*	هَذِهِ السَّيَارَةُ قَدِيمَةٌ.
This one (is) old. (predicate)	*hādhā qadīmun.*	هَذَا قَدِيمٌ.

Adjectives (attributes and predicates) agree in gender and number with the noun (or the subject of a nominal sentence):

(an) industrious student (m.)	*ṭālibun mujtahidun*	طَالِبٌ مُجتَهِدٌ
(an) industrious student (f.)	*ṭālibatun mujtahidatun*	طَالِبَةٌ مُجتَهِدَةٌ
industrious students (m.)	*ṭalabatun mujtahidūna*	طَلَبَةٌ مُجتَهِدُونَ
industrious students (f.)	*ṭālibātun mujtahidātun*	طَالِبَاتٌ مُجتَهِدَاتٌ

Nouns that denote things—that is, not persons or animals—are an exception. The adjectives that modify these nouns are in the feminine singular, regardless of the gender or number:

old books (m. pl.)	*kutubun qadīmatun*	كُتُبٌ قَدِيمَةٌ
old houses (f. pl.)	*buyūtun qadīmatun*	بُيُوتٌ قَدِيمَةٌ

Adjectives that function as attributes also agree with the noun in state (definite / indefinite) and case:

(a) pretty woman	*'imra'atun jamīlatun*	اِمرَأَةٌ جَمِيلَةٌ
the pretty woman	*al-mar'atul-jamilatu*	المَرأَةُ الجَمِيلَةُ
of the pretty woman (gen.)	*'indal-mar'atil-jamīlati*	عِندَ المَرأَةِ الجَمِيلَةِ

If an adjective follows a noun that is not declinable in the singular or in the plural, the adjectives nevertheless
G7 take the appropriate case ending:

the nice young man	*al-fatal-laṭīfu (nom. m. sing.)*	الفَتَى اللَطِيفُ
with the nice young man	*'indal-fatal-laṭīfi (gen. m. sing.)*	عِندَالفَتَى اللَطِيفِ
the two nice young men	*al-fatayāni al-laṭīfāni (nom. m. dual)*	الفَتَيَانِ اللَطِيفَانِ
with the nice young men	*'indal-fityāni al-laṭīfīna (gen. m. pl.)*	عِندَ الفِتيَانِ اللَطِيفِينَ

G2
G3
G5
G6

The gender, number, and case endings of adjectives are formed like the endings of nouns.

1 Match the adjectives with the nouns. The gender of the adjectives must agree with the gender of the nouns.

طَوِيلٌ	كَبِيرَةٌ	جَدِيدَةٌ	ذَكِيٌّ	ثَرْثَارَةٌ	حَارٌّ

1	هُوَ رَجُلٌ ________.	He is a … man.
2	هَذِهِ مَدِينَةٌ ________.	This is a … city.
3	هُوَ طَالِبٌ ________.	He is a … student.
4	هَذِهِ سَيَّارَةٌ ________.	This is a … car.
5	هِيَ بِنْتٌ ________.	She is a … girl.
6	الطَّقْسُ ________.	The weather is …

2 Listen to the sentences, and add the appropriate adjective at the right spot. Note that the order of the sentences on the CD does not match the order given here.

22

كَبِيرَةٌ	جَمِيلَةٌ	شَاهِقٌ	سَرِيعٌ	لَذِيذٌ	دِرَاسِيَّةٌ	بَيْضَاءُ	صَغِيرَةٌ

1	كَنْزَةٌ ________	a white sweater
2	غُرْفَةٌ ________	mall room
3	طَعَامٌ ________	asty food
4	حَقِيبَةٌ ________	a big bag
5	مِنْحَةٌ ________	cholarship
6	قِطَارٌ ________	a fast train
7	مَلَابِسُ ________	tty dresses
8	جَبَلٌ ________	n mountain

3 … rrect.

			incorrect	correct
1	صُورَةٌ جَمِيلَةٌ	a pretty picture	☐	☐
2	رَجُلٌ الْوَسِيمَ	od-looking man	☐	☐
3	الْفَتَاةُ مِصْرِيَّةٌ	an Egyptian girl	☐	☐
4	شَارِعٌ نَظِيفٌ	a clean street	☐	☐
5	السَّاعَةُ الذَّهَبِيَّةِ	the gold watch	☐	☐
6	أَرْضٌ زِرَاعِيَّةٌ	arable land	☐	☐
7	مُصَوِّرٌ صُحُفِيٌّ	ess photographer	☐	☐
8	قُمَاشٌ مُلَوَّنٌ	colored fabric	☐	☐

Grammar

Adjectives: Comparison اسمُ التَفضِيل

To compare the attributes of two or more nouns, you use the comparative or superlative degree of the adjectives (*ismu tafḍil*). In Arabic, the comparative and superlative are formed according to the patterns *'af'ala* أفعَل and
G30 *fu'lā* فُعلَى. These models follow the word formation rules based on the word stems.

Comparative

The comparative is invariable. It keeps the same form, regardless of gender, number, or case:

		comparative			adjective
bigger	*'akbaru*	أكبَرُ	big (m./f.)	*kabīrun / ~atun*	كَبيرٌ / كَبيرَة
smaller	*'aṣġaru*	أصغَرُ	small (m./f.)	*ṣaġīrun / ~atun*	صَغيرٌ / صَغيرَة
prettier	*'ajmalu*	أجمَلُ	pretty (m./f.)	*jamīlun / ~atun*	جَميلٌ / جَميلَة
uglier	*'aqbaḥu*	أقبَحُ	ugly (m./f.)	*qabīḥun / ~atun*	قَبيحٌ / قَبيحَة
longer	*'aṭwalu*	أطوَلُ	long (m./f.)	*ṭawīlun / ~atun*	طَويلٌ / طَويلَة
shorter	*'aqṣaru*	أقصَرُ	short (m./f.)	*qaṣīrun / ~atun*	قَصيرٌ / قَصيرَة
younger	*'aqdamu*	أقدَمُ	old (m./f.)	*qadīmun / ~atun*	قَديمٌ / قَديمَة

G27 As a comparison word, the preposition *min* مِنْ (than, as) follows the comparative:

Ali is bigger than Omar. *'aliyun 'akbaru min 'omar.* عَلِيٌّ أكبَرُ مِنْ عُمَر.

Superlative

Arabic has no morphologically distinct form for the superlative, which is formed by adding the definite article *al* ال to the comparative form of the adjective. The superlative is dependent on gender. The feminine form follows the model *fu'lā* فُعلَى:

		superlative			adjective
the biggest	*al-'akbar* (m.) / *al-kubrā* (f.)	الأكبَر / الكُبرَى	big (m./f.)	*kabīrun / ~atun*	كَبيرٌ / كَبيرَة
the smallest	*al-'aṣġar* (m.) / *as-ṣuġrā* (f.)	الأصغَر / الصُغرَى	small (m./f.)	*ṣaġīrun / ~atun*	صَغيرٌ / صَغيرَة

"Ali the biggest." (= Ali is the biggest.) *'aliyun al-'akbar.* عَلِي الأكبَر.

Kadija is the smallest. *khadīdyatun al-ṣuġrā.* خَديجَة الصُغرَى.

G9
G27 If the superlative is formed with the preposition *fī* فِي (in), it becomes part of a genitive construction (*idafa*) in combination with the noun. In this case, the superlative (masculine and feminine) is in the comparative form *'af'ala* (without *al* ال):

Atlanta International Airport is the biggest airport in the U.S. *maṭāru 'atlantā 'al duwali 'akbaru maṭārin fī 'alwilāiāti 'al muttahidati.* مَطَارُ أطلَنطا الدُوَلِي أكبَرُ مَطارٍ فِي الولايَاتِ المُتّحِدَة.

She is the oldest in the (school) class. *hiya 'akbaru ṭālibatin fis-ṣaffī.* هَيَ أكبَرُ طَالِبَةٍ فِي الصَفّ.

G26

To make a comparison of equality involving an attribute of two or more nouns, use the preposition *ka* كَ (as).

My car is as pretty as yours. *sayyāratuka jamīlatun kasayyāratī.* سَيارَتُكَ جَميلَةٌ كَسَيارَتي.

1 From the options provided, pick out the comparative and use it to complete the sentences.

1 هَذِهِ السَّيَارَةُ ______________ مِنْ تِلْكَ. A رَخِيصَةٌ B الرَّخِيصَةُ C أَرْخَصُ

This car is cheaper than that one.

2 هَذَا الطَّالِبُ ______________ مِنْ ذَاكَ. A أَذْكَى B ذَكِيٌّ C ذَكِيَّةٌ

This student is smarter than that one.

3 تِلْكَ الزَّهْرَةُ ______________ مِنْ هَذِهِ. A أَجْمَلُ B جَمِيلٌ C جَمِيلاً

The flower is prettier than that one.

4 هَذَا المَبْنَى ______________ مِنْ ذَاكَ. A الكَبِيرُ B أَكْبَرُ C الكَبِيرَةُ

This building is bigger than that one.

5 هَذَا القَمِيصُ ______________ مِنْ ذَاكَ. A أَبْيَضٌ B الأَبْيَضُ C أَبْيَضُ

This shirt is whiter than that one.

6 هَذِهِ الكُتُبُ ______________ مِنْ تِلْكَ. A ثَقِيلَةٌ B أَثْقَلُ C الثَّقِيلَةُ

These books are heavier than those.

2 Complete the sentences by using the comparative forms of the adjectives given in parentheses.

1 جَامِعَةُ الأَزْهَرِ ______________ (قَدِيمٌ) مِنْ جَامِعَةِ القَاهِرَةِ.
Al-Azhar University is older than the University of Cairo.

2 مَطَارُ دُبَي ______________ (حَدِيثٌ) مِنْ مَطَارِ الكُوَيت.
The airport of Dubai is more modern than the airport of Kuwait.

3 القِطَارُ ______________ (سَرِيعٌ) مِنَ السَيَارَةِ.
The train is faster than the car.

4 جَمَالٌ ______________ (طَوِيلٌ) مِنْ يُوسُفَ.
Jamal is bigger than Yussuf.

5 أَظُنُّ أَنَّ مَدِينَة كَيب ______________ (جَمِيلٌ) من جُوهَنِسبَارغ.
I think that Cape Town is prettier than Johannesburg.

6 النَّمْلَةُ ______________ (صَغِيرٌ) مِنَ العَنكَبُوتِ.
The ant is smaller than the spider.

3 Using the adjectives given, form the appropriate superlatives and fill in the blanks.

قَدِيمٌ	رَخِيصٌ	عَالٍ	حَسَنٌ	كَبِيرٌ	ذَكِيٌّ
old	cheap	high	good	big	smart

1 عَلِيٌّ ______________ طَالِبٍ فِي الصَّفِّ.
Ali is the smartest student in the class.

2 رُومَا ______________ مَدِينَةٍ فِي إِيطَالِيَا.
Rome is the oldest city in Italy.

3 مَطْعَمُ زَيدٍ ______________ المَطَاعِمِ فِي المَدِينَةِ.
Zaid's restaurant is the best restaurant in town.

4 كِلِمَنجَارُو ______________ جَبَلٍ فِي إِفرِيقِيَا.
Kilimanjaro is the highest mountain in Africa.

5 الخُبزُ ______________ طَعَامٍ فِي مِصر.
Bread is the cheapest food in Egypt.

6 مَطَارُ أَطلَنطَا الدُوَلِي ______________ مَطَارٍ فِي الوِلايَاتِ المُتَّحِدَةِ.
Atlanta International Airport is the biggest airport in the U.S.

Verbal Sentence الجُملةُ الفعلِية

G11 A verbal sentence is one in which the predicate is a verb. If the verb is intransitive (that is, requires no object),
G19 the sentence has this structure: predicate (verb) – subject (noun or pronoun). If the verb is transitive, the
G21 sentence structure is as follows: predicate (verb) – subject (noun or pronoun) – object (noun or pronoun).
Note that a verbal sentence often requires no independently (separately) expressed subject. The subject is expressed in the prefix or suffix of the conjugated verb.

Verbal Sentence with Intransitive Verb and Subject as Part of the Conjugated Verb Ending

To make Arabic sentence construction clear, the first example is always translated literally in the material below. The other examples are rendered in terms of their general sense.

"Traveled." (= I traveled.)	*sāfar**tu**.*	سَافَرتُ.
You (m. sing.) slept.	*nim**ta**.*	نِمتَ.
You (m. pl.) were successful.	*najaḥ**tum**.*	نَجَحتُم.

G25 An adverbial or prepositional phrase can be added to these simple verbal sentences:
G27

"Traveled to India."	*sāfartu 'ial-hind.*	سَافَرتُ إلَى الهِند.
You slept sitting up.	*nimta jālisan.*	نِمتَ جَالِساً.
You were successful in the project.	*najaḥtum fil-mashru'i.*	نَجَحتُم فِي المَشرُوع.

Verbal Sentence with Intransitive Verb and Independent Subject (Noun)

"Slept the baby."	*nāmat-ṭiflu.*	نَامَ الطِّفلُ.
The girl was successful.	*najaḥatil-bintu.*	نَجَحَتِ البِنتُ.
The dog barked.	*nabaḥal-kalbu.*	نَبَحَ الكَلبُ.

Verbal Sentence with Transitive Verb, Subject, and Direct Object

"Boarded the passengers the airplane."	*rakibal-musāfirūna at-ṭā'irata.*	رَكِبَ المُسَافِرُونَ الطَّائِرَةَ.
I read the book.	*qar'atu kitāban.*	قَرَأتُ كِتَاباً.
You bought a shirt.	*ishtarayta qamīṣan.*	اِشتَرَيتَ قَمِيصاً.

Verbal Sentence as Interrogative Sentence

G1 As in the case of the nominal sentence, a question word (such as *hal* هَلْ or *'a* أ) can be placed in front of the
G15 verbal sentence to form an interrogative. The sentence structure is retained in questions as well:

"Did sleep?" (= Did you sleep?)	*hal nimta?*	هَلْ نِمتَ؟
Were you (m. pl.) successful in the project?	*hal najaḥtum fil-mashrū'i?*	هَلْ نَجَحتُم فِي المَشرُوعِ؟
Has the baby slept?	*'anāmat-ṭiflu?*	أنَامَ الطِّفلُ؟

G10 Verbal sentences have this structure: predicate – subject (with intransitive verbs) or predicate – object (with transitive verbs). The subject is expressed by the conjugated verb ending. In questions, a question word is placed in front of the verbal sentence. The sentence structure remains unchanged.

1 Form simple sentences by attaching the conjugated verb endings (past tense) supplied below to the words. Then translate. G19

تَ	تُمْ	تُ	تِ	تْ
2nd person m. sing.	3rd person m. pl.	1st person sing.	2nd person f. sing.	3rd person f. sing.

to travel	I traveled.	سَافَرْتُ.	سَافَرَ	1
to eat		___________	أَكَلَ	2
to write		___________	كَتَبَ	3
to fall		___________	سَقَطَ	4
to be successful		___________	نَجَحَ	5
to make a joke		___________	مَزَحَ	6
to read		___________	قَرَأَ	7
to play		___________	لَعِبَ	8

2 Complete the sentences with the appropriate predicate. Note that in some cases the subject is contained in the verb ending!

نَبَحَ	نَامَ	شَاهَدْنَا	كَتَبْتُم	طَبَخْتَ	غَضِبَ	ضَحِكَ	اِشْتَرَى
barked	slept	we looked	they wrote	you (sing.) cooked	was angry	laughed	he bought

المُعَلِّمُ. ___________	5	الطِّفلُ. ___________	1
الدَّرسَ. ___________	6	الطَّعَامَ. ___________	2
الكَلبُ. ___________	7	قَمِيصاً. ___________	3
الفِلمَ. ___________	8	زَيدٌ. ___________	4

3 Reformulate the statements as questions, using هَلْ or أ.

	question	statement	
You (m. sing.) opened the door.	؟___________	فَتَحتَ البَابَ.	1
The bus stopped.	؟___________	وَقَفَ البَاصُ.	2
The traveler returned.	؟___________	رَجَعَ المُسَافِرُ.	3
The train departed.	؟___________	غَادَرَ القِطَارُ.	4
The mouse ran away from the cat.	؟___________	فَرَّ الفَأرُ مِنَ القِطَّةِ.	5
You (f. sing.) opened the window.	؟___________	فَتَحتِ النَّافِذَةَ.	6
Zaid came.	؟___________	جَاءَ زَيدٌ.	7
You (m. sing.) traveled to Cairo.	؟___________	سَافَرتَ إِلَى القَاهِرَةِ.	8

Verbs: Infinitive ردصملا ةغيص / Past Tense الماضي

G18 The verb in Arabic has four moods: indicative (fact or factual condition), subjunctive (condition that is doubtful
G20 or not factual), jussive (negation of the past tense form and the imperative), and imperative (command form).
G22 These, however, are expressed only with the present tense form of the verb. The verb tenses are past, present, and future. The grammatical voices are active and passive. A verb is also conjugated in accordance with gender and number. The various conjugational features are expressed in prefixes, suffixes, or changes in the vowel pattern. Therefore, there is no need to name the subject separately.

Infinitive

Arabic verbs have no infinitive (basic form). Instead, the 3rd person masculine singular past tense serves as the
G30 basic form. This is used, for example, in a dictionary as the main entry.

Past Tense (الماضي)

The past tense, also known as the perfect or perfective (*al-māḍī*), expresses an action (event or condition) that was completed in the past. It is not dependent on mood, so it uses a perfective form to express completion. Gender and number are indicated by attaching suffixes to the past tense stem.

past tense of the verb stem *jalasa* جَلَسَ (to sit)

plural		dual		singular		
*jalas**nā***	جَلَسنا			*jalas**tu***	جَلَسْتُ	1st person
*jalas**tum***	جَلَستُم	*jalas**tumā***	جَلَستُمَا	*jalas**ta***	جَلَسْتَ	2nd person (m.)
*jalas**tunna***	جَلَسْتُنَّ	*jalas**tumā***	جَلَسْتُمَا	*jalas**ti***	جَلَسْتِ	2nd person (f.)
*jalas**ū***	جَلَسُوا	*jalas**ā***	جَلَسَا	*jalasa*	جَلَسَ	3rd person (m.)
*jalas**na***	جَلَسْنَ	*jalas**atā***	جَلَسَتَا	*jalas**at***	جَلَسَتْ	3rd person (f.)

The Arabic past tense can be translated into English in several ways because the English and Arabic systems of tense do not correspond fully. Only one example is given below.

I sat on the sofa. / I have sat on the sofa.	*jalastu ʿalal-ʾarīkati.*	جَلَستُ عَلَى الأرِيكَةِ.
Zaid sold his camel.	*bāʿa zaidun nāqatahu.*	بَاعَ زَيدٌ نَاقَتَهُ.
Zarina traveled by airplane.	*sāfarat zarīna bi-ṭ-ṭāʾiratin.*	سَافَرَتْ زَرِينَة بِالطَّائِرَةِ.
We visited a friend.	*zurnā ṣadīqan.*	زُرنَا صَدِيقاً.
They (f.) went to the market.	*dhahabna ʾilas-sūqi.*	ذَهَبْنَ إلَى السُّوقِ.
You (m. pl.) drank coffee.	*sharibtum qahwatan.*	شَرِبْتُم قَهوَةً.

1 Mark the box to indicate which sentence correctly renders the English sentence.

3		2		1	
I slept.		We sat down.		They (m. pl.) went.	
☐	A نِمتُ.	☐	A جَلَستُمَا.	☐	A ذَهَبتَ.
☐	B نِمتَ.	☐	B جَلَستُم.	☐	B ذَهَبُوا.
☐	C نِمتِ.	☐	C جَلَسنَا.	☐	C ذَهَبنَ.

2 Complete the sentences by adding the appropriate past tense ending to the verb.

I wrote a letter.	1 كَتَبـــــ رِسَالَةً.
We traveled to Oman.	2 سَافَـرـــــ إلَى عُمَان.
They (m. pl.) went to the museum.	3 ذَهَبـــــ إلَى المَتحَفِ.
He bought a car.	4 اشتَرـــــ سَيَارَةً.
They (f. dual) played basketball.	5 لَعِبَـــــ كُرَةَ السَلَةِ.
She passed the test.	6 نَجَحـــــ فِي الإمتِحَانِ.
You (m. sing.) read a book.	7 قَرَأـــــ كِتَاباً.
They (f. pl.) traveled to India.	8 سَافَرـــــ إلَى الهِند.
You (f. sing.) cooked rice.	9 طَبَخَـــــ رُزاً.
They (m. dual) visited a friend.	10 زَارـــــ صَدِيقاً.

3 Using the first example as a guideline, restate the sentence in the past tense with different subjects. Replace the subjects with the corresponding conjugated forms of the verb.

Mohamed + Ali + Yussuf + travel + to Singapore.	سَافَرُوا إلَى سِينغَافُورة.	1 مُحَمَد + عَلِي + يُوسُف =
	______________________	2 رُقَيَّة =
	______________________	3 هَالَة + خَاتُمَة =
	______________________	4 مَالِك + نَعِيم =
	______________________	5 أنَا + زَيد + شَعبَان =
	______________________	6 إبرَاهِيم =
	______________________	7 نَادِيَة + زَمزَم + حَلِيمَة =
	______________________	8 أنتَ =

Verbs: Present المُضارِع – Indicative / Subjunctive

The present tense (also known as the imperfect or imperfective) (*al-muḍāriʿ*) expresses an uncompleted, ongoing action. In Arabic, the various moods (indicative, subjunctive, jussive, and imperative) are rendered only in the present. The present tense is formed by attaching prefixes and suffixes to the verb stem. The prefixes express gender, whereas the suffixes express number and mood.

Indicative المُضارِع المَرفوع

The indicative (*al-muḍāriʿ al-marfūʿ*) is used to depict an event objectively.

We are watching a film.	*nushāhidu filman.*	نُشَاهِدُ فِلماً.

In the present indicative, the subject of the verb is indicated by prefixes. These are formed from the letters *hamza* أ , *nūn* ن , *yā* ي, and *tā* ت.

They (m. pl.) sit.	***jajlisūna.***	يَجلِسُونَ	I sit.	***'ajlisu.***	أجْلِسُ
You (f. pl.) sit.	***tajlisna.***	تَجلِسْنَ	We sit.	***najlisu.***	نَجلِسُ

The conjugational prefixes and suffixes for the present indicative are:

present indicative of the verb stem *kataba* كَتَبَ (to write)

plural		dual		singular		
naktubu	نَكْتُبُ			***'aktubu***	أكْتُبُ	1st person
taktubūna	تَكْتُبُونَ	***taktubāni***	تَكْتُبَانِ	***taktubu***	تَكْتُبُ	2nd person (m.)
taktubna	تَكْتُبنَ	***taktubāni***	تَكْتُبَانِ	***taktubīna***	تَكْتُبِينَ	2nd person (f.)
yaktubūna	يَكْتُبُونَ	***yaktubāni***	يَكْتُبَانِ	***yaktubu***	يَكْتُبُ	3rd person (m.)
yaktubna	يَكْتُبنَ	***taktubāni***	تَكْتُبَانِ	***taktubu***	تَكْتُبُ	3rd person (f.)

The Subjunctive المُضارِع المَنصوب

In contrast to the indicative, the subjunctive (*al-muḍāri' al-manṣūb*) expresses subjectivity (doubts, wishes,
G23 intentions). The subjunctive always follows certain particles, such as *lan* لَنْ (negative particle), *ḥattā* حَتَى
G26 (so that, until), *'an* أنْ (that), and *li* لِ (in order to).

They won't come back.	*lan yarjiʿū.*	لَنْ يَرجِعُوا.
I'd like to ask you (m. sing.) to get it ready.	*'arjū minka 'an tukmila hādhā.*	أرجُو مِنْكَ أنْ تُكمِلَ هَذَا.

The subjunctive is formed from the present indicative. The suffixes change as follows: *ḍamma* ـُ (*-u*) becomes *fatha* ـَ (*-a*). In the case of *-ūna*, *īna*, and *āni*, the letter *nūn* ن with a short vowel is omitted; only the long vowels (*ū*, *ī*, *ā*) remain. The suffix *nūn* ن and *fatha* ـَ without a long vowel (*-an*) remains unchanged in the subjunctive. The prefixes for the indicative are also used for the subjunctive.

present subjunctive of the verb stem *kataba* كَتَبَ (to write)

plural		dual		singular		
naktuba	نَكْتُبَ			***'aktuba***	أكْتُبَ	1st person
taktubū	تَكْتُبُوا	***taktubā***	تَكْتُبَا	***taktuba***	تَكْتُبَ	2nd person (m.)
taktubna	تَكْتُبنَ	***taktubā***	تَكْتُبَا	***taktubī***	تَكْتُبِي	2nd person (f.)
yaktubū	يَكْتُبُوا	***yaktubā***	يَكْتُبَا	***yaktuba***	يَكْتُبَ	3rd person (m.)
yaktubna	يَكْتُبنَ	***taktubā***	تَكْتُبَا	***taktuba***	تَكْتُبَ	3rd person (f.)

1 Match the forms of the verb ضَحِكَ (to laugh) conjugated in the indicative with the corresponding grammatical person.

G10

1	أَنَا	I	→ 4	A	ضَحِكَ
2	أَنْتَ	you (m. sing.)		B	ضَحِكْتِ
3	أَنْتِ	you (f. sing.)		C	ضَحِكَتْ
4	هُوَ	he / it		D	ضَحِكْتُ
5	هِيَ	she / it		E	ضَحِكْتَ
6	نَحْنُ	we		F	ضَحِكْنَ
7	أَنْتُمَا	you (dual)		G	ضَحِكَا
8	أَنْتُم	you (m. pl.)		H	ضَحِكْتُمَا
9	أَنْتُنَّ	you (f. pl.)		I	ضَحِكْنَا
10	هُمَا	they (dual)		J	ضَحِكْتُم
11	هُم	they (m. pl.)		K	ضَحِكْتُنَّ
12	هُنَّ	they (f. pl.)		L	ضَحِكُوا

2 From the infinitive (past tense form of the verb), form the present indicative in the person required.

	infinitive	present indicative	
1	جَلَسَ	(1st pers. sing.) ______	to sit
2	أَكَلَ	(3rd pers. sing. f.) ______	to eat
3	ذَهَبَ	(2nd pers. dual m.) ______	to go
4	دَرَسَ	(3rd pers. pl. f.) ______	to study
5	نَظَرَ	(2nd pers. sing. m.) ______	to look
6	سَاقَ	(3rd pers. pl. m.) ______	to drive
7	لَعِبَ	(2nd pers. sing. m.) ______	to play
8	طَبَخَ	(1st pers. pl.) ______	to cook

3 Fill in the blanks with the missing verb in the required person of the present subjunctive. The verbs in parentheses are in the present indicative.

1 لَن ______ (ينسَونَ) المَوعِد. — They (m. pl.) will not forget the appointment.

2 عَلَيكِ أَن ______ (تَذهَبُ) إِلَى الطَّبِيب. — You (f. sing.) should go to the doctor.

3 اِمشِ عَلَى طُول حَتَى ______ (تَصِلُ) إِلَى إِشَارَةِ المُرُور. — Go straight ahead until you (m. sing.) come to the traffic light.

4 تَعَالَوا لِـ ______ (نَدرُسُ) مَعاً. — Let's go, in order to learn together.

5 لَن ______ (يَتَأَخَّرنَ) عَن الدَّرس. — They (f. pl.) won't come to class late.

6 عَلَينَا أَن ______ (نَكتُبُ) وَاجِبَاتِ المَنزِل. — We should do the homework.

4 Write these sentences in Arabic. Then write them in the plural of the appropriate person.

	singular	plural	
1	______	______	I'm reading a book.
2	______	______	He goes to the market.
3	______	______	She plays soccer.

Verbs: Present الْمُضَارِع – Jussive / Imperative

Jussive الْمُضَارِع الْمَجْزُوم

G20 The jussive, like the indicative and the subjunctive, is rendered only with the present tense form of the verb.
G23 In combination with the negative particle *lam* لَمْ (not), the jussive is used to negate a statement in the past tense (perfect). Then the verb is no longer in the past tense but in the present jussive. The statement, however, continues to refer to an action or a condition in the past.

	present jussive			past tense	
You didn't write the letter.	*lam taktubir-risālata.*	لَمْ تَكْتُبِ الرِّسَالَةَ.	You wrote the letter.	*katabtar-risālata.*	كَتَبْتَ الرِّسَالَةَ.

The jussive is formed from the present indicative. In the jussive, conjugation is characterized by the absence of the short vowel in the suffix. Whereas the indicative is conjugated with *ḍamma* ـُ and the subjunctive with *fatha* ـَ (-*a*), the jussive is conjugated with *sukūn* ـْ. The suffixes -*ūna*,- *īna*, and -*āni* change as in the subjunctive: The letter *nūn* ن with a short vowel is omitted, and only the long vowels remain (-*ū*, -*ī*, -*ā*). The suffix *nūn* ن and *fatha* ـَ without a long vowel (-*na*) is retained in the jussive. The prefixes for the indicative are also used for the jussive.

G20

present jussive of the verb stem *kataba* كَتَبَ (to write)

plural		dual		singular		
naktub	نَكْتُبْ			***'aktub***	أَكْتُبْ	1st person
taktubū	تَكْتُبُوا	***taktubā***	تَكْتُبَا	***taktub***	تَكْتُبْ	2nd person (m.)
taktubna	تَكْتُبْنَ	***taktubā***	تَكْتُبَا	***taktubī***	تَكْتُبِي	2nd person (f.)
yaktubū	يَكْتُبُوا	***yaktubā***	يَكْتُبَا	***yaktub***	يَكْتُبْ	3rd person (m.)
yaktubna	يَكْتُبْنَ	***taktubā***	تَكْتُبَا	***taktub***	تَكْتُبْ	3rd person (f.)

Imperative فِعْلُ الأَمْر

The imperative expresses a demand or an instruction. It normally is used in the 2nd person singular and 2nd person plural.

	present imperative			present indicative	
Remember! (m. sing.)	*tadhakar!*	تذكَرْ!	You remember.	*tatadhakaru.*	تتذكَرُ.

The imperative too is formed from the present indicative. The prefixes are omitted altogether. Note, however: If the first letter after the prefix in the indicative is a consonant, then in the imperative *hamza* (above or below *alif*) must be placed in initial position as an auxiliary vowel. The following applies to the suffixes: In the second person masculine singular, *ḍamma* ـُ is replaced by *sukūn* ـْ. The 2nd person feminine singular and the 2nd person dual / plural have the same suffixes as the jussive.

present imperative of the verb stem *kataba* كَتَبَ (to write)

plural		dual		singular		
'uktubū	أُكْتُبُوا!	***'uktubā***	أُكْتُبَا!	***'uktub***	أُكْتُبْ!	2nd person (m.)
'uktubna	أُكْتُبْنَ!	***'uktubā***	أُكْتُبَا!	***'uktubī***	أُكْتُبِي!	2nd person (f.)

The jussive of the verb is used to negate the present imperative.

G23

1 The sentences given here are in the past tense. Change them to the jussive.

They (m. pl.) drank.	________________	1 شَرِبُوا.
We built a house.	________________	2 بَنَينَا بَيتاً.
You (f. pl.) engaged in discussion.	________________	3 نَاقَشتُنَّ.
I cleaned the room.	________________	4 نَظَفتُ الغُرفَةَ.
You (dual) visited the patient.	________________	5 زُرتُمَا المَرِيضَ.

2 Match the verbs in the imperative with the appropriate person.

G10

سَاعِدَا	اِفتَحْ	أُنظُرُوا	قُولِي	حَاوِلنَ	قِفنَ	اِرجِعُوا	أُدخُلا	كُلِي	قُمْ
to help	to open	to see	to say	to try	to stop	to go back	to go in	to eat	to rise

1 أَنتَ ________________ ________________

2 أَنتِ ________________ ________________

3 أَنتُمَا ________________ ________________

4 أَنتُم ________________ ________________

5 أَنتُنَّ ________________ ________________

3 Using the verbs in parentheses, form imperatives and request a girlfriend:

1. to go to Abdulnasir — (ذَهَبَ) إِلَى عَبدِ النَاصِر. ________________
2. to bring Osman's cassette — (أَخَذَ) الشَرِيطَ مِنْ عُثمَان. ________________
3. to call you at the office — (اِتَّصَلَ) بِي فِي المَكتَبِ. ________________
4. to buy sugar at the store — (اِشتَرَى) لِي سُكَّراً مِنَ الدُكَانِ. ________________

4 Now ask several friends to do something:

1. to play soccer with you — (لَعِبَ) مَعِي كُرَةَ القَدَم. ________________
2. to speak Arabic with you — (تَحَدَّثَ) مَعِي بِالعَرَبِيَةِ. ________________
3. to go to the market with you — (ذَهَبَ) مَعِي إِلَى السُّوق. ________________
4. to go to Jordan with you — (سَافَرَ) مَعِي إِلَى الأُردُن. ________________

Grammar

Verbs: Future / Active and Passive

Future المُستَقبَل

The future tense expresses an event that has not happened yet. The future tense in Arabic is marked by the particles *sa* س (expressed by the letter *sin* س) and *sawfa* سوفَ. The future is formed by adding *sa* س as a prefix to the verb in the present indicative or by placing *sawfa* سوفَ before the verb in the present indicative.

G20

		future			present indicative
I will write.	sa'aktubu.	سَأكتُبُ.	I write.	'aktubu.	أكتُبُ.
I will go.	sawfa 'adhhabu.	سوفَ أذهبُ.	I go.	'adhhabu.	أذهبُ.

sa س and *sawfa* سوفَ can be used interchangeably:

I will write the letter.	*sa'aktubur-risālata.*	سَأكتبُ الرِّسَالَةَ.
	sawfa 'aktubur-risālata.	سَوفَ أكتبُ الرِّسَالَةَ.
I will go to school.	*sa'adhhabu 'ilal-madrasati.*	سَأذهبُ إلى المدرسةِ.
	sawfa 'adhhabu 'ilal-madrasati.	سَوفَ أذهبُ إلى المدرسةِ.

Active and Passive الفعل المبني للمعلوم والفعل المبني للمجهول

The active voice is used when the agent of an action is the subject of the verb. In the passive voice, however, the object of a sentence becomes the subject.

In Arabic, the passive is used primarily when the agent of an action is unknown. The passive voice of a verb is formed by a change in vocalization within the verb (in the active voice). The basic vowel changes are as follows:

- For the past tense: The first consonant carries *ḍamma* ـُ, and the second consonant carries *kasra* ـِ.

G19

		past passive			past active
The door was opened.	*futiḥal-bābu.*	فُتِحَ البَابُ.	The girl opened the door.	*fataḥatil-bintu al-bāba.*	فَتحتْ البِنتُ البَابَ.
The letter was written.	*kutibatir-risālatu.*	كُتِبَتِ الرِّسَالَةُ.	He wrote the letter.	*katabar-risālata.*	كَتَبَ الرِّسَالَةَ.

- For the present tense: The prefix carries *ḍamma* ـُ, and the middle consonant carries *fatḥa* ـَ.

G20

		present passive			present active
The letter is written.	*yuktabur-risālatu.*	تُكْتَبُ الرِّسَالَةُ.	He writes the letter.	*yaktubur-risālata.*	يَكتُبُ الرِّسَالَةَ.

G10

1 Match the forms of the verb لَبِسَ (to get dressed), which are conjugated in the future, with the appropriate grammatical person.

1	أَنَا	I	A سَتَلْبَسِينَ
2	أَنْتَ	you (m. sing.)	B سَتَلْبَسُ
3	أَنْتِ	you (f. sing.)	C سَأَلْبَسُ
4	هُوَ	he / it	D سَتَلْبَسُ
5	هِيَ	she / it	E سَيَلْبَسُ
6	نَحْنُ	we	F سَيَلْبَسْنَ
7	أَنْتُمَا	you (dual)	G سَيَلْبَسَانِ
8	أَنْتُم	you (m. pl.)	H سَيَلْبَسُونَ
9	أَنْتُنَّ	you (f. pl.)	I سَنَلْبَسُ
10	هُمَا	they (dual)	J سَتَلْبَسُونَ
11	هُم	they (m. pl.)	K سَتَلْبَسْنَ
12	هُنَّ	they (f. pl.)	L سَتَلْبَسَانِ

2 What will you do this weekend? Make plans for your family and yourself in Arabic. The verbs in parentheses are in the infinitive form.

1 ________ (نَامَ) طَوِيلاً. — I will sleep for a long time.

2 ________ (جَهَّزَ) .زَوجَتِي طَعَامَ الفُطُور. — My wife will prepare breakfast.

3 ________ (لَعِبَ) أَلِن كُرَةَ السَّلَّةِ. — Ellen will play basketball.

4 ________ (زَارَ) أَصدِقَاؤُنَا. — Our friends will visit us.

5 ________ (أَتَى) صَدِيقَةُ زَهرة لِتَلعَبَ مَعَهَا. — Sarah's girlfriend will come to play.

6 ________ (بَاتَ) الطِفلَانِ عِندَ جَدَّتِهِمَا. — The (two) children will stay with their grandmother.

7 ________ (ذَهَبَ) أَنَا وَزَوجَتِي إِلَى السِينَمَا. — My wife and I will go to a movie.

3 Fill in the blanks with verbs in the correct tense and in the passive voice. The verbs given below are infinitives.

صَلَّحَ	طَبَعَ	حَرَسَ	دَهَنَ	سَدَّ	عَزَمَ	أَقَامَ	فَتَحَ
to repair	to publish	to guard	to paint	to block	to invite	to hold (celebrate)	to open

1 ________ حَفلَةُ العِيدِ بَعدَ شَهرِ رَمَضَانَ. — An Eid party was held after Ramadan.

2 ________ سَيَارَتُنَا بَعدَ الحَادِثِ. — Our car was repaired after the accident.

3 ________ البَيتُ. — The apartment is being painted.

4 ________ البَابُ. — The door was opened.

5 ________ كِتَابُ رَفِيق شَامِي قَبلَ شَهرَينِ. — Rafik Shami's book was published two months ago.

6 ________ أَنَاسٌ كَثِيرُونَ لِلحَفلَةِ. — Many people are invited to the event.

7 ________ طُرُقٌ عَدِيدَةٌ بَعدَ الطُوفَانِ. — After the storm, many roads were blocked.

8 ________ المَطَارُ حِرَاسَةً شَدِيدَةً. — The airport is strictly guarded.

Verbs: Negation

The negation of a verb or a sentence follows simple rules. Depending on the mood and tense of the verb, various particles are added to a verb or a sentence.

Negation of the Past Tense

G19 The past tense form of a verb is negated by using the particle *lam* لَم (not). Then the verb is no longer in the
G21 past tense but in the present jussive. The statement, however, continues to refer to the past. The original sentence structure is retained, and the particle *lam* لَم is placed before the verb or before an entire sentence:

We didn't leave.	*lam nusāfir.*	لَم نُسَافِر.	We left.	*sāfarnā.*	سَافَرنَا.

Negation of the Present Indicative

G20 The present indicative is negated by placing the particle *lā* لا (not) in front of the verb. The verb remains in the indicative mood:

I don't understand what you're saying.	*'ana lā 'afhamu mā taqūlu.*	أَنَا لا أَفهَمُ مَا تَقُولُ.	I understand what you're saying.	*'ana 'afhamu mā taqūlu.*	أَنَا أَفهَمُ مَا تَقُولُ.

The present tense of the verb "to be" is negated with *laysa* لَيسَ (to not be). Note that although *laysa* لَيسَ
G24 reflects the present, it is in the past tense. In addition, it requires a predicate in the accusative:

The man is not a policeman.	*ar-rajulu laysa shurṭiyan.*	الرَّجُلُ لَيسَ شُرطِياً.	The man is a policeman.	*ar-rayulu schurṭiyyun.*	الرَّجُلُ شُرطِيٌّ.

G1 The verb *laysa* لَيسَ (to not be) can also be used to negate a nominal sentence. In this case, the predicate of the nominal sentence must also be in the accusative:

The room (is) not big.	*lajsatil-ġurfatu wāsiʿatan.*	لَيسَتِ الغُرفَةُ وَاسِعَةً.	The room (is) big.	*'al-ġurfatu wāsiʿatun.*	الغرفةُ واسعةٌ.

Negation of the Present Subjunctive

The present subjunctive is negated by using the particle *lā* لا (not). In this case, *lā* لا and the subjunctive particle
G20 *'an* أَن (that) become *'allā* ألاّ .

I ask you not to do this again.	*'arjū minka 'allā tafʿala hādhā marratan 'ukhrā.*	أَرجُو مِنكَ ألاّ تَفعَلَ هَذا مَرَّةً أُخرَى.

Negation of the Present Imperative

To negate the present imperative, the particle *lā* لا (not) is placed before the verb. The form of the verb changes;
G21 it is conjugated in the jussive:

Don't eat the food!	*lā t'akulit-ṭaʿāma!*	لا تَأكُلِ الطَعَامَ!	Eat the food!	*kulit-ṭaʿāma!*	كُلِ الطَعَامَ!

Negation of the Future Tense

The negative particle *lan* لَن negates the future. In this case, the affirmative sentence undergoes the following
G20 changes: The future particles *sa* س and *sawfa* سوف are omitted, and the verb is no longer in the future tense
G22 but in the subjunctive.

I will not go.	*lan 'adhhaba.*	لَن أَذهَبَ.	I will go.	*sa'adhhabu.*	سَأَذهَبُ.

1 Listen to the sentences, and decide whether they are affirmative or negative (negated) statements. Write the negative particles that you hear in the blanks provided. 23

negative particle	negative	affirmative	
____________	☐	☐	1
____________	☐	☐	2
____________	☐	☐	3
____________	☐	☐	4
____________	☐	☐	5
____________	☐	☐	6

2 Supply the correct form of the verb given in parentheses and the appropriate particle.

We didn't discuss the topic.	1 نَحنُ ____________ (نَاقَشَ) المَوضُوع.
He doesn't like soccer.	2 هُوَ ____________ (أَحَبَّ) كُرَةَ القَدَم.
He didn't have a city map.	3 ____________ (كَانَ) مَعَهُ خَرِيطَةٌ لِلمَدِينَةِ.
The city is not big.	4 ____________ (المَدِينَةُ) كَبِيرَةً.
It's better that you not travel by bus.	5 الأفضَل لَكَ ____________ (سَافَرَ) بِالبَاص.
Don't cook; we'll eat falafel at the Arab restaurant.	6 ____________ (طَبَخ) فَسَوفَ نَأكُلُ الفَلافِل فِي المَطعَمِ العَرَبِي.
I didn't understand what you said.	7 أَنَا ____________ (فَهِمَ) مَا قُلتَهُ.
He will not work here.	8 هُوَ ____________ (اشتَغَلَ) هُنَا.

3 Negate the sentences below.

I read this entertaining book.	____________ ____________	1 قَرَأتُ هَذَا الكِتَابَ المُمتِع.
This university is old.	____________	2 هَذِهِ الجَامِعَةُ قَدِيمَةٌ.
Come through this door.	____________	3 اُدخُلُوا مِنْ هَذَا البَاب.
Osman went away during the summer vacation.	____________ ____________	4 سَافَرَ عُثمَان فِي عُطلَةِ الصَيفِ.
It's possible for you to pay with a credit card.	____________ ____________	5 يُمكِنُ أن تَدفَعَ بِبِطَاقَةِ الإئتِمَانِ.
Arabic books are cheap in Cairo.	____________ ____________	6 الكُتُبُ العَرَبِيَةُ رَخِيصَةٌ فِي القَاهِرَة.
It's better that we take a walk now.	____________ ____________	7 الأَفَضَلُ أَن نَذهَبَ لِلتَّنَزُهِ الآنَ.
You have visited many cities.	____________	8 زُرتُم مُدُناً كَثِيرَةً.

Verbs: Verb "to be" / Modal Verbs

The Verb "to be" كَانَ وَأَخَواتُها

Arabic refers to verbs that express the state of "being" or "becoming" as "*kāna* كَانَ and its sisters" (*kāna wa 'akhawātuhā*). *kāna* كَانَ (to be) and *'aṣbaha* أصبَحَ (to become) have two special features: First, they are
G1 not used in the present tense; a nominal sentence does not require them. Second, they always require the accusative case for the predicate, which follows them:

The weather was cold.	*kānat-ṭaqṣu bāridan.*	كَانَ الطَّقسُ بَارداً.
The environment was polluted.	*'aṣbaḥatil-bay'atu mulawathatan.*	أصبَحَتِ البِيئَةُ مُلَوثَةً.
The weather will be rainy.	*sayakūnut-ṭaqsu mumṭiran.*	سَيَكُونُ الطَقسُ مُطِراً.

G19 The verb *laysa* لَيسَ (to not be)—although it is used with the past tense—reflects a negated state or condition
G23 in the present. It also requires a predicate in the accusative:

Shaban is not stingy.	*laysa sha'bānu bakhīlan.*	لَيسَ شَعبَانُ بَخِيلاً.

kāna كَانَ, although it is conjugated with regular conjugational endings, undergoes internal vowel changes in some cases. You will find the conjugated forms of the verb in the verb tables.

Modal Verbs

Modal verbs indicate your attitude toward an action, for example, whether you want to, must, or can do something. *'arāda* أرَاد (to want to), *yayibu* يَجِبُ (to have to, must), and *'amkana* أمكَنَ (to be possible, can) are the most common modal verbs in Arabic.

- *'arāda* أرَاد (to want / to want to)

The verb *'arāda* أرَاد can be followed either by the conjunction *'an* أنْ (that) or directly by a noun or pronoun.

He wanted the discussion to be continued.	*'arāda 'an tastamirra al-munāqashata.*	أراد أنْ تَستَمِرَّ المُنَاقَشَة.
I want to go to the market.	*'urīdudh-dhihāba 'ilas-sūqi.*	أُريدُ الذِّهابَ إلَى السُوقِ.

- *yajibu* يَجِبُ (to have to, must)

The verb *yajibu* يَجِبُ is always followed by the preposition *'alā* عَلَى (on, at) with a noun or pronoun, as well as the conjunction *'an* أنْ (that):

The driver must stop at the crosswalk. (Literally, "It is at the driver that he stops at the crosswalk.")	*yajibu 'alas-sā'iqi 'an yaqifa 'inda mamar-ril mushāti.*	يَجِبُ عَلَى السَّائِقِ أنْ يَقِفَ عِندَ مَمَرِّ المُشَاةِ.

If the sentence contains a pronoun, *yajibu* يَجِبُ can be omitted altogether, and the pronoun can be attached
A7 directly to the preposition *'alā* عَلَى. In this case, *'alif maqṣūra* in *'alā* عَلَى becomes *yā* ي.

He has to take the medications.	*'alayhi 'an yatanāwald-dawā'a.*	عَلَيهِ أنْ يَتَنَاوَلَ الدَوَاءَ.

- *'amkana* أمكَنَ (can, to be possible)

Can I pay with a credit card?	*hal yumkinu 'an 'adfa'a bi biṭāqatil-'itimāni?*	هَل يُمكِنُ أن أدفَعَ بِبِطَاقَةِ الإئتِمَانِ؟

1 Decide whether the sentences with كَانَ, أَصبَحَ and لَيسَ are correct or incorrect.
Then make the necessary corrections.

		incorrect	correct	
The food was delicious.	______	☐	☐	1 كَانَ الطَعَامُ لَذِيذاً.
This is not your (f. sing.) pen.	______	☐	☐	2 هَذَا لَيسَ قَلَمُكِ.
Shaban became minister.	______	☐	☐	3 أَصْبَحَ شَعبَانُ وَزِيراً.
This is not your (m. sing.) shirt.	______	☐	☐	4 لَيسَ هذَا قَمِيصُكَ.
This is not a new car.	______	☐	☐	5 السَيَارَةٌ هَذِهِ جَدِيدَةٌ لَيسَ.
He drove a red car.	______	☐	☐	6 كَانَ يَسُوقُ سَيَارَةً حَمرَاءَ.
The world has become a small village.	______	☐	☐	7 أصبَحَ العَالَمُ قَريَةً صَغِيرَةً.
The weather was sunny.	______	☐	☐	8 كَانَ الطَقسُ مُشمِساً.

2 Which modal verb should you use in the following everyday situations? Fill in the blanks.

يَجِبُ	أَرَادَ	أمكَنَ

You ask a friend whether he can watch your dog. ______ 1

You confide that you have to go to the doctor. ______ 2

You ask whether smoking is allowed in the restaurant. ______ 3

You inform someone that you want to go away on a trip. ______ 4

You say that you like dates. ______ 5

You think it's very important for children to have their own experiences. ______ 6

3 Fill in the blanks with the correct form of the appropriate modal verb. Note that you must also add the conjunction *'an* أَنْ.

You (f. sing.) have to go to school.	تَذهَبَ إِلَى المَدْرَسَةِ. ______	1
He would like to go home.	يَذهَبَ إِلَى البَيتِ. ______	2
She can help me.	تُسَاعِدَنِي. ______	3
They (m. dual) have to do homework.	تَعمَلا وَاجِبَات المَنزِل. ______	4
We would like to eat and drink.	نَأكُلَ وَنَشرَبَ. ______	5
You (f. pl.) must go shopping.	تَذهَبنَّ إِلَى التَّسَوُقِ. ______	6
I can go to the museum with you.	أذهَبَ مَعَكَ إِلَى المَتحَفِ. ______	7
I have to stay at home.	أمكُثَ فِي البَيتِ. ______	8

Grammar

G25
Adverbs الظُّروفُ

Adverbs (*ẓurūf*) modify, or qualify the meaning of, an action. They supply additional information about verbs,
G5 adverbs, other adverbs, or entire sentences. This information refers to place (where?), time (when? how often?),
G6 manner (how?), and quantity (how much?). In Arabic, most adverbs are in the accusative case.

Adverbs of Place

G26 In Arabic, some adverbs of place function as prepositions but are not classified as such: *taḥta* تَحْتَ (under),
G27 *fawqa* فَوقَ (over), *'amāma* أمَامَ (in front of), *khalfa* خَلفَ (behind), *muqābila* مُقَابِلَ (across from), *bayna* بَينَ
(*between*), *'inda* عِندَ (at, with), *qurba* قُربَ (near), *bu'da* بُعدَ (far), *khārija* خَارِجَ (outside), *yamīna* يَمِينَ (to/on
the right), *yasāra* يَسَارَ (to/on the left). With the exception of *hunā* هُنَا (here) and *hunāka* هُنَاكَ (there),
they modify a word in the genitive:

under the window	*taḥtan-nafidhati*	تَحتَ النَّافِذَةِ

The adverbs themselves agree in case only if they are used in combination with a preposition:

She came out (from) behind the curtain.	*kharajat min khalfis-sitāri.*	خَرَجتْ مِنْ خَلفِ السِتَارِ.

Adverbs of Time

Apart from *qabla* قَبلَ (before) and *ba'da* بَعدَ (after), most adverbs of time require no change in the case of the word modified: *al'āna* الآنَ (now), *thumma* ثُمَّ (then), *'akhīran* أخِيراً (finally), *'abadan* أبَداً (never), ahyānan أحيَاناً (sometimes), *dā'iman* دَائِماً (always), *'amsi* أمسِ (yesterday), *al-yawma* اليَومَ (today), *gadan* غَداً (tomorrow):

Sometimes I travel in summer.	*'aḥyānan 'usāfiru fis-ṣayfi.*	أحيَاناً أسَافِرُ فِي الصَيفِ.
What time is it now?	*kamis-sā'atul-'āna?*	كَم السَاعَةُ الآنَ؟

Adverbs of Manner

G2 *hākadhā* هَكَذَا (so, thus) and *kadhālika* كَذلكَ (also, too) are invariable. Most adverbs of manner, however, agree
G3 with the word modified in gender, number, and case: *biluṭfin* بِلُطفٍ (nicely, in a friendly way), *ṭayyiban* طَيِّباً
G5 (well), *ġayru ḥasanin* غَيرُ حَسَنٍ (not well, poorly), *sarī'an* سَرِيعاً (quickly, fast), *baṭī'an* بَطِيئاً (slowly).
G6

The train was fast.	*kānal-qiṭāru sarī'**an**.*	كَانَ القِطَارُ سَرِيعاً.
We came quickly (with).	*j'inā bisur'at**in**.*	جِئنَا بِسُرعَةٍ.

Adverbs of Quantity

Adverbs of quantity include *kathīran* كَثِيراً (much, very), *qalīlan* قَلِيلاً (little), *tamāman* تَمَاماً (all, entirely), *'ajma'a* أجمَعَ (all, entirely), *batātan* بَتَاتاً (not at all), *faqaṭ* فَقَط (only).

There was little food.	*kānat-ṭa'āmu qalīlan.*	كَانَ الطَعَامُ قَلِيلاً.
I don't like that at all.	*lā 'uḥibbu hādhā batātan.*	لاأُحِبُّ هَذا بَتَاتاً.

1 Mark the correct answer.

3		2		1	
كَيفَ حَالُكَ؟ How are you?		أينَ أنت؟ Where are you?		مَتَي تَأتِي؟ When are you coming?	
☐	A طَيِّب	☐	A طَيِّب	☐	A هُنَا
☐	B بَطِيئا	☐	B خَارِج	☐	B أمس
☐	C قُرب	☐	C أمس	☐	C غَداً

2 Rewrite the sentences given below to mean the opposite. Choose the appropriate adverb from those provided.

بِسُرعَةٍ	خَلفَ	كَثِيراً	غَداً

He is standing in front of the house.	.______	1 هُوَ وَاقِفٌ أمَامَ البَيتِ.
My mother is going away today.	.______	2 تُسَافِرُ أُمِي اليَومَ.
The ship moves slowly.	.______	3 السَّفِينَةُ تَسِيرُ بُبطءٍ.
She always eats little.	.______	4 هِيَ دَائِمًاتَأكُلُ قَلِيلاً.

3 Fill in the appropriate adverb.

مُقَابِل	أمَام	بِسُرعَةٍ	الخَارِج	جَيِّد	ألآن	قَلِيلٌ	دَائِماً	أمس

How are you?—Fine, thanks.	1 كَيفَ حَالُكَ؟ ______. شُكراً.
I tried to call you yesterday.	2 حَاوَلتُ أن أتَّصِلَ بِكَ ______.
I always go for a walk on Sunday.	3 أيَامَ الأحدِ أمشِي ______. لِلتَّنَزُه.
Do you possibly have time now?	4 هَل عِندَكَ وَقتٌ ______؟
I don't have much (have little) time, but we can quickly go have coffee.	5 الوَقتُ عِندِي ______. وَلَكِن يُمكِنُ أن نَذهَبَ وَنَشرَبَ قَهوَةً ______.
Gladly. Shall we meet in front of Café Lulu?	6 حَسَناً. هَل نَلتَقِي ______. مَقهَى لُؤلُؤ؟
Is that across from the train station?	7 هَل هُوَ ______. المَحَطَةِ؟
Yes. The weather is sunny; we can sit outside.	8 نَعَم. الطَقسُ مُشمِسٌ وَيُمكِنُ أن نَجلِسَ فِي ______.

4 Correct the sentences. Pay attention to the case and to the position of the adverb.

My sister came from Dubai yesterday.	______ ______	1 جَاءَتْ أُختِي أَمْسِ مِنْ دُبَي.
We always eat bread for breakfast.	______ ______	2 فِي وَقتِ الفُطُورِ نَأكُلُ الخُبزَ دَائِمٌ.
It's now three o'clock in the afternoon.	______ ______	3 السَاعَةُ الثَالِثَةُ بَعدَ الظُهرِ الآنَ.

Grammar

Prepositions حُرُوفُ الجَر (1)

Prepositions (*ḥurūf al-jar*) express relationships between two elements (person, thing, event, etc.). These relationships include the following: place (where?) direction (where to/from?), time (when?), intention (for what purpose?), cause (why?), manner (how?), and instrument (with what?). Arabic distinguishes among prepositions that consist of one, two, and three syllables. They appear mainly in connection with nouns and
G5 pronouns and determine their case. They always require the genitive. The prepositions that consist of a single
G6 letter are placed before the noun or pronoun as a prefix; that is, they become part of the word. An additional feature of all prepositions is that they never can be used with another preposition.

> The meaning of some English prepositions is expressed in Arabic with adverbs.

G25

bi بِ

The preposition *bi* بِ primarily expresses the place and manner of an action:

a student *at* the University of Mogadishu	*ṭālibun bi-jāmiʿati maqdīshu*	طَالِبٌ بِجَامِعَةِ مَقدِيشُو
Sit down *beside* me.	*ʾijlis bijānibī.*	اجلِس بِجَانِبِي.
The problem is being solved *by* peaceful means.	*ḥullatil-mushkilatu bi-ṭarīqatin silmiyatin.*	حُلَّتِ المُشكِلَة بِطَرِيقَةٍ سِلمِيَةٍ.

li لِ

li لِ expresses intention and cause. In addition, it indicates ownership (in the sense of the verb "to have"):

I'm struggling (in order) *to* exist.	*ʾajtahidu li-ʾanjaḥa.*	أجتَهِدُ لأنجَحَ.
He quit *for* unclear reasons.	*ʾistaqāla li-ʾasbābi ġāmiḍatin.*	اِستَقَالَ لأسبَابٍ غَامِضَةٍ.
The house *has* a back entrance.	*lil-bayti bābun khalfiyyun.*	لِلبَيتِ بَابٌ خَلفِيٌّ.

If *li* لِ precedes a (prefixed) personal pronoun, the short vowel *kasra* ـِ is replaced by *fatḥa* ـَ and *li* لِ becomes
G11 *la* لَ:

you have / she has (f. sing.)	*laka / lahā*	لَكَ / لَهَا

An exception is the 1st person singular; here *li* لِ is retained in its original form:

I have	*lī*	لِي

If *li* لِ precedes the definite article *al* ال, it replaces the letter *alif* ا in *al* ال:

G4

the woman has	*lil-marʾati*	لِلمَرأةِ	the woman	*al-marʾatu*	المَرأةُ

ka كَ

The preposition *ka* كَ is used in comparisons and expresses function. It can be used only in connection with
G10 independent personal pronouns or with demonstrative pronouns, but not with attached personal pronouns.

G12
G17

You (f. sing.) are *like* the radiant sun.	*ʾanti kash-shamsi fiḍiyāʾi.*	أنتِ كَالشَمسِ فِي الضِيَاءِ.
This man works *as* a teacher.	*hādhar-rajulu yaʿmalu ka-mudarrisin.*	هَذَا الرَجُلُ يَعمَلُ كَمُدَرِسٍ.

1 Underline the prepositions in the following sentences. Then decide what kind of relationship the preposition expresses, and make the correct matches.

١ 1	يَذهَبُونَ إِلَى المَكتَبَةِ لِيَقرَؤُوا.	A	Comparison ("like, as")
2	هُوَ مُوَظَّفٌ بِالبَرِيد.	B	Place ("at")
3	حِذَاؤُهُ كَحِذَائِكَ.	C	Ownership ("I have")
4	أَتِينَا بِسُرعَةٍ.	D	Intention ("in order to")
5	لِلسَّكَنِ شُرفَةٌ.	E	Manner ("with, by")

2 Fill in the blanks with بِ , لِ or كَ.

1 هُوَ أُستَاذٌ ____جَامِعَةِ القَاهِرَة. — He is a professor at the University of Cairo.

2 جِئنَا ____زِيَارَتِكُم. — We came (in order) to visit you.

3 سَافَرتُ ____سَيَارَةٍ. — I traveled by car.

4 فَتَحتُ الحَقِيبَةَ ____أَنظُرَ مَافِيهَا. — I opened the bag (in order) to see what is in it.

5 سَيَارَتُهَا ____سَيَارَتِكَ. — Your car is like their car.

6 ____لبَيتِ حَدِيقَةٌ كَبِيرَة. — The house has a big yard (garden).

7 المَطعَمُ ____جَانِبِ المَسرَحِ. — The restaurant is next to the theater.

8 هِيَ تَعمَلُ ____مُمَرِضَةٍ. — She works as a nurse.

3 Add the preposition لِ to the personal pronouns, and then translate. G11

1 لَ + هَا = لَهَا she has

2 لَ + هُمَا = ________ ____________

3 لِ + ي = ________ ____________

4 لَ + هُم = ________ ____________

5 لَ + هُنَّ = ________ ____________

6 لَ + نَا = ________ ____________

7 لَ + كُمَا = ________ ____________

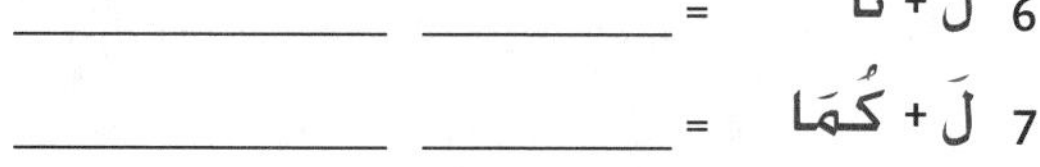

8 لَ + كَ = ________ ____________

9 لَ + هُ = ________ ____________

4 Complete the sentences by placing لِ before the (definite) nouns.

1 ____المَرأَةِ بَيتٌ.

2 ____الغُرفَةِ شُرفَةٌ.

3 ____القَمِيصِ جَيبٌ.

4 ____البَيتِ بَابٌ خَلفِيٌّ.

5 ____الشَجَرَةِ ثِمَارٌ.

6 ____السَيَارَةِ لَونٌ أَحمَر.

Grammar

Prepositions حُرُوفُ الجَر (2)

min مِنْ

G17 *min* مِنْ is used in comparisons (with an adjective in the comparative degree) and to indicate direction. In addition, it expresses quantity or tells what something is made of:

This shirt is cheaper *than* that one.	*hādhal-qamīṣu 'arkhaṣu min dhāka.*	هَذَا القَمِيصُ أَرخَصُ مِنْ ذَاكَ.
From where did you come?	*min 'ayna ji'ta?*	مِنْ أَينَ جِئتَ؟
Is he *one of the* students?	*hal huwa minat-ṭalabati?*	هَل هُوَ مِنَ الطَلَبَةِ؟
This pullover is *made of* wool.	*hādhil-kanzatu ṣuniʿat minas-ṣūfi.*	هَذِه الكَنزَةُ صُنِعَت مِنَ الصُوفِ.

Note: *min* مِنْ ends in *sukūn* ـْ. If it precedes the definite article *al* ال, then *fatḥa* ـَ must be inserted as an auxiliary vowel.

fī فِي

The preposition *fī* فِي expresses place and time and is used in the general sense of "about":

The juice is *in the* refrigerator.	*al-ʿaṣīru fith-thallājati.*	العَصِيرُ فِي الثَلاجَةِ.
We're meeting *at* six o'clock..	*naltaqī fils-sāʿatis-sādisati.*	نَلتَقِي فِي السَاعَةِ السَادِسَةِ.
We talked *about* the topic.	*taḥadathnā fī hādhal-mawḍūʿ.*	تَحَدَثنَا فِي هَذَا المَوضُوع.

ʿan عَنْ

The most important meanings of *ʿan* عَنْ are "on" (referring to direction) and "of, about":

The museum is *on* the right side.	*al-mathḥafu ʿan yamīnika.*	المَتْحَفُ عَنْ يَمِينِكَ.
Tell us *about* your trip to Germany.	*'akhbirnā ʿan safarika 'ilā 'almāniyā.*	أخبِرنَا عَن سَفَرِكَ إِلَى أَلمَانِيَا.

ʿalā عَلَى

The preposition *ʿalā* عَلَى means "on" and "with":

He sleeps *on* the bed.	*huwa nā'imun ʿalas-sarīri.*	هُوَ نَائِمٌ عَلَى السَرِيرِ.
Peace be *with* you.	*'as-salāmu ʿalaykum.*	السَلامُ عَلَيكُم.

'ilā إِلَى

'ilā إِلَى is primarily a preposition indicating direction:

Where (to where) are you going?	*'ilā 'ayna tadhhabu?*	إِلَى أينَ تَذهَبُ؟
I'm going *to the* market.	*'adhhabu 'ilas-sūqi.*	أذهَبُ إِلَى السُوق.

The most important Arabic prepositions:

at, beside, next to; with, by	*bi*	بِ	in; at; about	*fī*	فِي
in order to; for, because of; "to have"	*li*	لِ	on; of, about	*ʿan*	عَنْ
as, like	*ka*	كَ	on; with	*ʿalā*	عَلَى
than; (made) of; one of the; from (where)	*min*	مِنْ	to (where)	*'ilā*	إِلَى

Prepositions always require the genitive!

1 Which Arabic preposition would you use to express the following sentences? The prepositions may be used more than once.

1 Have you (sing.) already heard about his latest experience?	
2 I'm going to the university.	A مِنْ
3 He found it (m.) on the cabinet.	B فِي
4 The bakery opens at 5 o'clock.	C عَنْ
5 There is still soup in the kitchen.	D عَلَى
6 Where did you get the sweater?	E إِلَى
7 The parking garage is on the left side.	

2 Add مِنْ and عَنْ in the appropriate place.

The door is made of wood.	1 صُنِعَ البَابُ ________ الخَشَبِ.
Tell us about your job.	2 حَدِّثنَا ________ عَمَلِكَ.
He has come from school.	3 جَاءَ ________ المَدرَسَةِ.
Where do you come from?	4 ________ أَينَ جِئتَ؟
From when until when?	5 ________ مَتَى إِلَى مَتَى؟
Do you know anything about our friend?	6 هَل تَعرِفُ شَيئاً ________ صَاحِبِنَا
This skirt is prettier than that one.	7 هَذِهِ التَّنُّورَةُ أَجمَلُ ________ تِلكَ.

3 Translate, using the prepositions فِي , عَلَى and إِلَى . Make sure to make the appropriate changes in the case of the noun and the adjective.

in (into) the beautiful hotel	________ 1	in / on the train	________ 4
on the big table	________ 2	in the small room	________ 5
to the train station	________ 3	on foot (literally "on the feet")	________ 6

4 Using complete sentences, answer the following questions in Arabic. Use the appropriate preposition as well as the following items:

الرَّصِيف 5	دِمَشق	السَاعَة 3

1 مَتَى تُقلِعُ الطَائِرَةُ إِلَى رِيَاض؟
When does the airplane leave for Riyadh?
____

2 مِن أَيِّ رَصِيفٍ يُغَادِرُ القِطَارُ إِلَى الإِسكَندَرِيَّة؟
From which track does the train to Alexandria leave?
____

3 فِي أَيَّةِ مَدِينَةٍ عِشتَ فِي سُورِيَا؟
In which town in Syria did you live?
____

Grammar

Conjunctions حُرُوف العَطف

Conjunctions (*hurūf al-ʿatf*) connect words, groups of words, sentences, or parts of sentences. Some important Arabic conjunctions are:

- *wāw* و (and)

The letter *wāw* و is used in enumerations as the conjunction *wa* و. Note that *wa* و precedes all the listed elements:

The room has a shower and a toilet and a refrigerator. *al-ġurfatu mujahazatun bi-dūshin wa mirḥaḍin wa thallāja.* الغُرفَةُ مُجَهـّزَةٌ بِدُوشٍ و مِرحَاض وثَلاجَة.

- *mā … walā* ما ... ولا (neither … nor)

He has neither read it (himself) nor let anyone else read it. *mā qara'a walā taraka ġayrahu jaqra'.* مَاقَرَأَ وَلاتَرَكَ غَيْرَهُ يَقرأ.

- *lākinna* لَكِنَّ (but)

Maryam lives in Canada, but she comes from Somalia. *maryamun taʿīshu fī kanada lākinnahā minas-ṣūmāl.* مَريَمُ تَعِيشُ فِي كَندا لَكِنَّهَا مِنَ الصّومَال.

- *bal* بَلْ (but / rather)

I don't mean all the students, but some of them. *lam 'aqṣud kullat-ṭalabati bal baʿḍahum.* لَمْ أقصُد كُلَّ الطَلَبَةِ بَل بَعضَهُمْ.

- *ām* أم (or)

Are you going by train or by bus? *hal tusāfiru bil-qiṭāri am bil-bās?* هَل تُسَافِرُ بالقِطَارِ أم بالبَاص؟

- *'immā … wa 'immā* إمّا ... وإمّا (either … or)

Either we'll go by train or by car. *'immā 'an nusāfira bil-qiṭāri wa 'imma bis-sayārati.* إمَّا أَنْ نُسَافِرَ بِالقِطَارِ وإمَّا بِالسَيَارَة.

- *'anna* أَنَّ (that)

I believe that the train is late. *'aẓunnu 'annal-qiṭāra muta'akhirun.* أَظُنُّ أَنَّ القِطَارَ مُتَأخِرٌ.

- *fa* فـ (so, therefore)

They couldn't get a car, so they went by train. *lam yajidū sayāratan, fasāfarū bil-qiṭāri.* لَم يَجِدُوا سَيَارَةً فَسَافَرُوا بِالقِطَار.

- *thumma* ثُمَّ (then, after that)

We traveled to Egypt and then to Syria. *sāfarnā 'ilā miṣra thumma 'ilā sūriyā.* سَافَرنَا إلَى مِصرَ ثُمَّ إلَى سُوريَا.

- *li'anna* لأَنَّ (because)

I wasn't at work because I was sick. *lam adhhab 'ilal-ʿamali li'annī kuntu marīḍan.* لَمْ أذْهَبْ إلَى العَمَلِ لأنّي كُنتُ مَرِيضاً.

- *'idhā* إذا (in case, if)

If I find a job, I'll buy a car. *'idhā wajadtu ʿamalan fasa'ashtarī sayāratan.* إذَا وَجَدتُ عَمَلاً فَسَأشتَري سَيَارَةً.

- *mithla* مِثل (like)

I have a coat like the one you have. *ʿindī miʿṭafun mithlal-ladhī ʿindaka.* عِندِي مِعطَفٌ مِثْلُ الَذِي عِندَكَ.

1 How does the sentence continue? Mark the correct box.

I like to get exercise ... أُحِبُّ الرِيَاضَة ...

3	2	1
... and sleep a lot..	... but I don't always have time for it.	... because it's good for me.
A إمَا النَّومَ الكَثِيرَ. ☐	A إذَا لا أجِدُ لَهَا وَقت بِصِفَةٍ دَائِمَةٍ. ☐	A لأنَّهَا مُفِيدَةٌ لِلصِّحَةِ. ☐
B والنَّومَ الكَثِيرَ. ☐	B وَلكِنَّنِي لا أجِدُ لَهَا وَقتاً بِصِفَةٍ دَائِمَةٍ. ☐	B أن مُفِيدَةٌ لِلصِحَةِ. ☐

2 Use the conjunctions given to link the sentence provided with sentences 1–6.

فَـ	لَكِن	لأنَّنِي	ثُمَّ	إذَا

سَأذهَبُ لِلتَّنَزُه ... I will go for a walk ...

1 ________ لَم تَمطُر السَمَاء. ... if it doesn't rain today.

2 ________ كُنتُ فِي البَيتِ طُولَ اليَوم. ... because I was at home all day.

3 ________ أذهَبُ لِلأكلِ فِي المَطعَم العَرَبِي. ... and then I'll eat in an Arab restaurant.

4 ________ لَن أركُض. ... but not jog.

5 ________ أنَا غَيرُ مَوْجُودٍ فِي البَيتِ. ... so I will not be at home.

3 Put the items given in a meaningful order, so that they form complete sentences.

1 وَ إبنَتِي / ذَهَبنَا / وَزَوجِي / إلَى / أنَا / حَدِيقَة الحَيَوَانَات. — My husband, my daughter, and I went to the zoo. ________

2 أَسَداً / وقُرُوداً / وَوَحِيد القَرن / وَثَعَابِين / وَطُيُوراً كَثِيرَةً / فَرَأينَا. — We saw a lion, monkeys, a rhinoceros, snakes, and many birds. ________

3 زَرَافَةً / مَا رَأينَا / ولا فِيلاً. — We saw neither a giraffe nor an elephant. ________

4 رَجَعنَا / ثُمَّ / فِي مَركَزِ المَدِينَةِ / وَنَزَلنَا / بِالقِطَار. — That we came back by train and got off in the center of town. ________

5 إبنَتِي / نُرِيدُ / كُنَّا / إلَى السِينمَا / أن نَذهَبَ / كَانَت قَد تَعِبَت / ولكِن. — We wanted to go to the movies, but my daughter was tired. ________

6 فَلَم / إلَى السِينمَا / رَجَعنَا / بَل إلَى البَيتِ / نَذهَب. — So we didn't go to the movies but (rather) home. ________

7 أن تَطبَخَ / أن تَغسِلَ / قُلتُ / لِزَوجِي / إمَا / المَوَاعِين / وَإمَا. — I said to my husband, "Either you cook or you wash the dishes." ________

8 وَمَعكَرُنَة / فَطَبَختُ / لأنَّنَا / دَجَاجاً / نُحِبُّ الدجَاج. — So I made chicken and spaghetti because we like chicken. ________

Numerals الأرقام

V6 Note that the following table gives the masculine and feminine forms only for the single digits (ones).

Cardinal numbers								Ordinal numbers			
1–9 m./f.		11–19		10, 20 … 90		100, 1000 etc.		1st–9th		10th–19th	
1	وَاحِدٌ / وَاحِدَةٌ	11	أَحَدَ عَشَرَ	10	عَشَرَةٌ	100	مِئَةٌ	1st	أَوَّلٌ	10th/ 11th	عَاشِرٌ / حَادِيَ عَشَرَ
2	إِثْنَانِ / إِثْنَتَانِ	12	إِثْنَا عَشَرَ	20	عِشْرُونَ	200	مِئَتَانِ	2nd	ثَانٍ	12th	ثَانِيَ عَشَرَ
3	ثَلَاثٌ / ثَلَاثَةٌ	13	ثَلَاثَ عَشْرَةَ	30	ثَلَاثُونَ	300	ثَلَاثُمِئَةٍ	3rd	ثَالِثٌ	13th	ثَالِثَ عَشَرَ
4	أَرْبَعٌ / أَرْبَعَةٌ	14	أَرْبَعَ عَشْرَةَ	40	أَرْبَعُونَ	1000	أَلْفٌ	4th	رَابِعٌ	14th	رَابِعَ عَشَرَ
5	خَمْسٌ / خَمْسَةٌ	15	خَمْسَ عَشْرَةَ	50	خَمْسُونَ	1000 000	مَلْيُونٌ	5th	خَامِسٌ	15th	خَامِسَ عَشَرَ
6	سِتٌّ / سِتَّةٌ	16	سِتَّ عَشْرَةَ	60	سِتُّونَ			6th	سَادِسٌ	16th	سَادِسَ عَشَرَ
7	سَبْعٌ / سَبْعَةٌ	17	سَبْعَ عَشْرَةَ	70	سَبْعُونَ			7th	سَابِعٌ	17th	سَابِعَ عَشَرَ
8	ثَمَانٍ / ثَمَانِيَةٌ	18	ثَمَانِيَ عَشْرَةً	80	ثَمَانُونَ			8th	ثَامِنٌ	18th	ثَامِنَ عَشَرَ
9	تِسْعٌ / تِسْعَةٌ	19	تِسْعَ عَشْرَةَ	90	تِسْعُونَ			9th	تَاسِعٌ	19th	تَاسِعَ عَشَرَ

The most important features of the cardinal numbers are:

- The number "one" behaves like an adjective and agrees in gender and case with the noun being counted.
- The number "two" agrees in case with the noun being counted and thus follows the rules of declension for the dual.
- G6 The numbers 3 to 10 have a special feature: If the noun being counted is masculine, then the number is feminine. If the noun being counted is feminine, then the number is masculine. The noun being counted is always in the genitive case.
- The number "eleven" is invariable with regard to case and is always in the accusative. It is made up of the numbers "one" and "ten." If the noun being counted is masculine, then both parts of the number are masculine. If the noun being counted is feminine, then both parts of the number are feminine. The noun being counted is always in the accusative singular.
- The number "twelve" agrees in case with the noun being counted. The parts of the number ("two" and "ten") always agree in gender with the noun being counted.
- The numbers 13 to 19 are made up of two parts ("three" and "ten," etc.) They are invariable with regard to case. The noun being counted is always in the accusative singular. With regard to agreement in gender with the noun, this rule applies: The first part of the number always is opposite in gender from the noun (see above); the second part of the number agrees in gender with the noun.
- The numbers 20 to 90 are formed from the stem of the single-digit numbers (ones), combined with the ending *-ūna* of the sound masculine plural. They are invariable with regard to gender but agree in case. They follow G3 the rules for the sound masculine plural. They are followed by a noun in the accusative singular.
- G6 The numbers 100 and 200: The number "one hundred" is always feminine and is invariable with regard to case. 200 is the number "one hundred" in the dual, and it is declined according to the rules for the dual. Both form an *idafa* compound with the noun, and therefore the noun is always in the genitive singular.
- The numbers 300 to 900: The hundreds over 200 are formed from the corresponding ones (in the masculine) G9 and the number "hundred." "Hundred" is in the genitive singular here. The noun being counted is in the genitive singular.

The most important features of the ordinal numbers are:

- Ordinal numbers are formed from the stem of the cardinal numbers and are invariable.
- In contrast to the cardinal numbers, the ordinal numbers always follow the noun.

Grammar

1 Mark the noun that goes with the numeral. Pay attention to gender, number, and case.

3	2	1
أربَعَةُ	وَاحِد	سِتَّةُ
A دَرَاهِم ☐	A قَلَمٌ ☐	A مُهَنْدِسَاتٍ ☐
B مَحَطَّاتٍ ☐	B وَرَقَةٌ ☐	B مُهَندِسٍ ☐

6	5	4
ثَلاثُ	خَمْسَةُ	اثنَتَانِ
A رِجَالٍ ☐	A نُجُومٍ ☐	A طَالِبَانِ ☐
B بَنَاتٍ ☐	B سَاعَاتٍ ☐	B طَالِبَتَانِ ☐

2 Write out the numbers in words.

1
عَلَى الطَاوِلَةِ ...

On the table are lying ...

A 3 ____________ أقلام. pens

B 5 ____________ وَرَقَاتٍ. sheets of paper

2
عَلَى المَائِدَةِ ...

On the table are standing ...

A 14 ____________ كُوباً. cups

B 14 ____________ قَارُورَةً. bottles

3
مُعَلَّقٌ عَلَى الجِدَارِ ...

On the wall are hanging ...

A 11 ____________ صُورَةً. photos

B 7 ____________ رُسُومٍ. pictures

3 Write out the numbers and the sum in words.

1 16+21 ____________ + ____________ = ____________

2 67+153 ____________ + ____________ = ____________

3 232+355 ____________ + ____________ = ____________

4 Translate.

1 ____________ the fifth day

2 ____________ the seventeenth week

3 ____________ the ninth book

4 ____________ the third child

Grammar

Word Formation

In Arabic, words are formed on the basis of word stems (basic stem and expanded stems). The basic stem *al-mudjarad ath-thulāthī* الفِعل المُجَرَّد الثُلاثِي consists of three root consonants (see below). Through addition of other consonants or vowels, a word acquires expanded or completely different meanings. For example, the root *KTB*—made up of the consonants ك, ت, and ب —is the basis for the following words:

to write	*kataba*	كَتَبَ
book	*kitābun*	كِتَابٌ
library	*maktabatun*	مَكْتَبَةٌ

Understanding the word stems is an important starting point for learning the Arabic language or Arabic vocabulary. Moreover, it is a key requirement for working with a dictionary because the entries generally are arranged according to word stems (the basic stem of the word always comes first). In order to derive the basic stem of a word, you can use various patterns (*al-mīzān al-sarfī* المِيزَان الصَرفِي). This is demonstrated in the examples below, using verb stems.

Basic Stem مُجَرَّد

The basic stem (*mujarad*) of a verb consists of three root consonants. Generally these root consonants are represented by *fā* ف, *'ain* ع, and *lām* ل. The resulting word *fa'ala* فَعَلَ (to do, to make) represents the model structure. *fā* ف represents the first consonant of the word, *'ain* ع the second or middle consonant, and *lām* ل the third or last consonant. If you apply this model structure to the verb *kataba* كَتَبَ, it becomes clear that the three consonants ***KaTaBa*** exactly follow the pattern of ***Fa'aLa*** فَعَلَ. The derived root, therefore, is *KTB*.

Expanded Stem مَزِيد

Verbs that consist of more than three root consonants have an expanded stem (*mazīd*). In this case, one or more consonants or vowels are added to the basic stem. If you want to determine the basic stem of the expanded verbs, you also use the model structure *fa'ala* فَعَلَ. In this case, *fa'ala* فَعَلَ first must be expanded in accordance with the expanded stem:

	pattern (expanded)		verb (expanded stem)	
to teach	***Fa''aLa***	فَعَّلَ	***DaRRaSa***	دَرَّسَ
to win	***'iFta'aLa***	افتَعَلَ	***'iNtaṢaRa***	انتَصَرَ

The expanded verb and the expanded model structure exhibit the same rhythm of pronunciation. If you now remove the added consonants or vowels of the expanded stem, leaving only those that correspond to the model structure, you will obtain the basic stem of the verb.

	pattern		verb (basic stem)
to learn	***Fa'aLa***	فَعَلَ	***DaRaSa***
to help	***Fa'aLa***	فَعَلَ	***NaṢaRa***

In the verb tables, you will find examples of verbs that exhibit the basic stem, as well as additional examples of the most common expanded stems.

Grammar

1 Match the verbs (basic stem and expanded stem) with the corresponding model structure. The verb tables can help you get the correct answers.

		model structure	verb	
to ask, request	A	يَفْعَلُ	طَلَبَ	1
he sits	B	اِسْتَفْعَلَ	يَجْلِسُ	2
he asks	C	فَعُلَ	يَسْأَلُ	3
to age	D	فَعَّلَ	كَبُرَ	4
to think something is good	E	يَفْعِلُ	اِسْتَحْسَنَ	5
to become pale	F	تَفَعَّلَ	اِصْفَرَّ	6
to hesitate	G	فَعَلَ	تَرَدَّدَ	7
to arrange, organize	H	اِفْعَلَّ	رَتَّبَ	8

2 The following verbs exhibit the basic stem الفِعل المُجَرَّد الثُلاثِي. Determine the model structure of the verbs as in the first two examples. Each verb appears twice—first in the past, and then in the present. The verb tables can help you with this exercise.

model structure		verb	
فَعَلَ	=	ذَهَبَ	1
يَفْعَلُ	=	يَذْهَبُ	2
________________	=	شَرِبَ	3
________________	=	يَشْرَبُ	4
________________	=	جَلَسَ	5
________________	=	يَجْلِسُ	6
________________	=	كَتَبَ	7
________________	=	يَكْتُبُ	8

3 Determine the basic stem of these verbs, all of which exhibit an expanded stem. The verb tables can help you with this exercise.

basic stem		verb	
كَسَرَ	=	اِنْكَسَرَ	1
________________	=	تَكَاتَبَ	2
________________	=	دَرَّسَ	3
________________	=	أَكْرَمَ	4
________________	=	اِرْتَفَعَ	5
________________	=	اِسْتَفْسَرَ	6

Saying Hello / Inquiries into Each Other's Health / Saying Goodbye

24

Good afternoon, (Mr.) Adam!	*nahāruka saʿīd yā sayyid ādam.*	◄ نَهارُكَ سعيد يا سيِّد آدم!
Good afternoon, (Ms.) Samira!	*nahāruki saʿīd yā sayyida samīra!*	◁ نَهارُكِ سَعِيد يا سيِّدة سَميرَة!
How are you?	*kayfa ḥāluka?*	◄ كَيفَ حَالُكَ؟
Fine, and you?	*'ana bikhayrin, wa 'anti?*	◁ أَنا بِخَيرٍ، وَأَنتِ؟

G10

In Arabic, people often are addressed in the so-called vocative. In this case, *yā* يَا is always placed in front of the name (with or without a form of address). Literally translated, the term of address is "Oh Mr. (Sir) / Ms. (Ma'am). . . .!" or "Oh Hamid!"

	Vocative		Nominative
yā sayyid ādam!	يَا سيِّد آدم!	*'as-sayyid ādam*	السيِّد آدَم
yā sayyida samīra!	يَا سيِّدة سَميرَة!	*'as-sayyida samīra*	السيِّدة سَميرَة
yā ḥamīd!	يَاحَمِيد!	*ḥamīd*	حَمِيد

Saying Hello تَحِيَّة

Good morning.	*sabāḥul-khayr.*	صَباحُ الخير.
Good afternoon.	*nahāruka saʿīd.*	نَهارُكَ سَعِيد.
Good evening.	*masā 'ul-khayr.*	مَساءُ الخير.
Peace be with you!	*as-salāmu ʿalaykum!*	السَّلامُ عَلَيكُمْ!

In response, you say:

Peace be with you!	*wa ʿalaykumus-salām!*	وَعَلَيكُمْ السَّلام!

More informally, or among good friends, you use these greetings:

Hello! / Hi!	*marḥaban!*	مَرحَباً!
Welcome!	*'ahlan wa sahlan!*	أَهلاًوَسَهلاً!

Inquiries into Each Other's Health سُؤَالٌ عَنِ الحَالِ

How are things?	*kayfal-ḥāl?*	كَيفَ الحَال؟
How are you?	*kayfa ḥāluka? (m.) / kayfa ḥāluki? (f.)*	كَيفَ حالُكَ / كَيفَ حالُكِ؟
And you?	*wa 'anta? (m.) / wa 'anti? (f.)*	وأَنتَ / وأَنتِ؟

These questions are answered as follows:

Fine.	*bi khayr.*	بخير.
Thank God. (neutral)	*al-ḥamdu liLāh.*	الحَمدُ لِلّه.
Not bad. (if the state of health is really not so good)	*lā b'as.*	لابَأس.

Saying Goodbye وَدَاعٌ

Goodbye!	*maʿas-salāma!*	مَعَ السَّلامَة!
So long!	*i'lal-liqā'!*	إِلى اللِقاء!
All the best!	*'atamannā laka kulal-khayr!*	أَتَمنى لكَ كُلَ الخَير!
Good luck!	*ḥaẓan saʿīdan!*	حظاً سَعيداً!

1 What do you say as a greeting and what do you say as a farewell? Put the expressions in the appropriate column.

السَّلامُ عَلَيكُمْ!	حظاً سَعيداً!	أهلاًوَسَهلاً!	مَعَ السَّلامَة!
إلَى اللِقَاءِ!	أتَمَنَّى لكَ كُلَّ الخَيرِ!	مَسَاءُ الخَيرِ.	نَهَارُكَ سَعِيدٌ.

hello	goodbye

2 Complete the following two dialogues.

formal	informal
1 السَّلامُ عَلَيكُم يا سَيِّدَة سَمِيرَة!	1 مَرحَباً يَا آدَم!
2 ________ يَاسَيِّد آدَم.	2 ________ يَا سَمِيرَة!
3 كَيفَ ________ ؟	3 كَيفَ ________ ؟
4 ________ وَ ________ ؟	4 بِخَيرٍ. وَ ________ ؟

3 Say hello to the following persons. In some cases, several formulas of greeting are possible.

1. a good acquaintance in the evening ________
2. an unknown Arab woman in the morning ________
3. your girlfriend in the afternoon ________
4. several Arabs in a formal situation ________
5. several Arabs in an informal situation ________

4 How are you? – كَيفَ حَالُكَ؟ How do you respond to this question in the following frames of mind?

1 ☺ ________

2 😐 ________

3 ☹ ________

Introducing Yourself / Someone Else

25

Good afternoon! May I introduce myself? My name is Adnan ibn Akhmad. What is your name?	*nahāruka saʿīd! hal tasmahīna lī bi'an 'uqadima laki nafsī? ismī ʿadnān ibn 'aḥmad. masmukil karīm?*	◄ نَهارُكَ سَعيد! هَل تَسمَحِينَ لِي بِأن أُقدِمَ لَكِ نَفسي؟ إسمي عَدنَان ابن أحمَد. مَاسمُكِ الكَرِيم؟
I am Fatima Hassan.	*'ismī fāṭima ḥassan.*	◁ إسمي فَاطِمَة حَسَن.
(I'm) Pleased to meet you.	*furṣa saʿīda.*	◄ فُرصَة سَعِيدَة.
Likewise.	*wa 'ana asʿad.*	◁ وَأنَا أسعَد

V1 Introducing Yourself أن تُعَرِّفَ نَفسَك

May I introduce myself?	*ismaḥ lī bi'an 'uqadima laka nafsī?*	إسمَح لِي بِأن أُقدِمَ لَكَ نَفسي؟

Then you generally state your own name:

My name is …	*ismī …*	إسمي ...
I am …	*'ana …*	أنَا ...

and ask the name of the person you're talking to:

What's your name?	*masmuka?*	مَاسْمُكَ؟
What is your name?	*masmukal-karīm?*	مَاسْمُكَ الكَرِيم؟

Introducing Someone Else أَنْ تُعَرِّفَ شَخصاً آخَر

When introducing a third person, you say:

May I introduce you to each other?	*'ismaḥū lī 'an 'uʿarrifa baʿḍukum ʿalā baʿḍ?*	إسمَحُوا لِي أن أُعَرِّف بَعضَكُم عَلَى بَعض؟
Allow me to introduce you.	*hal tasmaḥu lī bi'an 'uqadima laka?*	هَل تَسمَحُ لِي بِأن أُقدِمَ لَكَ؟
This is Mr. / Mrs., Ms. / Miss …	*hādhā as-sayyid / hādhihis-sayyida / al-'anīsa …*	هَذا السيِّد / هذه السيِّدة / الآنِسَة ...

You respond to an introduction as follows:

(I'm) Pleased to meet you.	*furṣa saʿīda.*	فرصَة سَعِيدَة.
Likewise.	*wa 'ana asʿad.*	وَأنَا أسعد.

G1

In Arabic, you can omit the verb in simple sentences (nominal sentences) in the present tense:

My name (is) Warda.	*ismī warda.*	إسمي وَردَة.
I (am) Yussuf.	*'ana yūsuf.*	أنَا يُوسُف.
This (is) Malik.	*hādhā mālik.*	هَذا مَالِك.

1 Put this dialogue back in the correct order by numbering the sentences.

A [1] نَهارُكَ سَعيد!

B ☐ فرْصَةٌ سَعيدَة يا سَيِّدة فاطِمَة.

C ☐ إسمَحي لِي بِأن أُقَدِمَ لَكِ نَفسي؟ أنَا عَدنَان ابن أحمَد. مَاسمُكِ الكَريم؟

D ☐ أنَا أسعَد يَا سَيِّد عَدنَان.

E ☐ أنا فَاطمَة حَسَن.

F ☐ نَهارُكِ سَعيد!

2 A man would like to make your acquaintance. How do you respond?

you:	man:
1 ______________	مَسَاءُ الخَير.
2 اِسمي ______________	اِسمي نَعيم مَحمُود. ماسمُكَ الكَريم؟
3 ______________	فُرصَة سَعيدَة.

3 Now you want to introduce yourself to someone. Fill in the blanks.

woman:	you:
نَهارُكَ سَعيد!	1 نَهارُكِ ______________
أنَاهَالَة حَمدَان.	2 أنَا ______________. مَا ______________؟
وأنا أسعَد.	3 ______________.

4 Introduce the following persons in Arabic.

1. Your favorite singer (f.): ______________

2. Your neighbor (m.): ______________

3. Your best friend (f.) / (m.): ______________

Communication

Stating Your Age / Occupation / Address

26

How old are you?	*kam ʿumruka?*	كَم عُمرُكَ؟ ◂
I am thirty.	*ʿumrī thalāthūna sana.*	عُمري ثَلاثون سَنَة. ◃
What is your occupation?	*mā hiya ḥirfatuka?*	ما هِيَ حِرفَتُكَ؟ ◂
I'm an engineer. I work for an international company.	*'ana muhandis 'aʿmalu fī 'iḥdāsh-sharikātil-ʿālamiya.*	أنا مُهَندِس. اعمَلُ في إحدى الشَركات العَالَمِيةِ. ◃
What is your address?	*mā huwa ʿinwānuka?*	مَا هُوَ عِنوانُكَ؟ ◂
My address: P.O. Box 199665 Deira-Dubai – UAE	*ʿinwānī: ṣād ba 199665 …*	عِنوَاني: ص.ب. 199665 دِيرَه-دُبَي - الإمَارَات المُتَّحِدةِ. ◃

Stating Your Age أن تذكُرَعُمرَك

V6
G29

How old are you?	*kam ʿumruka?*	كَم عُمرُكَ؟
I …	*ʿumrī …*	عُمري ...
… am 24 years old.	*… 'arbaʿun wa ʿishrūna sana.*	... 24 سَنَة.
… am not yet 30.	*… lam 'abluġ 'ath-thalāthīna baʿdu.*	... لَم أبلغ 30 بَعدُ.
… just turned 40.	*… 'al-'āna balaġtul-'arbaʿīna sana.*	... الآنَ بَلَغتُ 40 سَنَة.
… am about to turn 19.	*… sa'uṣbiḥu tisʿa ʿashrata sana.*	... سَأصبِحُ تِسعَ عَشْرَةَ سَنَة.

Information About Your Occupation بَيَانُ المِهنَةِ

V2

What is your occupation?	*mā hiya ḥirfatuka / mā hiya mihnatuka?*	مَاهِيَ حِرفَتُكَ / مَاهِيَ مِهنَتُكَ؟
I'm a businessman / businesswoman.	*'ana tājir / tājira.*	أنا تَاجِر / تَاجِرَة.
I work as a teacher (m.) / (f.).	*'ana muʿalim / muʿalima.*	أنا مُعَلِم / مُعَلِمَة.
I go to school / college.	*'ana ṭalib / 'adrus.*	أنا طالِب / أدرُس.
Where do you work?	*'ajna tashtaġil?*	أينَ تَشتَغِل؟
I work at a company / a school / an institute.	*'ana 'ashtaġilu fī 'iḥdash-sharikāt / al-madāris / fī 'iḥdal-maʿāhid.*	أنا اشتَغِلُ فِي إحدى الشَركَات / المَدَارس / فِي إحدى المَعَاهِد.

Information About Your Address تَفَاصِيل عَن العِنوَانِ / مَكَان السَكَنِ

V1

What is your address?	*mā huwa ʿinwānuka?*	مَاهُوَ عِنوانُكَ؟
My address is P.O. Box 199665, Deira-Dubai – UAE	*ʿinwānī: ṣād ba 199665 …*	عِنوَانِي: ص.ب: 199665 دِيرَه-دُبَي - الإمَارَات المُتَّحِدةِ.
I live on al-Baladiya Street behind the big mosque.	*'ana 'askunu fī shāriʿ al-baladiya khalfal-masjidil-kabīri.*	أنا أسكُنُ فِي شَارع البَلَدِيَة خَلفَ المَسجِدِ الكَبِير.

1 Can you answer these questions by giving information about yourself? In sections V2 (Occupations) and V6 (Numbers), you'll find words that help with this exercise.

1 كَم عُمرُكَ؟ ______

2 مَا هُوَ عِنوانُكَ؟ ______

3 ما هِيَ حِرفتُكَ؟ ______

4 أينَ تَشتَغِل؟ ______

2 How do you give the following information about your age? Mark the correct expressions.

1. I am twenty years old.

A ☐ عُمري عِشرُونَ سَنَة.

B ☐ سَأصبِحُ عِشرينَ سَنَة.

C ☐ لَم أبلُغ العِشرينَ بَعدُ.

2. I just turned forty.

A ☐ سَأصبِحُ أربَعِينَ سَنَة.

B ☐ لَم أبلُغ الأربَعِينَ بَعدُ.

C ☐ الآن بَلَغتُ أربَعِينَ سَنَة.

3. I'm about to be thirty-three.

A ☐ عُمري ثَلاثٌ وَ ثلاثُونَ سَنَة.

B ☐ سَأصبِحُ ثلاثٌ وَثلاثِينَ سَنَة.

C ☐ الآن بَلَغتُ ثَلاثاً وثَلاثِينَ سَنَة.

3 Translate these questions into Arabic.

1. What is your occupation? ______

2. How old are you? ______

3. What is your address? ______

Communication

Stating Your Nationality / Origin / Place of Residence

 27

Are you American?	*hal 'anti 'amrikiyya?*	◄ هَل أَنتِ أمريكية؟
Yes, I'm from the United States. And you?	*na'am, 'ana min 'amerika. wa 'anta?*	< نَعَم، أنا مِن أمريكا. وأَنتَ؟
I'm Egyptian. Where do you live?	*'ana miṣri. 'ayna taskunīna?*	◄ أنا مِصريّ. أينَ تَسكُنينَ؟
I live in Chicago. And you?	*'ana 'askunu fī 'shikāgo. wa 'anta?*	< أنا أسكُنُ فِي شيكاغو. وأنتَ؟
I live in Cairo.	*'ana 'askunu fil-qāhira.*	◄ أنا أسكُنُ فِي القَاهِرَة.

V3 Stating Your Nationality / Origin الجنسية / بَيانُ النَسَب

What is your nationality?	*mā hija jinsiyatuka?*	مَا هِيَ جِنسِيتُكَ؟
Are you American?	*hal 'anta 'amriki (m.) / 'anti 'amrikiyya (f.)?*	هَلْ أنتَ أمريكي / أَنتِ أمريكية؟
I am Egyptian (m.) / (f.).	*'ana miṣri / miṣriya.*	أنا مِصريّ / مِصريَّة
... English (m.) / (f.).	*... 'inyilīzi / 'injilīziyya*	... إنجليزيّ / إنجليزيّة
... French (m.) / (f.).	*... faransi / faransiyya*	... فَرَنسِيّ / فَرَنسِيَّة
Where do you come from?	*min 'ayyi baladin 'anta?*	مِن أيّ بَلَدٍ أنتَ؟
Are you from Egypt / the U.S.?	*hal 'anta min miṣra / 'amrikā?*	هَل أنتَ مِن مِصرَ / أمريكا؟
I come from England / France ...	*'ana min 'injiltarā / faransā ...*	أنا مِن إنْجِلتَرَة / فَرَنسَا ...

Stating Your Place of Residence تَفَاصِيلٌ عَن السُكنى

Where do you live?	*'ayna taskun?*	أينَ تَسكُن؟
Where are you staying? (for a short stay, for example, in a hotel)	*'ayna tuqīm?*	أينَ تُقِيم؟
I live in ...	*'ana 'askunu fī ...*	أنا أسكُنُ فِي ...
... Egypt / the U.S.	*... miṣra / 'amerika.*	... مِصرَ / أمريكا
... in Cairo / New York / Miami.	*... fil-qāhira / 'nyu york / mayami.*	... فِي القَاهِرَة / نيويورك / مَيامي.
I'm staying at the al-Hijaz Hotel.	*'ana 'askunu fī funduq al-ḥijāz.*	أنا أسكُنُ فِي فُندُق „الحِجاز".
I live in town / in the country.	*'ana 'askunu fil-madīna / fir-rīf.*	أنا أسكُنُ فِي المَدينَة / فِي الرِّيف.
I live / I'm staying with my parents / friends.	*'ana 'askunu 'inda wālidayya / 'aṣdiqā'ī.*	أنا أسكُنُ عِندَ وَالِدَيَّ / أصدِقَائِي.

Communication

1 How do you ask for information about …? Match the items below.

1. … place of residence
2. … nationality
3. … country of origin
4. … a particular nationality

A مِنْ أيِّ بَلَدٍ أنتَ؟
B مَا هِيَ جنسِيتُك؟
C أينَ تَسكُنُ؟
D هَل أنتَ ألمَانِي؟

2 Where do these people come from, and what is their nationality? Use the following model to write about each person. Pay attention to the masculine and feminine endings for the designations of nationality!

يُوسُف عَبدالنَاصِر أردُن	يُوسُف مِن الأردُن. هُوَ أُردُنِيٌّ.
Barbara Smith أمرِيكَا	1 Barbara مِن __________________. هِيَ __________________.
سُمَيا حُسَين كُوَيت	2 سُمَيا مِن __________________. هِيَ __________________.
Henri Chapuis فَرنسَا	3 Henri مِن __________________. هُوَ __________________.

3 Use the words given below to form the following sentences:

أنَا أقِيم	بَاكِستَان	فِي القَاهِرَة	أنَا أسكُنُ
أنَا أُقِيم	عِندَ أصدِقَائِي	فِي فُندُق	أنَا مِن

1. I live in Cairo. ________________________________
2. I'm staying in a hotel. ________________________________
3. I come from Pakistan. ________________________________
4. I'm staying with friends. ________________________________

Communication

Talking About Your Family

Do you have a family?	*hal laki ʿāʾila?*	◂ هَل لَكِ عَائِلة؟
Yes, I have a father and a mother.	*naʿam, lī ʾab wa ʾum.*	◃ نَعَم، لِي أَب وأُم.
I have a sister; she isn't married yet.	*lī ʾukht wāḥida wahya lam tatazawwaj baʿd.*	◂ لِي أُخت واحِدة. وهِيَ لَمْ تَتَزَوَّج بَعد.
My older brother is married; he has two children.	*ʾachī al-ʾakbar mutazawwij wa lahu waladān.*	◃ أَخِي الأَكبَر مُتَزَوِّج. ولَهُ وَلَدان.

Inquiring about Family Relationships أن تَسأَلَ عَنِ الوضع العَائِلي

V4

Do you have …	*hal laka (m.) / hal laki (f.) …*	هَل لَكَ / هَل لَكِ ...
… a family / a husband / a wife?	*… ʿāiʾla / zawj / zawja?*	... عَائِلَة / زَوج / زَوجَة؟
… brothers and sisters / children?	*… ʾikhwa / ʾakhawāt / ʾawlād?*	... إخوَة / أَخَوَات / أولاد؟
… a son / a daughter?	*… ibn / ibna?*	... اِبن / اِبنَة؟
How many children / brothers / sisters do you have?	*kam ʿadadu ʾawlādika / ʾikhwatika / ʾakhawātika?*	كَم عَدَدُ أولادِكَ / إخوَتكَ / أَخَواتكَ؟
Are you …	*hal ʾanta (m.) / hal ʾanti (f.) …*	هَل أَنتَ / هَل أَنتِ ...
… married?	*… mutazawwij (m.) / mutazawwija (f.)?*	... مُتَزَوِّج / مُتَزَوِّجَة؟
… divorced?	*… muṭallaq (m.) / muṭallaqa (f.)?*	... مُطَلَق / مُطَلَقَة؟
… single?	*… aʿzab (m.) / ʿazbāʾ (f.)?*	... أعزَب / عَزبَاء؟

Describing Family Relationships أن تَصِفَ الوَضع العَائِلي

I have two sisters / daughter.	*lī ʾukhtān / bintān.*	لِي أُختَان / بِنتَان.
I have three brothers / sons / daughters.	*lī thalātha minal-ikhwa / ʾabnāʾ / ʾawlād.*	لِي ثَلاثَة مِن الإخوَة / أَبنَاء / أولاد.
I don't have any sisters / brothers.	*laysa lī ʾakhawāt / ʾikhwa.*	لَيسَ لِي أَخَوَات / إخوَة.
… daughters / sons / children.	*… banāt / ʾabnāʾ / ʾawlād.*	... بَنَات / أَبنَاء / أولاد.
I have a wife / a husband.	*lī zawja / zawj.*	لِي زَوجَة / زَوج.
I don't have a wife / a husband.	*laysa lī zawja / laysa lī zawj.*	لَيسَ لِي زَوجَة / لَيسَ لِي زَوج.

Who's who in an Arab family? Arabic names usually consist of three names. The name gives information about the person's own given name (the first name), the father's given name (the second name), and the grandfather's given name (the third name). As a rule, married couples thus have different "last names." In the case of sons, the names often are combined with *ibn* إبن (son of …), whereas daughters' names include *bint* بنت (daughter of …). Akhmed ibn Hassan is "Akhmed, son of Hassan."

1 Which sentences are identical in meaning? Mark the correct box.

1 أَنَا مُتَزَوِّج.
A ☐ لِـي أُخْتَان.
B ☐ لِـي زَوْجَـة.
C ☐ لِـي أَب.

2 لِـي أولاد.
A ☐ لِـي أُم.
B ☐ لِـي زَوج.
C ☐ لِـي اِبنَان.

3 انَا أعزَب.
A ☐ لِـي أخ.
B ☐ لَيس لِـي زَوجَـة.
C ☐ لِـي اِبنَـة.

2 Here you see four answers. What are the questions they answer? Fill in the blanks, following this pattern:
Question: هَل لَكَ عَائِلَة ؟ – Answer: نَعَم، لِـي عَائِلَة.

1 ________________ ؟ نَعَم، لِـي أخ.
2 ________________ ؟ نَعَم، أنَا مُتَزَوِّج.
3 ________________ ؟ نَعَم، أنَا مُطَلَق.
4 ________________ ؟ نَعَم، لِـي أَولاد.

3 How would Zaid Ali Mohammed (the father) describe his family? Complete the sentences. The information in the box on the previous page can help you with this exercise.

عَبدُ الرحمَن بن زَيد	خَديجَة عَلِي مُحَمد	لِي
هَالَة حَسَن عُثمَان	بِشَارَة بِنت زَيد	زَيد عَلِي مُحَمد

1 اِسمِي ________________. اِسمُ زَوجَتِي ________________.
2 لِي ________________ و ________________. اِسمُ اِبنَتِي:
________________ واسمُ اِبْنِي: ________________.
3 ________________ أختٌ. اسمُهَا ________________.

4 And what is your family like? Describe the makeup of your family. If you need additional vocabulary, you can also look at section V4 (Family).

لِي ____

Communication

Apologizing / Asking for Something / Saying Thank You

Excuse me, can you please tell me the time?	*law samaḥta, 'akhbirnī kamis-sa'a?*	◄ لَو سَمَحتَ. أخبِرني كَم السَاعة؟
It's now 12 o'clock.	*as-sā'atul-'ān 'ath-thāniyata 'ashara ẓuhran.*	◁ السَاعَةُ الآن 12 ظُهراً.
Thanks very much!	*shukran jazīlan!*	◄ شُكراً جَزيلاً!
You're welcome!	*'afwan!*	◁ عَفواً!

Apologizing اعتِذار

You can use the following expressions as civilities when you address someone or when you actually are apologizing for something:

Excuse me. / Sorry. / Pardon me.	*min faḍlika / 'afwan / law samaḥt!*	مِن فَضلِكَ / عَفواً / لَو سَمَحت!
Sorry that I'm late.	*'a'tadhiru 'an ta'akhurī.*	اعتَذِرُعَن تَأخُري.
Pardon me for bothering you.	*sāmiḥnī 'alal-'iz'āj.*	سَامِحني عَلى الإزعَاج.

As a polite response to an apology, you say:

Don't mention it. / It was nothing.	*lā tubāli!*	لاتُبالِ!
Don't worry about it. / It doesn't matter.	*lā yuhimuk!*	لا يُهِمُك!

Asking for Something عِندَمَا تَطلُبَ شَيئاً مِن غَيرِك

A very polite request is expressed this way:

Can / Could you help me?	*hal yumkinuka 'an tusā'idanī?*	هَل يُمكِنُكَ أن تُسَاعِدَنِي؟
Could you explain / give (something) …	*hal bi'imkānika 'an tuwaḍiḥa / tu'ṭīnī …*	هَل بِإمكَانِكَ أن تُوضِحَ / تُعطِيني ...

More informally, you can also say:

Please tell / show / give …	*min faḍlika qul lī / dullanī 'alā / 'a'ṭinī …*	مِن فَضلِكَ قُل لِي / دُلَّني عَلَى / أعطِنِي ...

Saying Thank You عِندَمَا تَشكُرُ

Here's how to express your gratitude:

Thanks. / Thanks very much.	*shukran! / shukran jazīlan!*	شُكراً! / شُكراً جَزيلاً!
I thank you.	*'ashkuruka!*	أشكُرُك!

Polite responses to "thank you" are:

You're welcome. / You're very welcome.	*'afwan! / tafaḍal!*	عَفواً! / تَفَضَل!
Don't mention it.	*lā shukra 'alal-wājib!*	لاشُكرَ عَلى الوَاجِب!

1 Which expressions belong to which category? Write them in the correct column.

مِن فَضلِكَ قُل لِي ...　　لاتُبالِ!　　لَو سَمَحتَ!　　هَل يُمكِنُكَ ...

شُكراً!　　لاشُكرَ عَلى الوَاجِب!　　أشكُرُكَ!　　لا يُهِمُكَ!

apology	thank you	request

2 What is the polite response to the following statements? Write your answers in the balloons.

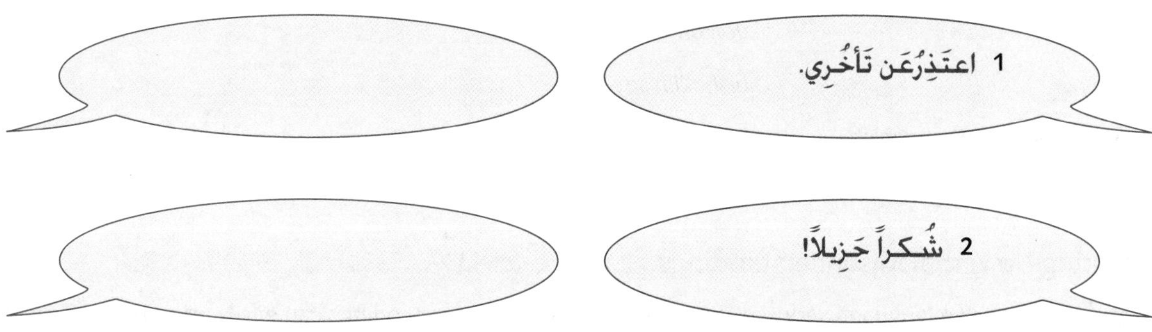

3 How would you formulate the following requests?

1. You want someone to give you the newspaper.

Direct request: ______________ الجَريدَة.

Very polite request: ______________ الجَريدَة.

2. You would like to know what time it is now.

Direct request: ______________ كَم السَّاعَة الآن.

Very polite request: ______________ كَم السَّاعَة الآن.

Knowledge of a Language / Clearing Up Misunderstandings

30

You really speak Arabic well!	*'innaka tujīdul-ʿarabiyya!*	◄ إنَّكَ تُجِيدُ العَرَبِيَّة!
Thanks. And do you speak English?	*shukran. wa hal 'anti tatakalamīnal-'indjilīziyya?*	◁ شُكراً. وَهَل أنتِ تَتَكَلَّمِينَ الإنْجِليزِية؟
Unfortunately, I don't. But I know a little German and French.	*lā maʿal 'asaf. walākinnī 'aʿrifu qalīlan minal-'injilīziyya wal-faransiyya.*	◄ لا مَعَ الأسف. ولكِنِّي أعرِفُ قَلِيلاً مِن الإنْجِلِيزيَّة والفَرَنسِيَّة.

Knowledge of a Language تَفاصِيلٌ حَولَ مَعرِفَةِ اللُّغاتِ

V3

Here's how to ask about a person's knowledge of languages:

Do you speak Arabic?	*hal tatakalamul-ʿarabiyya?*	هَل تَتَكَلَّمُ العَرَبِيَّة؟
Do you know English?	*hal taʿriful-l 'indjilīziyya?*	هَل تَعرِفُ الإنجِليزيَّة؟

Possible answers to these questions are:

Yes, I speak Arabic.	*naʿam 'ana 'atakalamul-ʿarabiyya.*	نَعَم، أنَاأتَكَلَّمُ العَرَبِيَّة.
proficiently / very well / well	*bishaklin mumtāz / jayyid jidan / jayyid*	بِشَكل مُمتَاز/ جَيِّد جِداً / جَيِّد
a little	*qalīlan*	قَلِيلاً
poorly	*bishaklin sayi'*	بِشَكل سَيء
I understand a little Spanish.	*'ana 'afhamul-'isbāniyya qalīlan.*	أنا أفهَمُ الإسبَّانِيَة قَلِيلاً.
I don't know (any) …	*'ana lā 'aʿrifu …*	أنَا لا أعرِفُ ...

Clearing Up Verbal Misunderstandings تَوْضِيحٌ لما فُهِمَ خَطَأً

If you don't speak a language very well, language-related misunderstandings can easily arise. Here's how to explain your communication problems in Arabic:

Excuse me, I didn't understand that.	*'afwan, 'ana lam 'afham hādhā.*	عَفواً، أنَا لَم أفهَم هَذا.
Sorry, I didn't catch (hear) that.	*afwan, 'ana lam 'asmaʿ dhālika jayyidan.*	عَفواً، أنَا لَم أسمَع ذلِكَ جَيِّداً.
Please repeat that.	*law samaḥt 'aʿid marratan 'ukhrā.*	لَوسَمَحت أعِد مَرَّةً أُخرَى.
Please speak more slowly.	*min faḍlika takalam bibuṭ'in.*	مِن فَضلِكَ تَكَلَم بِبُطئٍ.
I don't know what the word … means.	*'ana lā 'aʿrifu maʿnā hādhihil-kalima …*	أنَا لا أعرِفُ معنَى هَذِه الكَلِمَة ...
Can you explain to me what … means?	*hal bi 'imkānika 'an tuwaḍiḥa lī maʿnā …*	هَل بِإمكانِكَ أن تُوَضِحَ لِي مَعنى ... ؟
How do you say … in Arabic?	*mā maʿnā … bil ʿarabiyya?*	مَامَعنَى ... بِالعَرَبِيَّة؟

1 Write the words given below in the correct blank. Make sure that the verbs for أَنتَ (you) and أَنَا (I) have different prefixes. G20

1 هَل ________________ الإنجليزيَّة؟
2 هَل ________________ الألمانيَّة؟
3 أَنتَ ________________ العَرَبِيَّة!
4 أَنَا ________________ الفَرنسِيَّة قَلِيلاً.

2 Hassan is learning various languages. How would you rate his proficiency in these languages in Arabic? Fill in the blanks.

English: 1.0
French: 1.2
German: 2
Italian: 4
Spanish: 6
Russian: no knowledge

1 حَسَن يَتَكَلَّمُ الإنجليزيَّة بِشَكل مُمتَاز.
2 حَسَن يَتَكَلَّمُ الفَرَنسِيَّة ________________.
3 هُوَ يَتَكَلَّمُ الألمَانِيَّة ________________.
4 حَسَن يَتَكَلَّمُ الإيطَالِيَّة ________________.
5 حَسَن يَتَكَلَّمُ الأسبَانِيَّة ________________.
6 هُوَ ________________ يعرِفُ الرُوسِيَّة.

3 Which sentences would you use in which situation? Match the items below.

1. Your partner in conversation is talking too fast, and you want him to speak more slowly.
2. You didn't catch (hear) what was said.
3. You want your partner in conversation to repeat what was said.
4. You didn't understand what was said.
5. You don't know what a certain Arabic word means.
6. You would like to know how to say a certain English word in Arabic.

A عَفواً, أَنَا لَم أَفهَم هَذا.
B عَفواً, أَنَا لَم أَسمَع ذلِكَ جَيداً.
C أَنَا لا أَفهَمُ معنَى هَذه الكَلِمَة ...
D لَوسَمَحتَ أَعِد مَرَّةً أُخرَى.
E مِن فَضلِكَ تَكَلَم بِبُطئٍ.
F كَيفَ تَقولُ ... بِالعَربِيَّة؟

Talking About Habits / Preferences / Dislikes

 31

What do you like to do in your free time?	*mādhā tuḥibbu 'an taf'ala fī waqti farāġika?*	◄ مَاذَا تُحِبُّ أن تَفعَلَ فِي وَقتِ فَرَاغِكَ؟
I really like to play basketball. I often go to basketball games.	*'ana 'uḥibbu 'an 'al'aba kuratas-sala. kathīrammā 'al'abu kuratas-sala.*	◁ أَنَا أُحِبُّ أَن أَلعَبَ كُرَةَ السَّلَةِ. كَثِيراً مَا أَلعَبُ كُرَةَ السّلة.
And what do you like best?	*wa mādhā tufaḍilu 'alal-'aġlabi?*	◄ وَمَاذَا تُفَضِلُ عَلَى الأغلَبِ؟
I like traveling most of all. Usually I travel in the summer.	*'ufaḍilus-siyyāḥata 'ādatan 'usāfiru fis-ṣayf.*	◁ أُفَضِلُ السَّياحة. عَادَةً أُسَافِرُ فِي الصيف.
And what don't you enjoy so much?	*wa mal-ladhī lā tuḥibbuhu?*	◄ وَمَا الذي لا تُحِبُّهُ؟
I don't like soccer.	*'ana lā 'uḥibbu kuratal-qadam.*	◁ أَنَا لا أُحِبُّ كُرَةَ القَدَم.

Describing Habits وَصفُ العَادَات

G25

Habits are frequently expressed by using the following general indications of time and/or adverbs:

in the morning(s)	*sabāḥan*	صَبَاحاً
on weekends	*fī 'uṭalil-'usbū'iya*	فِي عُطلِ الأسبُوعِيَة
(on) Monday(s)	*kullu yawmi ithnayni*	كُلَّ يَوم اثنَين
most often	*kathīrammā*	كَثِيراً مَا
usually, as a rule	*'ādatan*	عَادَةً
We often go to the theater.	*naḥnu kathīrammā nadhhabu 'ilal-masraḥ.*	نَحنُ كَثِيراً مَا نَذهَبُ إِلَى المَسرَح.
Normally I ride my bike to work.	*'ādatan 'adhhabu ilal-'amali biddarāja.*	عَادَةً أَذهَبُ إِلَى العَمَلِ بِالدَّرَاجَة.

Expressing Preferences / Dislikes تَعبِيرٌ عَمَّا تُحِبُّهُ / تُفَضِلُهُ / ومَا لا تُحِبُّه

V5

I like music (very much).	*'ana 'uḥibbul-mūsīqā (kathīran).*	أَنَا أُحِبُّ المُوسِيقَى (كَثِيراً).
I like film best.	*'ana 'ufaḍilus-sīnimā.*	أَنَا أُفَضِلُ السِينِمَا.
I like theater most of all.	*'ana 'ufaḍilul-masraḥ.*	أَنَا أُفَضِلُ المَسرَح.
I don't like soccer.	*'ana lā 'uḥibbu kuratal-qadam.*	أَنَا لا أُحِبُّ كُرَةَ القَدَم.
I don't like soccer at all.	*'ana lā 'uḥibbu kuratal-qadami 'abadan.*	أَنَا لا أُحِبُّ كُرَةَ القَدَم أَبَداً.
I like soccer least of all.	*'aqalla mā 'uḥibbu kuratal-qadam.*	أَقَلَّ مَا أُحِبُّ كُرَةَ القَدَم.
I like to read. / I enjoy reading.	*'ana 'uḥibbul-qara'a.*	أَنَا أُحِبُّ القِرَاءَةَ.

1 Arabic has several ways of expressing preferences and /or dislikes. Complete the sentences below.

أُفَضِّل أُحِبُّ لا أُحِبّ

1. I really enjoy riding my bike to work. — أنا ________ الذِهَابَ إلَى العَمَلِ بالدَّرَاجَة.
2. I don't like to ride my bike to work. — أنا ________ الذِهَابَ إلَى العَمَلِ بالدَّرَاجَة.
3. Most of all I like riding my bike to work. — أنا ________ الذِهَابَ إلَى العَمَلِ بالدَّرَاجَة.

2 These sentences express preferences. Reword them to express dislikes.

1 أنَا أُحِبُّ المُوسِيقَى. ________

2 أنَا أُفَضِلُ المَسرَح. ________

3 أنَا أُحِبُّ الرِيَاضَةَ كَثِيراً. ________

3 Here you see the list of Hassan's likes and dislikes. Put them in order, from 1, "likes," to 6, "doesn't like at all."

A [1] حَسَن يُفَضِلُ السِينَمَا.

B [ ] هُو لا يُحِب المَسرَح.

C [ ] حَسَن لا يُحِبُّ كُرَةَ السَّلَة أبَداً.

D [ ] هُوَ يُحِبُّ القِرَاءَة.

E [ ] حَسَن يُحِبُّ كُرَةَ القَدَم كَثِيراً.

F [ ] هُوَ أقَلَّ مَا يُحِب المُوسِيقَى.

4 Reword these sentences so that they express habits. Use the words provided.

كَثِيراً مَا عَادَةً

1 ________ أُسَافِرُ فِي الصِيف.

2 ________ ألعَبُ كَرَةَ القَدَم فِي عُطلَةِ الأسبُوع.

C9

On the Telephone

32

Hello. (I'm listening.)	*'ana 'asma'.*	◂ أَنَا أَسمَع.
Good morning. May I speak to Sumaya, please?	*ṣabāhul khairi, 'awaddu 'an 'atakallama ma'a sumayā?*	◃ صَبَاحُ الخَير. أَوَدُّ أَن أَتَكَلَمَ مَعَ سُمَيَا؟
She's not here. Who's speaking?	*hiya laysat mawjūda. manil-mutakalim?*	◂ هِيَ لَيسَت مَوجُودَة. مَنِ المُتَكَلِم؟
My name is Hassan. Can you tell her that I called?	*'ismī ḥassan. hal bi 'imkāniki an tubliġīhā bi'annanī 'ittasalt?*	◃ اِسمِي حَسَن. هَل بِإمكَانِكِ أَن تُبلِغِيهَا بِأَنَّنِي اتَّصَلت؟
I'll pass on the message. Goodbye.	*sawfa 'ubliġuhā dhālika. ma'as-salāma.*	◂ سَوفَ أُبلِغُهَا ذَلِكَ. مَعَ السَّلامَة.

Answering the Phone عِندَمَا تُجِيبُ المُتَّصِل بِالهَاتِف

Hello.	*halū.*	هَلُو.
Who's calling / speaking?	*manil-muttaṣil / manil-mutakalim?*	مَنِ المُتَّصِل / مَنِ المُتَكَلِم؟

Asking for Someone أَن تَسأَلَ عَن شَخص

Is … there? / Can I speak to …?	*hal … mawjūd / hal yumkinunī 'an 'atakalama ma'a…*	هَل ... مَوجُود / هَل يُمكِنُنِي أَنْ أَتَكَلَمَ مَعَ ...
I'll call him / her, just a minute, please.	*sa'ad'ūhu / sa'ad'ūha, laḥẓa law samaḥt.*	سَأَدعُوهُ / سَأَدعُوهَا. لَحظَة لَو سَمَحت.
He's not here right now. / She's not here right now.	*huwa ġayru mawjūd ḥāliyan. / hiya ġayru mawjūda ḥāliyan.*	هُوَ غَيرُ مَوجُود حَالِياً. / هِيَ غَيرُ مَوجُودَة حَالِياً.

Wrong Number رَقمٌ خَطَأ

That person doesn't live here.	*hādhāsh-shakhṣ lā yaskunu hunā.*	هَذا الشَخص لايَسكُنُ هُنَا.
You have the wrong number.	*laqad 'ittaṣalta bi raqmin khaṭ'a.*	لَقَد اتَّصَلتَ بِرَقمٍ خَطَأ.

Leaving a Message أَن تَترُكَ خَبَراً

Can I leave a message?	*hal turīdu 'an 'ubliġahu 'anka shay'an?*	هَل تُرِيدُ أَن أُبلِغَهُ عَنكَ شَيأً؟
Can you please tell him / her …	*hal bi 'imkānika 'an tukhbirahu / tukhbirahā …*	هَل بِإمكَانِكَ أَنْ تُخبِرَهُ / تُخبِرَهَا ...
… he should call me? / she should call me?	*… 'alayhi 'an yat-taṣila bī / 'alayhā 'an tat-taṣila bī?*	... عَلَيهِ أَن يَتَّصِلَ بِي / عَلَيهَاأَن تَتَصِلَ بِي؟
… that I called him / her?	*… bi'annanī ittaṣaltu bihi / bihā?*	... بِأَنِنِي اتَّصلتُ بِهِ / بِهَا؟

Communication

1 When do you hear what? Match the items in the two columns.

1. When you pick up a ringing telephone.
2. The person you want to speak to is not there.
3. To say goodbye.
4. When you have the wrong number.
5. When someone asks who is calling.
6. When the person asked for is being called to the phone.

A هَذا الشَّخص لايَسكُنُ هُنَا.
B مَن المتَّصِل؟
C مَعَ السَّلامة.
D هَلُو.
E سَأدعُوهَا. لَحظَة لَو سَمَحت.
F هِيَ غَيرُ مَوجُودَة حَالِياً.

2 The following dialogue is out of order. Number the sentences to show the correct order.

A ☐ هَلُو.
B ☐ سَأدعُوه. لَحظَة لَو سَمَحت.
C ☐ صَبَاحُ الخَير. أَوَدُّ أن أَتَكَلَّمَ مَعَ سَمَيا؟
D ☐ إسمِي حَسن.
E ☐ مَنِ المُتَكَلِم؟

3 You are phoning someone. Fill in the missing parts of the dialogue.

هَلُو.	1 صَبَاحُ الخَير. ____________؟ (You would like to speak to Monica.).
مَنِ المُتَكَلِم؟	2 .____________ (You introduce yourself.)
هِيَ غَيرُ مَوجُودَة حَالِياً.	3 هَل بِإمكَانِكَ أَنْ تُخبِرَهَا ____________؟ .____________ (You would like Monica to call you back and you say goodbye.)

Arranging to Meet / Making, Accepting, Turning Down Suggestions

33

Hello, Sumaya. What are you doing this evening?	*'ahlan yā sumayā. mādhā taʿmalīna hādhal masā'?*	◄ أهلاً يَا سُمَيَا. ماذا تَعمَلِينَ هَذَا المَسَاءِ؟
Nothing. Do you have an idea?	*lā shay'. hal ʿindaka fikra?*	◁ لاشَيْء. هَل عِندَكَ فِكرَة؟
Shall we go to the theater? There's a good play now.	*hal nadhhabu 'ilal-masraḥ? hunāka masraḥiya jayyida.*	◄ هَل نَذهَبُ إلَى المَسْرَحِ؟ هناكَ مَسرَحِيَة جَيِّدة.
With pleasure. When and where should we meet?	*bikulli surur. 'ayna wa matā naltaqī?*	◁ بِكُلِّ سُرُور. أينَ ومَتَى نَلتَقِي؟
At six? At the entrance?	*fis-sāʿatis-sādisa? 'amāmal-madkhal?*	◄ فِي السَّاعَةِ السَّادِسة؟ أَمَامَ المَدخَل؟
Fine. See you then!	*ḥasanan. ilal-liqā'!*	◁ حَسَناً. إلَى اللِقَاءِ!

Making, Accepting, Turning Down Suggestions أن تَقتَرِحَ شَيئاً / تَأخُذَ / تَرفُضَ مَا أُقتُرِح

V5

Shall we meet?	*mā r'ayuka 'an naltaqī?*	مَارَأيُكَ أن نَلتَقِي؟
Shall we go to …, perhaps?	*mā r'ayuka 'an nadhhaba ilā …?*	مَارَأيُكَ أن نَذهَبَ إلَى ...؟
Would you possibly like …	*laʿalaka turīdu …*	لَعَلَكَ تُرِيدُ ...
… to go to the movies / concert?	*… 'adh-dhihāba ilas-sīnimā / ḥaflat mūsīqā?*	... الذِّهَابَ إلَى السِينمَا / حَفلَة مُوسِيقَى؟
… to watch a movie / a soccer game?	*… 'an tushāhida filman / mubārāt kuratal-qadam?*	... أن تُشَاهِدَ فِلماً / مُبَارَاة كُرَة القَدمِ؟
Shall we get together, maybe?	*hal yumkinu 'an naltaqiya?*	هَل يُمكِنُ أن نَلتَقِيَ؟
Good idea!	*fikra jayyida!*	فِكرَة جَيِّدة!
Unfortunately, I can't tonight.	*maʿal 'asaf lā 'astaṭīʿu hādhal masā'.*	مَعَ الأسفِ لا أستَطِيعُ هَذَا المَسَاء.
Unfortunately, I'll be busy tomorrow.	*maʿal 'asaf ġadan sa'akūnu mashġūlan.*	مَعَ الأسَفِ غَداً سَأكُونُ مَشغُولاً.
Maybe another day / on Saturday?	*'ufaḍilu yawman 'ākhara / yawmas-sabt?*	أُفَضِلُ يَوماً آخَرَ / يَوم السَّبت؟

Arranging the Place and Time أن تَتفِقَ عَلَى وَقت ومَكَانِ المَوعِدِ

V7
V8
G15

Where shall we meet?	*'ayna naltaqī?*	أينَ نَلتَقِي؟
Maybe we can meet …	*yumkinu 'an naltaqiya …*	يُمكِنُ أن نَلتَقِيَ ...
… at the entrance / exit?	*… 'amāmal madkhal / 'al-makhradj?*	... أمَامَ المَدخَل / المَخرَج؟
… at the (bus, streetcar) stop?	*… ʿinda mawqifil-bāṣ?*	... عِندَ مَوقِفِ البَاص؟
When shall we meet?	*mattā naltaqī?*	مَتَى نَلتَقِي؟
How would six o'clock be?	*kayfa fis-sāʿati 'as-sādisa?*	كَيفَ فِي السَّاعَةِ السَّادِسَة؟
Six o'clock is a little too early / too late.	*'as-sāʿatus-sādisa waqt mubakir / muta'akhir baʿḍash-shay'.*	السَّاعَةُ السَّادِسَة وقت مُبَكِر / مُتَأخِر بَعض الشَّيء.

1 Match the questions and suggestions on the right with the appropriate response on the left.

1 ماذاتعمَلُ هَذَا المَسَاء؟
2 لَعَلّكَ تُريدُ أن تَذهَبَ إلَى السينمَا؟
3 مَتَى نَلتَقِي؟
4 أينَ نَلتَقِي؟
5 مَارَأيُكَ أن نَذهَبَ إلَى المَسرَحِيَة غَداً؟

A يُمكِنُ أن نَلتَقِيَ أمَامَ المَدخَل؟
B فِكرَة جَيِّدة!
C مَعَ الأسف غَداً لا أستَطِيعُ .
D لاشَيْء.
E كَيفَ فِي السّاعَةِ السّادِسَة؟

2 A friend suggests that you could do something together on Friday. Respond to the suggestion by using the information in parentheses.

1 مَارَأيُكَ أن نَذهَبَ إلَى السينمَا يَومَ الجُمعَة؟

________________________!

(You think it's a good idea.)

2 مَعَ الأسفِ لا ____________ يَومَ الجُمعَة. ____________ يَومَ السَّبت؟

(You turn down the suggestion because you can't do it on Friday. Suggest Saturday as an alternative.)

3 ____________ و ____________ نَلتَقِي؟

(You want to know when and where you should meet.)

3 Here you see an excerpt from the calendar of events for this Friday. Suggest to a friend (m.) some things you could do together.

نُشَاهِد نَذهَبُ لَعَلّكَ تُريدُ

1 **السينمَا:**
فِلم "Titanic"

____

____

2 **مَركَزُ الرِيَاضَة:**
مُبَارَاة كُرَة القَدم

____

____

3 **قَاعَة المَسرَح:**
مَسرَحِيَة "Mozart"

____

____

Asking for Directions / Giving Directions

34

Excuse me, can you please tell me where the National Museum is?	*law samahti, hal yumkinu ʼan tukhbirīnī ʼajnal-mathaf ʼal-shaʿbī?*	◀ لَو سَمَحتِ، هَل يُمكِنُ أن تُخبِرينِي أَينَ المَتحَف الشَّعبِي؟
Yes, go straight down this street, and then turn left. The museum is on the right.	*naʿam, ʼimshi fī hādhasch-shāriʿ ʼilal-ʼamām thumma tawajyah ilal-jasār, ʼal-matḥafu ʿalā jihatil-yamīni.*	◁ نَعَم، إمشِ فِي هَذا الشَّارِع إلَى الأَمَام ثُمَّ تَوَجَّه إلَى اليَسَار. المَتحَفُ عَلَى جِهَةِ اليَمِين.

Asking for Directions أَن تَسأَلَ مَن يَدُلُّكَ عَلَى الطَّرِيق

Excuse me, where is …?	*law samaḥt, ʼayna …?*	لَو سَمَحت، أَينَ ...؟
Can you …	*ʼayumkinuka …*	أَيُمكِنُكَ ...
… tell me how to get to …?	*… ʼan tukhbiranī kayfal-wuṣūlu ilā …?*	... أَن تُخبِرَنِي كَيفَ الوُصُول إلَى ...؟
… show me the way to …?	*… ʼan tadullanī ʿalāṭarīqi ʼilā …?*	... أن.تَدُلَّنِي عَلَى الطَّرِيقِ إلَى ...؟
How do you get to … on foot / by car?	*kayfa ʼaṣilu ʼilā / kayfa ʼasūqu ʼilā …?*	كَيفَ أَصِلُ إلَى / كَيفَ أَسُوقُ إلَى ...؟
Does this bus / train go to …?	*hal yadhhabu hādhal-bāṣ / al-qiṭār ʼilā …?*	هَل يَذهَبُ هَذَا البَاص / القِطَارإلَى ...؟
Do you have to transfer?	*hal ʿalayya ʼan ʼubaddilal-bāṣ?*	هَل عَلَيَّ أَن أُبَدِّلَ البَاص؟

Giving Directions أَن تَدُلَّ عَلَى الطَّرِيق

V8 ↑ V13 Go straight ahead / back / down this street.	*ʼimshi ʼilal-ʼamām / ʼirjiʿ ʼilal warāʼ / hādhaṭarīq ʿalā ṭūl.*	إمشِ إلَى الأَمَام / إرجِع إلَى الوَرَاء / هَذَا الطَّرِيق عَلَى طُول.
Go 200 meters straight ahead.	*ʼimshi ʼilal-ʼamām miʼatay mitr.*	إمشِ إلَى الأَمَام مِئَتَي مِتر.
Go to the intersection / traffic light.	*ʼimschi ḥattā muftariqṭ-ṭuruq / ʼishāratal-murūr.*	إمشِ حَتَى مُفتَرَق الطُّرق / إشَارَةَ المُرُور.
Cross the street.	*ʼuʿburi-ṭarīqa.*	أُعبُر الطَّرِيقَ.
Turn left / right.	*tawajah ʼilal-yasār / al-yamīn.*	تَوَجَّه إلَى اليَسَار / اليَمِين.
At the post office, you turn onto Hamdan Street.	*ʿindal-barīdi kḥudh shāriʿ ḥamdān.*	عِندَ البَرِيد خُذ شَارِع حَمدَان.
The train station is there / here …	*hunāka maḥaṭatul-qiṭār / hunā …*	هُنَاكَ مَحَطَةُ القِطَار / هُنَا ...
… on the right / left / other side of the street.	*… ʿalā jihatil-yamīn / al-yasār / ʿalal-jānib ʼal-ʼākhari minash-shāriʿ.*	... عَلَى جِهَةِ اليَمِين / اليَسَار / عَلَى الجَانِب الآخرِ مِن الشَّارِع.
Take Bus No. 5 to …	*khudhil-bāṣ raqam khamsa ḥattā …*	خُذِ البَاص رَقَم 5 حَتّى ...
Get out at the …. stop.	*ʼinzil fī maḥaṭati …*	انزل فِي مَحَطَةِ ...
Transfer to Bus No. 1.	*baddil bāṣ wa khudh al-bāṣ raqam wāḥid.*	بَدِّل البَاص وخُذ البَاص رَقَم 1.

1 What direction do the arrows indicate? Mark the correct box.

1
A ☐ إرجع إلَى الوَرَاء
B ☐ إمشِ إلَى الأمَام
C ☐ تَوَجَّه إلَى اليَسَار

2
A ☐ إمشِ إلَى الأمَام
B ☐ تَوَجَّه إلَى اليَمين
C ☐ تَوَجَّه إلَى اليَسَار

3
A ☐ تَوَجَّه إلَى اليَمين
B ☐ تَوَجَّه إلَى اليَسَار
C ☐ إرجع إلَى الوَرَاء

2 Match the expressions with the translations.

1 عِندَ إشَارَةِ المُرُور تَوَجَّه إلَى اليَسَار
2 تَوَجَّه إلَى اليَمين
3 أُعبُر الشَارِع
4 إمشِ إلَى الأمَام عَلَى طُول
5 إركَب البَاص رَقْمْ 5
6 عَلَى يَسَارِالشّارِع
7 بَدِّل البَاص وخُذْ البَاص رَقم 6
8 تَسُوقْ حَتَى مَركَزِ المَدينَة

A Go straight ahead
B Cross the street
C Go (by vehicle) to the center of town
D Transfer to Bus No. 6
E Turn left at the traffic light
F Turn right
G On the left side of the street
H Take Bus No. 5

3 Complete this dialogue, using the words provided. The translation will help you.

تَوَجَّه إلَى اليَمين	تَوَجَّه إلَى اليَسَار	كَيفَ الوُصُول	الشَارِع	مئة متر	المَحَطَة

1 لَوسَمَحتَ، أخبِرني ____________ إلَى مَحَطَةِ القِطَار؟

Excuse me! Can you please tell me how to get to the train station?

2 أُعبُر__________ ثُمَّ __________.

Cross the street and turn left.

3 إمشِ عَلَى طُول ____________.

Go 100 meters straight ahead.

4 عِندَ إشَارَةِ المُرُور____________.

Turn right at the traffic light.

5 ____________ عَلَى يَمينِ الشَارِع.

The train station is on the right side of the street.

Communication

At a Restaurant

35

Could I order, please?	*'urīdu 'an 'aṭlubaṭ-ṭa'āma law samaḥta?*	◄ أُرِيدُ أن أَطلُبَ الطَعَام لَوسَمَحتَ؟
Yes, please. What would you like?	*na'am, tafaḍalī, mādhā taṭlubīna?*	◁ نَعَم، تَفَضَلِي. مَاذَا تَطلُبِينَ؟
I would like chicken and salad.	*'aṭlubu dajāj wa salaṭa.*	◄ أَطلُبُ دَجَاج وسَلطَة.
What would you like to drink?	*mādhā turīdīna 'an tashrabī?*	◁ مَاذا تُرِيدِينَ أن تَشرَبِي؟
A glass of lemonade.	*'aṣīral-laymūn.*	◄ عَصِيرالَلَّيمُون.

Menu / Ordering Food كَيفَ تَطلُب طَعَاماً / وَجبَة طَعَام

V9

V10

May I have the menu, please?	*'urīd qā'imatat-ṭa'āmi law samaḥta?*	أُرِيدُ قَائِمَةَ الطَعَام لَوسَمَحتَ؟
What can you recommend?	*bimādhā tanṣaḥunī?*	بِمَاذَا تَنْصَحُنِي؟
I would like (more) / (less) …	*'urīd (ziyāda / qalīlan min) …*	أُرِيدُ (زِيَادَة / قَلِيلاً مِن) ...

A waiter / a waitress asks:

What would you like?	*mādhā taṭlub?*	مَاذَا تَطلُب؟
Would you like …?	*hal turīd …?*	هَل تُرِيد ...

Talking About the Meal الكَلَامُ عَن الطعَام

Does it taste good? / Are you enjoying it?	*hal kānat-ṭa'āmu ṭayyiban?*	هَل كَانَ الطَعَامُ طَيِّباً؟
Very good!	*jayyid jidan!*	جَيِّد جِداً!
Too sweet / sour / salty / spicy.	*ḥulwun / ḥāmiḍun / māliḥun / ḥāddun.*	حُلوٌ / حَامِضٌ / مَالِحٌ / حَادٌّ.
It needs sugar / salt.	*'innahu bilā sukkar / milḥ.*	إِنَّهُ بِلا سُكَّر / مِلح.

Paying الدَفعُ

(May I have the) Check, please!	*al-ḥisāb law samaḥt!*	الحِساب لَوسَمَحت!
Here you are.	*tafaḍal.*	تَفَضَل.

Toasts and Related Expressions

Bon appétit! / Enjoy your meal!	*shahiyya ṭayyiba!*	شَهِيَّة طَيِّبَة!
Cheers! / To your health!	*fī ṣihatik!*	فِي صِحَتِك!

Communication

1 This dialogue is out of order. Number the sentences in their logical order.

A [1] مَاذَا تَطلُبُ؟
B ☐ الحِسابُ لَوسَمَحتَ!
C ☐ أَطلُبُ سَلطَة.
D ☐ مَاذا تُريدُ أن تَشرَبَ؟
E ☐ شَهيَّة طَيِّبَة!
F ☐ عَصِيرَ اللَّيمُون.
G ☐ تَفَضل.

2 Match the two columns. What do you say about your food if …

1. it is very good.	A إنَّهُ بِلا مِلح.
2. it is too salty.	B إنَّهُ بِلا سُكَّر.
3. it is very sweet.	C مَالِح.
4. it needs salt.	D جَيِّد جداً!
5. it needs sugar.	E حُلْوٌ كَثِيراً.

3 Translate the sentences, using the words provided.

مِن عَصِيرِ اللّيمُون	أُرِيدُ	شَهِيَّة طَيِّبَة
قَائِمةَ الطَعَام	فِي صِحَتِك	الطَعَامُ طَيِّباً

1. Bon appétit! ________________!
2. Cheers! ________________!
3. I would like more lemonade. ________ زِيَادَةَ ________.
4. Does it taste good? هَلْ كَانَ ________________؟
5. Could I have the menu? أُرِيدُ ____________ لَوسَمَحتَ؟

C13

Shopping

36

How much does this white sweater cost?	*kam qīmatu hādhihil-kanzatil-bayḍā'?*	◀ كَم قِيمَةُ هَذِهِ الكَنزَةِ البَيضَاء؟
It costs 100 dirham.	*qīmatuhā mi'atu dirham.*	◁ قِيمَتُهَا مِئَةُ دِرهَم.
Oh, that's a little too expensive.	*'awh, hādhā ġālin baʿḍash-schay'.*	◀ أوه. هَذَا غَال بَعضَ الشَيء.
How do you like this green one here? It's a little cheaper.	*kayfa tarā hādhihil-chaḍrā'? 'innahā 'arkhạṣu baʿḍash-shay'.*	◁ كَيفَ تَرَيهَذِهِ الخَضرَاء؟ إنَّهَا أرخَصُ بَعضَ الشَيْء.
It doesn't look bad. Where can I try it on?	*tabdū lā b'asa bihā. 'ayna ġurfatul-qiyas?*	◀ تَبدُو لابَأسَ بِهَا. أينَ غُرفَة القِيَاس؟

In a Store فِي الدُكَان

V8
V11

Do you have …?	*hal ʿindaka …?*	هَل عِندَكَ ...؟
I would like …	*'ana 'urīd …*	أنَا أُرِيد ...
I'm just looking (around).	*'ana 'urīdu 'an 'anẓura faqaṭ.*	أنَا أُرِيدُ أن أنظُرَ فَقَط.

Asking the Price أن تَسألَ عَنِ القِيمَة

How much does … cost?	*kam qīmatu …?*	كَم قِيمَةُ ...؟
The jacket costs 100 dirham.	*qīmatus-sutrati mi'atu dirham.*	قِيمَةُ السُترَةِ 100 دِرهَم.
Would you have something less expensive?	*'aturīdu (m.)/'aturīdīna (f.) shay'an 'arkhaṣ?*	أتُرِيدُ / أتُرِيدِينَ شَيئاً أرخَص؟

G16
G17

Comparing and Evaluating Things أن تُقَارِنَ الأشيَاء وَتُقِيمَهَا

How do you like …?	*hal yuʿjibuka …?*	هَل يُعجِبُكَ ...؟
I like it quite well / don't like it at all.	*'innahu yuʿjibunī kathīran / lā yuʿjibunī.*	إنَّهُ يُعجِبُنِي كَثِيراً / لا يُعجِبُنِي.
This jacket is prettier than that one.	*hādhihis-sutratu 'ajmalu min tilk.*	هَذِه السُترَةُ أجمَلُ مِن تِلك.
This coat is better looking than that one.	*hādhal miʿṭafu 'ajmalu min dhāk.*	هَذا المِعطَفُ أجمَلُ مِن ذَاك.
That shirt is the nicest.	*hādhal-qamīsu 'ajmalu minal-kul.*	هَذا القَمِيصُ أجمَلُ مِن الكُلِ.
I like this dress better.	*hādhāth-thaubu yuʿjibunī 'akthar.*	هَذَا الثَّوبُ يُعجِبُنِي أكثَر.
That is a little too expensive / too cheap.	*hādhā ġālin baʿḍa-shay' / raḥīṣ baʿḍa-shay'.*	هَذاغَالٍ بَعض الشَيء / رَخِيص بَعض الشَيء.
… too big	*… kabīr (m.)/kabīra (f.) jiddan.*	كَبِير / كَبِيرَة جداً.
… too small	*… ṣaġīr (m.)/ṣaġīra (f.) jiddan.*	صَغِير / صَغِيرَة جداً.
Do you have these shoes one size bigger / smaller?	*hal ʿindaka min hādhihil-'aḥdhiya 'akbar/'aṣġar bimaqāsin wāḥid?*	هَل عِندَكَ مِن هَذِهِ الأحذِيَة أكبَر / أصغَر بِمَقَاس وَاحِد؟

Paying الدَفع

How much do I owe?	*kam ʿalayya 'an 'adfaʿ?*	كَم عَلَيَّ أن أدفَع؟
Where is the checkout / cash desk?	*'aynaṣ-ṣundūq?*	أينَ الصُندُوق؟
Can I pay by credit card?	*hal yumkinu bi'an 'adfaʿa bi biṭāqatil-'itimān?*	هَل يُمكِنُ أنْ أدفَعَ بِبِطَاقَةِ الإئتِمَان؟

Communication

1 Translate into English.

1 أَنَا أُرِيدُ هَذَا الثَّوبُ.

_______________.

2 أَنَا أُرِيدُ أن أَنْظُرَ فَقَط.

_______________.

3 كَم قِيمَةُ هَذِه الكَنزَة؟

_______________.

4 هَذَا القَمِيص غَال جِداً.

_______________.

5 كَم عَلَيَّ أن أدفَع؟

_______________.

6 هَل عِندَكَ مِن هَذِهِ الأحذِيَة أَكبَر بِمَقَاس وَاحِد؟

_______________.

2 Match these items with their opposites.

1	غَال جِداً	A	يُعجِبُنِي
2	كَبِير جِداً	B	غَال
3	لايُعجِبُنِي	C	صَغِيرَة جِداً
4	رَخِيص	D	رَخِيص جِداً
5	كَبِيرَة جِداً	E	صَغِير جِداً

3 Complete the sentences with the words provided. The translation will help you with this exercise.

صَغِير جِدا	جِداً	هَذِهِ	لا تُعجِبُنِي	أَجمَلُ	غَالِيَة جِداً	يُعجِبُنِي

1 _______________ الكَنزَة _______________. This sweater is too expensive.

2 هَذَا المِعطَفُ _______________. This coat is too small.

3 هَذِهِ الأحذِيَة _______________. I don't like these shoes.

4 هَذَا القَمِيصُ _______________ مِن ذَاكَ. This shirt is nicer than that one.

5 هَذَا الثَّوبُ _______________ _______________. I like this dress very much.

Communication

At a Hotel

37

Good afternoon. I would like a room.	*nahāruka saʿīd. 'urīdu ġurfa min faḍlika.*	◄ نَهارُكَ سَعيد. أُريدُ غُرفَة مِن فَضلِك.
A single or a double?	*ġurfa lishakhṣin wāḥid 'am lishakhṣayn?*	◁ غُرفَة لِشَخصٍ واحِد أم لِشَخصَين؟
A single room. How is it equipped?	*lishakhṣ wāḥid. bimādhā mujahaza?*	◄ لِشَخص واحِد. بِماذا مُجَهزة؟
It has a shower, toilet, color TV, and refrigerator. How long do you want to stay?	*fīhā dūsh wa mirḥāḍ wa tilfiẓyūn mulawan wa thallāja. kam turīdīna 'an tuqīmī?*	◁ فيهَا دُوش ومِرحَاض وتِلفِزيون مُلَوَن وثَلاّجَة. كَم تُريدينَ أن تُقيمي؟
One week.	*'usbūʿan wāḥidan.*	◄ أُسبُوعاً واحِداً.

Reserving a Room حَجزُ غُرفَةٍ

V7 I would like / would like to reserve ...	*'ana 'urīdu 'an 'aḥjiza ...*	أنَا أُريدُ أن أحجِزَ ...
... a single / double room	*... lishakhṣin wāḥid / ġurfa lishakhṣayn*	... لِشَخصٍ واحِد / غُرفَة لِشَخصَين
... for one night / two nights	*... lilayla wāḥida / lilaylatayn*	لِلَيلَة وَاحِدَة / لِلَيلَتَين
... one week / two weeks	*... li'usbūʿin wāḥid / li'usbūʿayn*	لِأُسبُوعٍ واحِد / لأسبُوعَين
From when until when?	*min matā 'ilā matā?*	مِن مَتَى إلَى مَتَى؟
From August 20 to September 1.	*min ʿishrīna 'aġusṭus 'ilā 'awali sibtambir.*	مِن 20 أغسطس إلَى 1 سِبتَمبِر.
Unfortunately, we have no vacant rooms.	*maʿal 'asaf laysat ladaynā ġurfa fāriġa.*	مَعَ الأسَف لَيسَت لَدينَا غُرفَة فَارِغَة.

Describing a Room أن تَصِفَ الغُرفَة

The room has a shower / a bath / a bathtub V12	*lil ġurfati dūshun / ḥamām / ḥawḍu 'istiḥmām*	لِلغُرفَةِ دُوشٌ / حَمَام / حَوض اِستِحمَام
... a color TV	*... tilfiẓyūn mulawan*	... تِلفِزيون مُلَوَن
... a refrigerator	*... thallaja*	... ثلاّجَة
... a telephone	*... hātif*	... هَاتِف
... a balcony	*... dhātu shurfa*	...ذَاتُ شُرفَة
... a beautiful view	*... 'iṭlāla jamīla*	... إطلالة جَميلَة
A room with breakfast /	*ġurfat maʿal-fuṭūr*	غُرفَة مَعَ الفُطور
lunch / dinner	*'al-ġadhā' / 'al-ʿashā'*	... الغَذاء / العَشاء

1 What questions do you ask when reserving a hotel room? Mark the boxes.

1 هَل أَنتَ مُتَزَوِّج؟ ☐
2 مِن مَتَى إلَى مَتَى؟ ☐
3 كَم عُمرُكَ؟ ☐
4 أينَ تَسكُنُ؟ ☐
5 كَم تُريدُ أن تُقيمَ؟ ☐
6 غُرفَة لِشَخص واحِد أم لِشَخصَين؟ ☐

2 You want to reserve a room. How do you say …? Match the items below.

I would like a room …	أُريدُ غُرفَةً وَاحِدَة مِن فَضلِكَ …
1. with a bathtub	A مَعَ فُطُور
2. with a balcony	B مَعَ هَاتِف
3. with a telephone	C مَعَ دُوش
4. with a color TV	D إطلالة جَميلَة
5. with a shower	E مَعَ تِلفِزيون
6. with breakfast	F ذَاتُ شُرفَة
7. with a beautiful view	G مَعَ حَوض اِستِحمَام

3 Translate the following questions and wishes. The dialogue on the opposite page will help you.

I would like a single room. 1

____

I would like a room with breakfast. 2

____

How is the room equipped? 3

____

I would like a room for one week. 4

____

Communication

Traveling

38

Good afternoon. One ticket to Cairo, please.	*nahāruki sa'īd. 'urīdu tadhkira wāḥida 'ilal-qāhira min faḍliki.*	◄ نَهَارُكِ سَعِيد. أُرِيدُ تَذكَرَة وَاحِدَة إِلَى القَاهِرَة مِن فَضلِكِ.
One way or round-trip?	*dhihāban faqaṭ 'am dhihāban wa 'iyāban?*	◁ ذَهَاباً فَقط أم ذَهاباً وإِيَاباً؟
One way. When and from where does the train leave?	*dhihāban faqaṭ. matā wa min 'ayna yuġādirul-qiṭār?*	◄ ذَهَاباً فَقَط. مَتَى ومِن أَينَ يُغَادِرُ القِطَار؟
The train departs from Track 5 at 12:10.	*'al-qiṭāru yuġādiru fis-sā'ati 'ath-thāniyyati 'ashara wa 'ashri daqā'iqa ba'da-ẓuhr min'ar-raṣīfil-khāmis.*	◁ القِطَارُ يُغَادِرُ فِي السَاعَة 12 وعَشر دَقَائِق بَعد الظُهر مِن الرَصِيف 5.

Buying a Ticket أن تَشتَرِي تَذكِرَة

Where is the ticket window?	*'ayna maktabut-tadhākir?*	أينَ مَكتَبُ التَذَاكِر؟
A ticket to …, please.	*tadhkaratan wāḥida 'ilā … min faḍlika.*	تَذكَرَةً وَاحِدَة إِلَى ... مِن فَضلِكَ.
A one-way ticket, please.	*tadhkaratan lidh-dhihābi faqaṭ law samaḥt.*	تَذكَرَةً لِلذّهَابِ فَقَط لَو سَمَحت.
… a round-trip ticket.	*… tadhkaratan lidh-dhihābi wal-'iyābi.*	... تَذكَرَةً لِلذّهَابِ والإِيَابِ.

Asking for Travel Information أن تَسأَلَ عَن مَعلُومَاتٍ تَتَعَلَّقُ بِالسَّفر

V7
V13
G15

When does the train leave?	*matā yuġādirul qiṭār?*	مَتَى يُغادِرُ القِطَار؟
… does the bus leave?	*… yuġādirul-bāṣ?*	... يُغَادِرُ البَاص؟
… does the flight take off?	*… waqtul 'iqlā'?*	... وَقتُ الإقلاع؟
When does the train arrive?	*matā yaṣilul-qiṭār?*	مَتَى يَصِلُ القِطَار؟
When does the bus arrive?	*matā yaṣilul-bāṣ?*	مَتَى يَصِلُ البَاص؟
When does the plane land?	*matā tahbuṭut-tā'ira?*	مَتَى تَهبِطُ الطَائِرَة؟
The train is 10 minutes late.	*sawfa jata'akharul-qiṭāru 'ashra daqā'iq.*	سَوفَ يَتَأخَرُ القِطَارُ 10 دَقَائِق.
From where does the train / bus leave?	*min 'ayna yuġādirul-qiṭār / al-bāṣ?*	مِن أَينَ يُغَادِرُ القِطَار / البَاص ؟
The train leaves / departs from Track 3.	*yuġādirul-qiṭaru minar-raṣīf 'ath-thālith.*	يُغَادِرُ القِطَارُ مِن الرَّصِيف 3.
Does this bus go to …?	*hal yadh-habu hādhal-bāṣ 'ilā …?*	هَل يَذهَبُ هَذَا البَاص إِلَى ...؟
Where does this train go?	*'ilā 'ayna yadh-habu hādhal qiṭār?*	إِلَى أَينَ يَذهَبُ هَذَا القِطَار؟
Does the train stop at every station?	*hal yaqiful-qiṭāru fī kulil-maḥaṭāt?*	هَل يَقِفُ القِطَارُ فِي كُلِ المَحَطَات؟
Have a good trip!	*riḥla sa'īda!*	رِحلَة سَعِيدَة!

1 Compose the sentences below, using the words provided.

أينَ	سَوفَ يتأخّرُ	القِطارُ	هَل	إلَى القَاهِرَة	مَكتَبُ التَذاكِر
هَذا القِطارُ	إلَى القَاهِرَة	يَذهَبُ	تَذكِرَة واحِدَة	لَوسَمَحت	

1. A ticket to Cairo, please.

____

2. Where is the ticket window?

____

3. The train is late.

____

4. Does this train go to Cairo?

____

2 Look at these answers. What questions do they answer? The question words in parentheses will give you a hint.

1 (When) ______________________________؟

يُغادِرُ القِطار فِي السّاعَةِ الوَاحِدَة بَعدَ الظُهر.

2 (Where (to)) ______________________________؟

يَذهَبُ القِطارُ إلَى رَمسِيس.

3 (From where) ______________________________؟

يُغادِرُ القِطارُ مِن الرَّصِيف 3.

4 (When) ______________________________؟

يَصِلُ القِطارُ فِي السّاعَةِ الثَالِثَةِ بَعدَ الظُهر.

5 (Whether the bus goes to the center of town) ______________________________؟

نَعَم، يَذهَبُ القِطارُ إلَى مَركَزِ المَدِينَة.

3 What do you wish someone who's going away on a trip?

______________________________!

Communication

Tables

G30 On the following pages, each verb table is accompanied by the corresponding model structure. The first model structure refers to the past tense, the second to the present indicative.
Note that the verb forms are not separated according to grammatical number, but are listed in order according to person (1st, 2nd, 3rd) in their singular, dual, and plural forms. This corresponds to the standard arrangement in Arabic.

Basic Stem I

dhahaba ذَهَبَ (to go) Model structure *faʿala / yafʿalu* فَعَلَ / يَفْعَلُ

الأمر	المُضارِع المَجزوم	المُضارِع المَنصوب	المُضارِع المَرفوع	المَاضِي		الضَمِير
Imperative	Present Jussive	Present Subjunctive	Present Indicative	Past	Personal Pronouns	
	أَذْهَبْ	أَذْهَبَ	أَذْهَبُ	ذَهَبْتُ	I	أَنَا
	نَذْهَبْ	نَذْهَبَ	نَذْهَبُ	ذَهَبْنَا	we	نَحْنُ
اِذْهَبْ	تَذْهَبْ	تَذْهَبَ	تَذْهَبُ	ذَهَبْتَ	you (m.)	أَنْتَ
اِذْهَبِي	تَذْهَبِي	تَذْهَبِي	تَذْهَبِينَ	ذَهَبْتِ	you (f.)	أَنْتِ
اِذْهَبَا	تَذْهَبَا	تَذْهَبَا	تَذْهَبَانِ	ذَهَبْتُمَا	you (m./f. dual)	أَنْتُمَا
اِذْهَبُوا	تَذْهَبُوا	تَذْهَبُوا	تَذْهَبُونَ	ذَهَبْتُمْ	you (m. pl.)	أَنْتُمْ
اِذْهَبْنَ	تَذْهَبْنَ	تَذْهَبْنَ	تَذْهَبْنَ	ذَهَبْتُنَّ	you (f. pl.)	أَنْتُنَّ
	يَذْهَبْ	يَذْهَبَ	يَذْهَبُ	ذَهَبَ	he / it	هُوَ
	تَذْهَبْ	تَذْهَبَ	تَذْهَبُ	ذَهَبَتْ	she / it	هِيَ
	يَذْهَبَا	يَذْهَبَا	يَذْهَبَانِ	ذَهَبَا	they (m. dual)	هُمَا
	تَذْهَبَا	تَذْهَبَا	تَذْهَبَانِ	ذَهَبَتَا	they (f. dual)	هُمَا
	يَذْهَبُوا	يَذْهَبُوا	يَذْهَبُونَ	ذَهَبُوا	they (m. pl.)	هُمْ
	يَذْهَبْنَ	يَذْهَبْنَ	يَذْهَبْنَ	ذَهَبْنَ	they (f. pl.)	هُنَّ

jalasa جَلَسَ (to sit) Model structure *faʿala/yafʿilu* فَعَلَ / يَفْعِلُ

الأَمر	المُضَارِع المَجْزُوم	المُضَارِع المَنصُوب	المُضَارِع المَرفُوع	المَاضِي	الضَمِير	
Imperative	Present Jussive	Present Subjunctive	Present Indicative	Past	Personal Pronouns	
	أجلِسْ	أجلِسَ	أجلِسُ	جَلَستُ	I	أَنَا
	نَجلِسْ	نَجلِسَ	نَجلِسُ	جَلَسنَا	we	نَحنُ
اِجلِسْ	تَجلِسْ	تَجلِسَ	تَجلِسُ	جَلَستَ	you (m.)	أَنتَ
اِجلِسِي	تَجلِسِي	تَجلِسِي	تَجلِسِينَ	جَلَستِ	you (f.)	أَنتِ
اِجلِسَا	تَجلِسَا	تَجلِسَا	تَجلِسَانِ	جَلَستُمَا	you (m./f. dual)	أَنتُمَا
اِجلِسُوا	تَجلِسُوا	تَجلِسُوا	تَجلِسُونَ	جَلَستُم	you (m. pl.)	أَنتُم
اِجلِسْنَ	تَجلِسنَ	تَجلِسنَ	تَجلِسنَ	جَلَستُنَّ	you (f. pl.)	أَنتُنَّ
	يَجلِسْ	يَجلِسَ	يَجلِسُ	جَلَسَ	he / it	هُوَ
	تَجلِسْ	تَجلِسَ	تَجلِسُ	جَلَسَتْ	she / it	هِيَ
	يَجلِسَا	يَجلِسَا	يَجلِسَانِ	جَلَسَا	they (m. dual)	هُمَا
	تَجلِسَا	تَجلِسَا	تَجلِسَانِ	جَلَسَتَا	they (f. dual)	هُمَا
	يَجلِسُوا	يَجلِسُوا	يَجلِسُونَ	جَلَسُوا	they (m. pl.)	هُم
	يَجلِسنَ	يَجلِسنَ	يَجلِسنَ	جَلَسنَ	they (f. pl.)	هُنَّ

kataba كَتَبَ (to write) Model structure *faʿala / yafʿulu* فَعَلَ / يَفْعُلُ

الأَمر	المُضَارِع المَجزُوم	المُضَارِع المَنصُوب	المُضَارِع المَرفُوع	المَاضِي	الضَمِير	
Imperative	Present Jussive	Present Subjunctive	Present Indicative	Past	Personal Pronouns	
	أَكْتُبْ	أَكْتُبَ	أَكْتُبُ	كَتَبْتُ	I	أَنَا
	نَكْتُبْ	نَكْتُبَ	نَكْتُبُ	كَتَبْنَا	we	نَحنُ
أُكْتُبْ	تَكْتُبْ	تَكْتُبَ	تَكْتُبُ	كَتَبْتَ	you (m.)	أَنتَ
أُكْتُبِي	تَكْتُبِي	تَكْتُبِي	تَكْتُبِينَ	كَتَبْتِ	you (f.)	أَنتِ
أُكْتُبَا	تَكْتُبَا	تَكْتُبَا	تَكْتُبَانِ	كَتَبْتُمَا	you (m./f. dual)	أَنتُمَا
أُكْتُبُوا	تَكْتُبُوا	تَكْتُبُوا	تَكْتُبُونَ	كَتَبْتُمْ	you (m. pl.)	أَنتُم
أُكْتُبْنَ	تَكْتُبْنَ	تَكْتُبْنَ	تَكْتُبْنَ	كَتَبْتُنَّ	you (f. pl.)	أَنتُنَّ
	يَكْتُبْ	يَكْتَ	يَكْتُبُ	كَتَبَ	he / it	هُوَ
	تَكْتُبْ	تَكْتُبَ	تَكْتُبُ	كَتَبَتْ	she / it	هِيَ
	يَكْتُبَا	يَكْتُبَا	يَكْتُبَانِ	كَتَبَا	they (m. dual)	هُمَا
	تَكْتُبَا	تَكْتُبَا	تَكْتُبَانِ	كَتَبَتَا	they (f. dual)	هُمَا
	يَكْتُبُوا	يَكْتُبُوا	يَكْتُبُونَ	كَتَبُوا	they (m. pl.)	هُم
	يَكْتُبْنَ	يَكْتُبْنَ	يَكْتُبْنَ	كَتَبْنَ	they (f. pl.)	هُنَّ

الأمر Imperative	المُضَارِع المَجزُوم Present Jussive	المُضَارِع المَنصُوب Present Subjunctive	المُضَارِع المَرفُوع Present Indicative	المَاضِي Past	الضَمِير Personal Pronouns	
	أَطلُبْ	أَطلُبَ	أَطلُبُ	طَلَبْتُ	I	أَنَا
	نَطلُبْ	نَطلُبَ	نَطلُبُ	طَلَبْنَا	we	نَحنُ
أُطلُبْ	تَطلُبْ	تَطلُبَ	تَطلُبُ	طَلَبْتَ	you (m.)	أَنتَ
أُطلُبِي	تَطلُبِي	تَطلُبِي	تَطلُبِينَ	طَلَبتِ	you (f.)	أَنتِ
أُطلُبَا	تَطلُبَا	تَطلُبَا	تَطلُبَانِ	طَلَبتُمَا	you (m./f. dual)	أَنتُمَا
أُطلُبُوا	تَطلُبُوا	تَطلُبُوا	تَطلُبُونَ	طَلَبْتُمْ	you (m. pl.)	أَنتُم
أُطلُبْنَ	تَطلُبْنَ	تَطلُبْنَ	تَطلُبْنَ	طَلَبْتُنَّ	you (f. pl.)	أَنتُنَّ
	يَطلُبْ	يَطلُبَ	يَطلُبُ	طَلَبَ	he / it	هُوَ
	تَطلُبْ	تَطلُبَ	تَطلُبُ	طَلَبَتْ	she / it	هِيَ
	يَطلُبَا	يَطلُبَا	يَطلُبَانِ	طَلَبَا	they (m. dual)	هُمَا
	تَطلُبَا	تَطلُبَا	تَطلُبَانِ	طَلَبَتَا	they (f. dual)	هُمَا
	يَطلُبُوا	يَطلُبُوا	يَطلُبُونَ	طَلَبُوا	they (m. pl.)	هُم
	يَطلُبْنَ	يَطلُبْنَ	يَطلُبْنَ	طَلَبْنَ	they (f. pl.)	هُنَّ

الأمر	المُضَارِع المَجزُوم	المُضَارِع المَنصُوب	المُضَارِع المَرفُوع	المَاضِي	الضَمِير	
Imperative	Present Jussive	Present Subjunctive	Present Indicative	Past	Personal Pronouns	
	أَشْرَبْ	أَشْرَبَ	أَشْرَبُ	شَرِبْتُ	I	أَنَا
	نَشْرَبْ	نَشْرَبَ	نَشْرَبُ	شَرِبْنَا	we	نَحْنُ
اِشْرَبْ	تَشْرَبْ	تَشْرَبَ	تَشْرَبُ	شَرِبْتَ	you (m.)	أَنْتَ
اِشْرَبِي	تَشْرَبِي	تَشْرَبِي	تَشْرَبِينَ	شَرِبْتِ	you (f.)	أَنْتِ
اِشْرَبَا	تَشْرَبَا	تَشْرَبَا	تَشْرَبَانِ	شَرِبْتُمَا	you (m./f. dual)	أَنْتُمَا
اِشْرَبُوا	تَشْرَبُوا	تَشْرَبُوا	تَشْرَبُونَ	شَرِبْتُمْ	you (m. pl.)	أَنْتُم
اِشْرَبْنَ	تَشْرَبْنَ	تَشْرَبْنَ	تَشْرَبْنَ	شَرِبْتُنَّ	you (f. pl.)	أَنْتُنَّ
	يَشْرَبْ	يَشْرَبَ	يَشْرَبُ	شَرِبَ	he / it	هُوَ
	تَشْرَبْ	تَشْرَبَ	تَشْرَبُ	شَرِبَتْ	she / it	هِيَ
	يَشْرَبَا	يَشْرَبَا	يَشْرَبَانِ	شَرِبَا	they (m. dual)	هُمَا
	تَشْرَبَا	تَشْرَبَا	تَشْرَبَانِ	شَرِبَتَا	they (f. dual)	هُمَا
	يَشْرَبُوا	يَشْرَبُوا	يَشْرَبُونَ	شَرِبُوا	they (m. pl.)	هُم
	يَشْرَبْنَ	يَشْرَبْنَ	يَشْرَبْنَ	شَرِبْنَ	they (f. pl.)	هُنَّ

الأمر	المُضارِع المَجزوم	المُضارِع المَنصوب	المُضارِع المَرفوع	الماضي	الضمير	
Imperative	Present Jussive	Present Subjunctive	Present Indicative	Past	Personal Pronouns	
	أكبُرْ	أكبُرَ	أكبُرُ	كَبِرتُ	I	أنا
	نَكبُرْ	نَكبُرَ	نَكبُرُ	كَبِرنا	we	نَحنُ
اُكبُرْ	تَكبُرْ	تَكبُرَ	تَكبُرُ	كَبِرتَ	you (m.)	أنتَ
اُكبُري	تَكبُري	تَكبُري	تَكبُرينَ	كَبِرتِ	you (f.)	أنتِ
اُكبُرا	تَكبُرا	تَكبُرا	تَكبُرانِ	كَبِرتُما	you (m./f. dual)	أنتُما
اُكبُروا	تَكبُروا	تَكبُروا	تَكبُرونَ	كَبِرتُم	you (m. pl.)	أنتُم
اُكبُرنَ	تَكبُرنَ	تَكبُرنَ	تَكبُرنَ	كَبِرتُنَّ	you (f. pl.)	أنتُنَّ
	يَكبُرْ	يَكبُرَ	يَكبُرُ	كَبُرَ	he / it	هُوَ
	تَكبُرْ	تَكبُرَ	تَكبُرُ	كَبِرَتْ	she / it	هِيَ
	يَكبُرا	يَكبُرا	يَكبُرانِ	كَبِرا	they (m. dual)	هُما
	تَكبُرا	تَكبُرا	تَكبُرانِ	كَبِرتا	they (f. dual)	هُما
	يَكبُروا	يَكبُروا	يَكبُرونَ	كَبِروا	they (m. pl.)	هُم
	يَكبُرْنَ	يَكبُرْنَ	يَكبُرْنَ	كَبِرنَ	they (f. pl.)	هُنَّ

dalla دَلَّ (to show, to point to / out) Model structure *fa'ala / yaf'ulu* فَعَلَ / يَفْعُلُ

dalla دَلَّ belongs to the category of *al-fi'l al-muda'af* الفِعل المُضَعَف (doubled verb roots). In verbs of this type, the second and third root consonants are identical.

الأمر	المُضارِع المَجزوم	المُضارِع المَنصوب	المُضارِع المَرفوع	الماضي	الضمير	
Imperative	Present Jussive	Present Subjunctive	Present Indicative	Past	Personal Pronouns	
	أَدُلَّ	أَدُلَّ	أَدُلُّ	دَلَلْتُ	I	أَنَا
	نَدُلَّ	نَدُلَّ	نَدُلُّ	دَلَلْنَا	we	نَحْنُ
دُلَّ	تَدُلَّ	تَدُلَّ	تَدُلُّ	دَلَلْتَ	you (m.)	أَنْتَ
دُلِّي	تَدُلِّي	تَدُلِّي	تَدُلِّينَ	دَلَلْتِ	you (f.)	أَنْتِ
دُلَّا	تَدُلَّا	تَدُلَّا	تَدُلَّانِ	دَلَلْتُمَا	you (m./f. dual)	أَنْتُمَا
دُلُّوا	تَدُلُّوا	تَدُلُّوا	تَدُلُّونَ	دَلَلْتُمْ	you (m. pl.)	أَنْتُم
اُدْلُلْنَ	تَدْلُلْنَ	تَدْلُلْنَ	تَدْلُلْنَ	دَلَلْتُنَّ	you (f. pl.)	أَنْتُنَّ
	يَدُلَّ	يَدُلَّ	يَدُلُّ	دَلَّ	he / it	هُوَ
	تَدُلَّ	تَدُلَّ	تَدُلُّ	دَلَّتْ	she / it	هِيَ
	يَدُلَّا	يَدُلَّا	يَدُلَّانِ	دَلَّا	they (m. dual)	هُمَا
	تَدُلَّا	تَدُلَّا	تَدُلَّانِ	دَلَّتَا	they (f. dual)	هُمَا
	يَدُلُّوا	يَدُلُّوا	يَدُلُّونَ	دَلُّوا	they (m. pl.)	هُم
	يَدْلُلْنَ	يَدْلُلْنَ	يَدْلُلْنَ	دَلَلْنَ	they (f. pl.)	هُنَّ

sa'ala سَأَلَ (to ask) Model structure fa'ala/yaf'alu فَعَلَ/يفعَلُ

sa'ala سَأَلَ belongs to the category of *al-fi'l al-mahmūz* الفِعل المَهمُوز. In these verbs, *hamza* ء is one of the three root consonants.

الأمر	المُضارِع المَجزُوم	المُضارِع المَنصوب	المُضارِع المَرفُوع	المَاضِي	الضَمير	
Imperative	Present Jussive	Present Subjunctive	Present Indicative	Past	Personal Pronouns	
	أسألْ	أسألَ	أسألُ	سَألتُ	I	أنَا
	نَسألْ	نَسألَ	نَسألُ	سَألنَا	we	نَحنُ
اِسألْ	تَسألْ	تَسألَ	تَسألُ	سَألتَ	you (m.)	أنتَ
اِسألِي	تَسألِي	تَسألِي	تَسألِينَ	سَألتِ	you (f.)	أنتِ
اِسألا	تَسألا	تَسألا	تَسألانِ	سَألتُمَا	you (m./f. dual)	أنتُمَا
اِسألُوا	تَسألُوا	تَسألُوا	تَسألُونَ	سَألتُم	you (m. pl.)	أنتُم
اِسألْنَ	تَسألْنَ	تَسألْنَ	تَسألْنَ	سَألتُنَّ	you (f. pl.)	أنتُنَّ
	يَسألْ	يَسألَ	يَسألُ	سَألَ	he / it	هُوَ
	تَسألْ	تَسألَ	تَسألُ	سَألَتْ	she / it	هِيَ
	يَسألا	يَسألا	يَسألانِ	سَألا	they (m. dual)	هُمَا
	تَسألا	تَسألا	تَسألانِ	سَألَتَا	they (f. dual)	هُمَا
	يَسألُوا	يَسألُوا	يَسألُونَ	سَألُوا	they (m. pl.)	هُم
	يَسألْنَ	يَسألْنَ	يَسألْنَ	سَألْنَ	they (f. pl.)	هُنَّ

Tables

waṣala وَصَلَ (to arrive) Model structure *fa'ala / yaf'ilu* فَعَلَ / يَفْعِلُ

Verbs with an assimilated verb root (*al-fi'l al-mithāli* الْمِثَالِي الفِعل) begin with a semiconsonant, that is, with *wāw* و or *yā* ي. In the present tense, these verbs often omit *wāw* و; it merges with the prefix.

الأَمر	المُضارِع المَجزوم	المُضارِع المَنصوب	المُضارِع المَرفوع	الماضِي	الضَمير	
Imperative	Present Jussive	Present Subjunctive	Present Indicative	Past	Personal Pronouns	
	أَصِلْ	أَصِلَ	أَصِلُ	وَصَلْتُ	I	أَنا
	نَصِلْ	نَصِلَ	نَصِلُ	وَصَلْنا	we	نَحنُ
صِلْ	تَصِلْ	تَصِلَ	تَصِلُ	وَصَلْتَ	you (m.)	أَنتَ
صِلِي	تَصِلِي	تَصِلِي	تَصِلِينَ	وَصَلْتِ	you (f.)	أَنتِ
صِلا	تَصِلا	تَصِلا	تَصِلانِ	وَصَلْتُما	you (m./f. dual)	أَنتُما
صِلُوا	تَصِلُوا	تَصِلُوا	تَصِلُونَ	وَصَلْتُم	you (m. pl.)	أَنتُم
صِلْنَ	تَصِلْنَ	تَصِلْنَ	تَصِلْنَ	وَصَلْتُنَّ	you (f. pl.)	أَنتُنَّ
	يَصِلْ	يَصِلَ	يَصِلُ	وَصَلَ	he / it	هُوَ
	تَصِلْ	تَصِلَ	تَصِلُ	وَصَلَتْ	she / it	هِيَ
	يَصِلا	يَصِلا	يَصِلانِ	وَصَلا	they (m. dual)	هُما
	تَصِلا	تَصِلا	تَصِلانِ	وَصَلَتا	they (f. dual)	هُما
	يَصِلُوا	يَصِلُوا	يَصِلُونَ	وَصَلُوا	they (m. pl.)	هُم
	يَصِلْنَ	يَصِلْنَ	يَصِلْنَ	وَصَلْنَ	they (f. pl.)	هُنَّ

qāla قَالَ (to say) — Model structure *fa'ala / yufa'ilu* فَعَلَ / يُفعِلُ

qāla قَالَ is one of the so-called hollow verb roots, *al-fi'l al-'aywaf* الفِعل الأجوَف. Here the second root consonant is *wāw* و or *yā* ي.

الأمر	المُضارِع المَجزُوم	المُضارِع المَنصُوب	المُضارِع المَرفُوع	المَاضِي		الضَمِير
Imperative	Present Jussive	Present Subjunctive	Present Indicative	Past		Personal Pronouns
	أقُلْ	أقُولَ	أقُولُ	قُلْتُ	I	أنَا
	نَقُلْ	نَقُولَ	نَقُولُ	قُلْنَا	we	نَحنُ
قُلْ	تَقُلْ	تَقُولَ	تَقُولُ	قُلْتَ	you (m.)	أنتَ
قُولِي	تَقُولِي	تَقُولِي	تَقُولِينَ	قُلْتِ	you (f.)	أنتِ
قُولا	تَقُولا	تَقُولا	تَقُولانِ	قُلْتُمَا	you (m./f. dual)	أنتُمَا
قُولُوا	تَقُولُوا	تَقُولُوا	تَقُولُونَ	قُلْتُم	you (m. pl.)	أنتُم
قُلْنَ	تَقُلْنَ	تَقُلْنَ	تَقُلْنَ	قُلْتُنَّ	you (f. pl.)	أنتُنَّ
	يَقُلْ	يَقُولَ	يَقُولُ	قَالَ	he / it	هُوَ
	تَقُلْ	تَقُولَ	تَقُولُ	قَالَتْ	she / it	هِيَ
	يَقُولا	يَقُولا	يَقُولانِ	قَالا	they (m. dual)	هُمَا
	تَقُولا	تَقُولا	تَقُولانِ	قَالَتَا	they (f. dual)	هُمَا
	تَقُولُوا	تَقُولُوا	يَقُولُونَ	قَالُوا	they (m. pl.)	هُم
	يَقُلْنَ	يَقُلْنَ	يَقُلْنَ	قُلْنَ	they (f. pl.)	هُنَّ

Tables

jāʼa جَاءَ (to come) Model structure *faʻala/yafʻilu* فَعَلَ / يَفعِلُ

Hollow verbs can also appear in combination with *hamza* ء. In the imperative, they have a completely different form.

الضَمِير		المَاضِي	المُضَارِع المَرفُوع	المُضَارِع المَنصُوب	المُضَارِع المَجزُوم	الأمر
Personal Pronouns		Past	Present Indicative	Present Subjunctive	Present Jussive	Imperative
أَنَا	I	جِئْتُ	أَجِيءُ	أَجِيءَ	أَجِئْ	
نَحنُ	we	جِئْنَا	نَجِيءُ	نَجِيءَ	نَجِئْ	
أَنتَ	you (m.)	جِئْتَ	تَجِيءُ	تَجِيءَ	تَجِئْ	تَعَالَ
أَنتِ	you (f.)	جِئْتِ	تَجِيئِينَ	تَجِيئِي	تَجِيئِي	تَعَالَي
أَنتُمَا	you (m./f. dual)	جِئْتُمَا	تَجِيئَانِ	تَجِيئَا	تَجِيئَا	تَعَالَا
أَنتُم	you (m. pl.)	جِئْتُم	تَجِيئُونَ	تَجِيئُوا	تَجِيئُوا	تَعَالَوا
أَنتُنَّ	you (f. pl.)	جِئْتُنَّ	تَجِئْنَ	تَجِئْنَ	تَجِئْنَ	تَعَالَينَ
هُوَ	he / it	جَاءَ	يَجِيءُ	يَجِيءَ	يَجِئْ	
هِيَ	she / it	جَاءَتْ	تَجِيءُ	تَجِيءَ	تَجِئْ	
هُمَا	they (m. dual)	جَاءَا	يَجِيئَانِ	يَجِيئَا	يَجِيئَا	
هُمَا	they (f. dual)	جَاءَتَا	تَجِيئَانِ	تَجِيئَا	تَجِيئَا	
هُم	they (m. pl.)	جَاؤُوا	يَجِيئُونَ	يَجِيئُوا	يَجِيئُوا	
هُنَّ	they (f. pl.)	جِئْنَ	يَجِئْنَ	يَجِئْنَ	يَجِئْنَ	

nasiya نَسِيَ (to forget) Model structure *faʿila/yafʿalu* فَعِلَ / يَفْعَلُ

In the case of verbs with a defective verb root (*al-fiʿl al-nāqiṣ* الفِعل النَاقِص), the third consonant is *wāw* و or *yā* ي. The semiconsonants, however, can assume different forms or even vanish altogether. In the past tense, for example, this rule applies: If *yā* ي is the third root consonant, then the past tense of the verb ends in *yā* ي or *alif maqṣūra*. If *wāw* و is the third root consonant, then the past tense of the verb ends in *alif ṭawīla*.

الأمر	المُضارِع المَجزوم	المُضارِع المَنصوب	المُضارِع المَرفوع	المَاضي	الضَمير	
Imperative	Present Jussive	Present Subjunctive	Present Indicative	Past	Personal Pronouns	
	أَنْسَ	أَنسَى	أَنسَى	نَسِيتُ	I	أَنَا
	نَنْسَ	نَنْسَى	نَنْسَى	نَسِينَا	we	نَحنُ
اِنْسَ	تَنْسَ	تَنْسَى	تَنْسَى	نَسِيتَ	you (m.)	أَنتَ
اِنْسَيْ	تَنْسَيْ	تَنْسَيْ	تَنْسَيْنَ	نَسِيتِ	you (f.)	أَنتِ
اِنْسَيَا	تَنسَيَا	تَنسَيَا	تَنْسَيَانِ	نَسِيتُمَا	you (m./f. dual)	أَنتُمَا
اِنْسَوا	تَنْسَوا	تَنْسَوا	تَنْسَونَ	نَسِيتُم	you (m. pl.)	أَنتُم
اِنْسَيْنَ	تَنْسَيْنَ	تَنْسَيْنَ	تَنْسَيْنَ	نَسِيتُنَّ	you (f. pl.)	أَنتُنَّ
	يَنْسَ	يَنْسَى	يَنسَى	نَسِيَ	he / it	هُوَ
	تَنْسَ	تَنْسَى	تَنْسَى	نَسِيَتْ	she / it	هِيَ
	يَنْسَيَا	يَنْسَيَا	يَنْسَيَانِ	نَسِيَا	they (m. dual)	هُمَا
	تَنْسَيَا	تَنْسَيَا	تَنْسَيَانِ	نَسِيَتَا	they (f. dual)	هُمَا
	يَنْسَوا	يَنْسَوا	يَنْسَونَ	نَسُوا	they (m. pl.)	هُم
	يَنسَينَ	يَنسَينَ	يَنسَينَ	نَسِينَ	they (f. pl.)	هُنَّ

الضَمِير		المَاضِي	المُضَارِع المَرفُوع	المُضَارِع المَنصُوب	المُضَارِع المَجزُوم	الأَمر
Personal Pronouns		Past	Present Indicative	Present Subjunctive	Present Jussive	Imperative
أَنَا	I	كُنتُ	أَكُونُ	أَكُونَ	أَكُنْ	
نَحنُ	we	كُنّا	نَكُونُ	نَكُونَ	نَكُنْ	
أَنتَ	you (m.)	كُنتَ	تَكُونُ	تَكُونَ	تَكُنْ	كُنْ
أَنتِ	you (f.)	كُنتِ	تَكُونِينَ	تَكُونِي	تَكُونِي	كُونِي
أَنتُمَا	you (m./f. dual)	كُنتُمَا	تَكُونَانِ	تَكُونَا	تَكُونَا	كُونَا
أَنتُم	you (m. pl.)	كُنتُم	تَكُونُونَ	تَكُونُوا	تَكُونُوا	كُونُوا
أَنتُنَّ	you (f. pl.)	كُنتُنَّ	تَكُنَّ	تَكُنَّ	تَكُنَّ	كُنَّ
هُوَ	he / it	كَانَ	يَكُونُ	يَكُونَ	يَكُنْ	
هِيَ	she / it	كَانَتْ	تَكُونُ	تَكُونَ	تَكُنْ	
هُمَا	they (m. dual)	كَانَا	يَكُونَانِ	يَكُونَا	يَكُونَا	
هُمَا	they (f. dual)	كَانَتَا	تَكُونَانِ	تَكُونَا	تَكُونَا	
هُم	they (m. pl.)	كَانُوا	يَكُونُونَ	يَكُونُوا	يَكُونُوا	
هُنَّ	they (f. pl.)	كُنَّ	يَكُنَّ	يَكُنَّ	يَكُنَّ	

Expanded Stem II

kassara كَسَّرَ (to beat to pieces) Model structure *fa''ala / yufa''ilu* فَعَّلَ / يُفَعِّلُ

الأَمر	المُضَارِع المَجزُوم	المُضَارِع المَنصُوب	المُضَارِع المَرفُوع	المَاضِي	الضَمِير	
Imperative	**Present Jussive**	**Present Subjunctive**	**Present Indicative**	**Past**	**Personal Pronouns**	
	أُكَسِّرْ	أُكَسِّرَ	أُكَسِّرُ	كَسَّرْتُ	I	أَنَا
	نُكَسِّرْ	نُكَسِّرَ	نُكَسِّرُ	كَسَّرْنَا	we	نَحْنُ
كَسِّرْ	تُكَسِّرْ	تُكَسِّرَ	تُكَسِّرُ	كَسَّرْتَ	you (m.)	أَنْتَ
كَسِّرِي	تُكَسِّرِي	تُكَسِّرِي	تُكَسِّرِينَ	كَسَّرْتِ	you (f.)	أَنْتِ
كَسِّرَا	تُكَسِّرَا	تُكَسِّرَا	تُكَسِّرَانِ	كَسَّرْتُمَا	you (m./f. dual)	أَنْتُمَا
كَسِّرُوا	تُكَسِّرُوا	تُكَسِّرُوا	تُكَسِّرُونَ	كَسَّرْتُمْ	you (m. pl.)	أَنْتُمْ
كَسِّرْنَ	تُكَسِّرْنَ	تُكَسِّرْنَ	تُكَسِّرْنَ	كَسَّرْتُنَّ	you (f. pl.)	أَنْتُنَّ
	يُكَسِّرْ	يُكَسِّرَ	يُكَسِّرُ	كَسَّرَ	he / it	هُوَ
	تُكَسِّرْ	تُكَسِّرَ	تُكَسِّرُ	كَسَّرَتْ	she / it	هِيَ
	يُكَسِّرَا	يُكَسِّرَا	يُكَسِّرَانِ	كَسَّرَا	they (m. dual)	هُمَا
	تُكَسِّرَا	تُكَسِّرَا	تُكَسِّرَانِ	كَسَّرَتَا	they (f. dual)	هُمَا
	يُكَسِّرُوا	يُكَسِّرُوا	يُكَسِّرُونَ	كَسَّرُوا	they (m. pl.)	هُمْ
	يُكَسِّرْنَ	يُكَسِّرْنَ	يُكَسِّرْنَ	كَسَّرْنَ	they (f. pl.)	هُنَّ

Expanded Stem III

sāʿada سَاعَدَ (to help) Model structure *fāʿala / yufāʿilu* فَاعَلَ / يُفَاعِلُ

الأمر	المُضارع المَجزوم	المُضارع المَنصوب	المُضارِع المَرفوع	المَاضِي	الضَمير	
Imperative	Present Jussive	Present Subjunctive	Present Indicative	Past	Personal Pronouns	
	أُسَاعِدْ	أُسَاعِدَ	أُسَاعِدُ	سَاعَدْتُ	I	أَنَا
	نُسَاعِدْ	نُسَاعِدَ	نُسَاعِدُ	سَاعَدْنَا	we	نَحنُ
سَاعِدْ	تُسَاعِدْ	تُسَاعِدَ	تُسَاعِدُ	سَاعَدْتَ	you (m.)	أَنتَ
سَاعِدِي	تُسَاعِدِي	تُسَاعِدِي	تُسَاعِدِينَ	سَاعَدْتِ	you (f.)	أَنتِ
سَاعِدَا	تُسَاعِدَا	تُسَاعِدَا	تُسَاعِدَانِ	سَاعَدْتُمَا	you (m./f. dual)	أَنتُمَا
سَاعِدُوا	تُسَاعِدُوا	تُسَاعِدُوا	تُسَاعِدُونَ	سَاعَدْتُم	you (m. pl.)	أَنتُم
سَاعِدْنَ	تُسَاعِدْنَ	تُسَاعِدْنَ	تُسَاعِدْنَ	سَاعَدْتُنَّ	you (f. pl.)	أَنتُنَّ
	يُسَاعِدْ	يُسَاعِدَ	يُسَاعِدُ	سَاعَدَ	he / it	هُوَ
	تُسَاعِدْ	تُسَاعِدَ	تُسَاعِدُ	سَاعَدَتْ	she / it	هِيَ
	يُسَاعِدَا	يُسَاعِدَا	يُسَاعِدَانِ	سَاعَدَا	they (m. dual)	هُمَا
	تُسَاعِدَا	تُسَاعِدَا	تُسَاعِدَانِ	سَاعَدَتَا	they (f. dual)	هُمَا
	يُسَاعِدُوا	يُسَاعِدُوا	يُسَاعِدُونَ	سَاعَدُوا	they (m. pl.)	هُم
	يُسَاعِدْنَ	يُسَاعِدْنَ	يُسَاعِدْنَ	سَاعَدْنَ	they (f. pl.)	هُنَّ

Expanded Stem IV

'arsala أَرسَلَ (to send) Model structure *af'ala / yuf'ilu* أَفعَلَ / يُفْعِلُ

الأَمر	المُضارِع المَجزوم	المُضارِع المَنصوب	المُضارِع المَرفوع	المَاضي	الضَمير	
Imperative	Present Jussive	Present Subjunctive	Present Indicative	Past	Personal Pronouns	
	أُرسِلْ	أُرسِلَ	أُرسِلُ	أَرسَلتُ	I	أَنا
	نُرسِلْ	نُرسِلَ	نُرسِلُ	أَرسَلنا	we	نَحنُ
أَرسِلْ	تُرسِلْ	تُرسِلَ	تُرسِلُ	أَرسَلتَ	you (m.)	أَنتَ
أَرسِلي	تُرسِلي	تُرسِلي	تُرسِلينَ	أَرسَلتِ	you (f.)	أَنتِ
أَرسِلا	تُرسِلا	تُرسِلا	تُرسِلانِ	أَرسَلتُما	you (m./f. dual)	أَنتُما
أَرسِلوا	تُرسِلوا	تُرسِلوا	تُرسِلونَ	أَرسَلتُم	you (m. pl.)	أَنتُم
أَرسِلنَ	تُرسِلنَ	تُرسِلنَ	تُرسِلنَ	أَرسَلتُنَّ	you (f. pl.)	أَنتُنَّ
	يُرسِلْ	يُرسِلَ	يُرسِلُ	أَرسَلَ	he / it	هُوَ
	تُرسِلْ	تُرسِلَ	تُرسِلُ	أَرسَلَتْ	she / it	هِيَ
	يُرسِلا	يُرسِلا	يُرسِلانِ	أَرسَلا	they (m. dual)	هُمَا
	تُرسِلا	تُرسِلا	تُرسِلانِ	أَرسَلَتا	they (f. dual)	هُمَا
	يُرسِلوا	يُرسِلوا	يُرسِلونَ	أَرسَلوا	they (m. pl.)	هُم
	يُرسِلنَ	يُرسِلنَ	يُرسِلنَ	أَرسَلنَ	they (f. pl.)	هُنَّ

Expanded Stem V

taḥarraka تَحَرَّكَ (to move) Model structure *tafa‘‘ala / yatafa‘‘alu* تَفَعَّلَ / يَتَفَعَّلُ

الأمر	المُضارِع المَجزوم	المُضارِع المَنصوب	المُضارِع المَرفوع	المَاضِي	الضَمِير	
Imperative	Present Jussive	Present Subjunctive	Present Indicative	Past	Personal Pronouns	
	أَتَحَرَّكْ	أَتَحَرَّكَ	أَتَحَرَّكُ	تَحَرَّكْتُ	I	أَنَا
	نَتَحَرَّكْ	نَتَحَرَّكَ	نَتَحَرَّكُ	تَحَرَّكْنَا	we	نَحنُ
تَحَرَّكْ	تَتَحَرَّكْ	تَتَحَرَّكَ	تَتَحَرَّكُ	تَحَرَّكْتَ	you (m.)	أَنتَ
تَحَرَّكِي	تَتَحَرَّكِي	تَتَحَرَّكِي	تَتَحَرَّكِينَ	تَحَرَّكْتِ	you (f.)	أَنتِ
تَحَرَّكَا	تَتَحَرَّكَا	تَتَحَرَّكَا	تَتَحَرَّكَانِ	تَحَرَّكْتُمَا	you (m./f. dual)	أَنتُمَا
تَحَرَّكُوا	تَتَحَرَّكُوا	تَتَحَرَّكُوا	تَتَحَرَّكُونَ	تَحَرَّكْتُم	you (m. pl.)	أَنتُم
تَحَرَّكْنَ	تَتَحَرَّكْنَ	تَتَحَرَّكْنَ	تَتَحَرَّكْنَ	تَحَرَّكْتُنَّ	you (f. pl.)	أَنتُنَّ
	يَتَحَرَّكْ	يَتَحَرَّكَ	يَتَحَرَّكُ	تَحَرَّكَ	he / it	هُوَ
	تَتَحَرَّكِي	تَتَحَرَّكِي	تَتَحَرَّكُ	تَحَرَّكَتْ	she / it	هِيَ
	يَتَحَرَّكَا	يَتَحَرَّكَا	يَتَحَرَّكَانِ	تَحَرَّكَا	they (m. dual)	هُمَا
	تَتَحَرَّكَا	تَتَحَرَّكَا	تَتَحَرَّكَانِ	تَحَرَّكَتَا	they (f. dual)	هُمَا
	يَتَحَرَّكُوا	يَتَحَرَّكُوا	يَتَحَرَّكُونَ	تَحَرَّكُوا	they (m. pl.)	هُم
	يَتَحَرَّكْنَ	يَتَحَرَّكْنَ	يَتَحَرَّكْنَ	تَحَرَّكْنَ	they (f. pl.)	هُنَّ

Expanded Stem VI

takātaba تَكَاتَبَ (to write each other) Model structure *tafāʿala / yatafāʿalu* تَفَاعَلَ / يَتَفَاعَلُ

الأَمر	المُضارِع المَجزُوم	المُضارِع المَنصُوب	المُضارِع المَرفُوع	المَاضِي	الضَمِير	
Imperative	Present Jussive	Present Subjunctive	Present Indicative	Past	Personal Pronouns	
	أَتَكَاتَبْ	أَتَكَاتَبَ	أَتَكَاتَبُ	تَكَاتَبْتُ	I	أَنَا
	نَتَكَاتَبْ	نَتَكَاتَبَ	نَتَكَاتَبُ	تَكَاتَبْنَا	we	نَحنُ
تَكَاتَبْ	تَتَكَاتَبْ	تَتَكَاتَبَ	تَتَكَاتَبُ	تَكَاتَبْتَ	you (m.)	أَنتَ
تَكَاتَبِي	تَتَكَاتَبِي	تَتَكَاتَبِي	تَتَكَاتَبِينَ	تَكَاتَبْتِ	you (f.)	أَنتِ
تَكَاتَبَا	تَتَكَاتَبَا	تَتَكَاتَبَا	تَتَكَاتَبَانِ	تَكَاتَبْتُمَا	you (m./f. dual)	أَنتُمَا
تَكَاتَبُوا	تَتَكَاتَبُوا	تَتَكَاتَبُوا	تَتَكَاتَبُونَ	تَكَاتَبْتُمْ	you (m. pl.)	أَنتُم
تَكَاتَبْنَ	تَتَكَاتَبْنَ	تَتَكَاتَبْنَ	تَتَكَاتَبْنَ	تَكَاتَبْتُنَّ	you (f. pl.)	أَنتُنَّ
	يَتَكَاتَبْ	يَتَكَاتَبَ	يَتَكَاتَبُ	تَكَاتَبَ	he / it	هُوَ
	تَتَكَاتَبْ	تَتَكَاتَبَ	تَتَكَاتَبُ	تَكَاتَبَتْ	she / it	هِيَ
	يَتَكَاتَبَا	يَتَكَاتَبَا	يَتَكَاتَبَانِ	تَكَاتَبَا	they (m. dual)	هُمَا
	تَتَكَاتَبَا	تَتَكَاتَبَا	تَتَكَاتَبَانِ	تَكَاتَبَتَا	they (f. dual)	هُمَا
	يَتَكَاتَبُوا	يَتَكَاتَبُوا	يَتَكَاتَبُونَ	تَكَاتَبُوا	they (m. pl.)	هُم
	يَتَكَاتَبْنَ	يَتَكَاتَبْنَ	يَتَكَاتَبْنَ	تَكَاتَبْنَ	they (f. pl.)	هُنَّ

Expanded Stem VII

inkasara اِنْكَسَرَ (to be broken) Model structure *infaʿala/yanfaʿilu* اِنْفَعَلَ / يَنْفَعِلُ

الأمر	المُضَارِع المَجْزُوم	المُضَارِع المَنصُوب	المُضَارِع المَرفُوع	المَاضِي	الضَمِير	
Imperative	Present Jussive	Present Subjunctive	Present Indicative	Past	Personal Pronouns	
	أَنْكَسِرْ	أَنْكَسِرَ	أَنْكَسِرُ	اِنْكَسَرْتُ	I	أَنَا
	نَنْكَسِرْ	نَنْكَسِرَ	نَنْكَسِرُ	اِنْكَسَرْنَا	we	نَحنُ
اِنْكَسِرْ	تَنْكَسِرْ	تَنْكَسِرَ	تَنْكَسِرُ	اِنْكَسَرْتَ	you (m.)	أَنتَ
اِنْكَسِرِي	تَنْكَسِرِي	تَنْكَسِرِي	تَنْكَسِرِينَ	اِنْكَسَرْتِ	you (f.)	أَنتِ
اِنْكَسِرَا	تَنْكَسِرَا	تَنْكَسِرَا	تَنْكَسِرَانِ	اِنْكَسَرْتُمَا	you (m./f. dual)	أَنتُمَا
اِنْكَسِرُوا	تَنْكَسِرُوا	تَنْكَسِرُوا	تَنْكَسِرُونَ	اِنْكَسَرْتُمْ	you (m. pl.)	أَنتُم
اِنْكَسِرْنَ	تَنْكَسِرْنَ	تَنْكَسِرْنَ	تَنْكَسِرْنَ	اِنْكَسَرْتُنَّ	you (f. pl.)	أَنتُنَّ
	يَنْكَسِرْ	يَنْكَسِرَ	يَنْكَسِرُ	اِنْكَسَرَ	he / it	هُوَ
	تَنْكَسِرْ	تَنْكَسِرَ	تَنْكَسِرُ	اِنْكَسَرَتْ	she / it	هِيَ
	يَنْكَسِرَا	يَنْكَسِرَا	يَنْكَسِرَانِ	اِنْكَسَرَا	they (m. dual)	هُمَا
	يَنْكَسِرَا	يَنْكَسِرَا	يَنْكَسِرَانِ	اِنْكَسَرَتَا	they (f. dual)	هُمَا
	يَنْكَسِرُوا	يَنْكَسِرُوا	يَنْكَسِرُونَ	اِنْكَسَرُوا	they (m. pl.)	هُم
	يَنْكَسِرْنَ	يَنْكَسِرْنَ	يَنْكَسِرْنَ	اِنْكَسَرْنَ	they (f. pl.)	هُنَّ

Expanded Stem VIII

ijtama'a اِجتَمَعَ (to meet) Model structure *ifta'ala / yafta'ilu* اِفْتَعَلَ / يَفْتَعِلُ

الضَمير		المَاضِي	المُضارِع المَرفُوع	المُضارِع المَنصُوب	المُضارِع المَجزُوم	الأمر
Personal Pronouns		Past	Present Indicative	Present Subjunctive	Present Jussive	Imperative
أَنا	I	اِجْتَمَعْتُ	أَجْتَمِعُ	أَجْتَمِعَ	أَجْتَمِعْ	
نَحنُ	we	اِجْتَمَعْنا	نَجْتَمِعُ	نَجْتَمِعَ	نَجْتَمِعْ	
أَنتَ	you (m.)	اِجْتَمَعْتَ	تَجْتَمِعُ	تَجْتَمِعَ	تَجْتَمِعْ	اِجْتَمِعْ
أَنتِ	you (f.)	اِجْتَمَعْتِ	تَجْتَمِعِينَ	تَجْتَمِعِي	تَجْتَمِعِي	اِجْتَمِعِي
أَنتُمَا	you (m./f. dual)	اِجْتَمَعْتُمَا	تَجْتَمِعَانِ	تَجْتَمِعَا	تَجْتَمِعَا	اِجْتَمِعَا
أَنتُم	you (m. pl.)	اِجْتَمَعْتُم	تَجْتَمِعُونَ	تَجْتَمِعُوا	تَجْتَمِعُوا	اِجْتَمِعُوا
أَنتُنَّ	you (f. pl.)	اِجْتَمَعْتُنَّ	تَجْتَمِعْنَ	تَجْتَمِعْنَ	تَجْتَمِعْنَ	اِجْتَمِعْنَ
هُوَ	he / it	اِجْتَمَعَ	يَجْتَمِعُ	يَجْتَمِعَ	يَجْتَمِعْ	
هِيَ	she / it	اِجْتَمَعَتْ	تَجْتَمِعُ	تَجْتَمِعِي	تَجْتَمِعِي	
هُمَا	they (m. dual)	اِجْتَمَعَا	يَجْتَمِعَانِ	يَجْتَمِعَا	يَجْتَمِعَا	
هُمَا	they (f. dual)	اِجْتَمَعَتَا	تَجْتَمِعَانِ	تَجْتَمِعَا	تَجْتَمِعَا	
هُم	they (m. pl.)	اِجْتَمَعُوا	يَجْتَمِعُونَ	يَجْتَمِعُوا	يَجْتَمِعُوا	
هُنَّ	they (f. pl.)	اِجْتَمَعْنَ	يَجْتَمِعْنَ	يَجْتَمِعْنَ	يَجْتَمِعْنَ	

Expanded Stem IX

iḥmarra اِحْمَرَّ (to blush) — Model structure *ifʿalla / yafʿallu* اِفْعَلَّ / يَفْعَلُّ

الأمر	المُضَارِع المَجْزُوم	المُضَارِع المَنصُوب	المُضَارِع المَرفُوع	المَاضِي		الضَمِير
Imperative	Present Jussive	Present Subjunctive	Present Indicative	Past	Personal Pronouns	
	اَحْمَرَّ	اَحْمَرَّ	اَحْمَرُّ	اِحْمَرَرْتُ	I	أَنَا
	نَحْمَرِرْ	نَحْمَرَّ	نَحْمَرُّ	اِحْمَرَرْنَا	we	نَحنُ
اِحْمَرِرْ	تَحْمَرِرْ	تَحْمَرَّ	تَحْمَرُّ	اِحْمَرَرْتَ	you (m.)	أَنتَ
اِحْمَرِّي	تَحْمَرِّي	تَحْمَرِّي	تَحْمَرِّينَ	اِحْمَرَرْتِ	you (f.)	أَنتِ
اِحْمَرَّا	تَحْمَرَّا	تَحْمَرَّا	تَحْمَرَّانِ	اِحْمَرَرْتُمَا	you (m./f. dual)	أَنتُمَا
اِحْمَرُّوا	تَحْمَرُّوا	تَحْمَرُّوا	تَحْمَرُّونَ	اِحْمَرَرْتُمْ	you (m. pl.)	أَنتُم
اِحْمَرِرْنَ	تَحْمَرِرْنَ	تَحْمَرِرْنَ	تَحْمَرِرْنَ	اِحْمَرَرْتُنَّ	you (f. pl.)	أَنتُنَّ
	يَحْمَرِرْ	يَحْمَرَّ	يَحْمَرُّ	اِحْمَرَّ	he / it	هُوَ
	تَحْمَرِرْ	تَحْمَرَّ	تَحْمَرُّ	اِحْمَرَّتْ	she / it	هِيَ
	يَحْمَرَّا	يَحْمَرَّا	يَحْمَرَّانِ	اِحْمَرَّا	they (m. dual)	هُمَا
	تَحْمَرَّا	تَحْمَرَّا	تَحْمَرَّانِ	اِحْمَرَّتَا	they (f. dual)	هُمَا
	يَحْمَرُّوا	يَحْمَرُّوا	يَحْمَرُّونَ	اِحْمَرُّوا	they (m. pl.)	هُم
	يَحْمَرِرْنَ	يَحْمَرِرْنَ	يَحْمَرِرْنَ	اِحْمَرَرْنَ	they (f. pl.)	هُنَّ

Expanded Stem X

istafsara اِسْتَفْسَرَ (to inquire, to ask) Model structure *istafʿala / yastafʿilu* اِسْتَفْعَلَ / يَسْتَفْعِلُ

الأَمر	المُضَارِع المَجْزُوم	المُضَارِع المَنصُوب	المُضَارِع المَرفُوع	المَاضِي	الضَمِير	
Imperative	Present Jussive	Present Subjunctive	Present Indicative	Past	Personal Pronouns	
	أَسْتَفْسِرْ	أَسْتَفْسِرَ	أَسْتَفْسِرُ	اِسْتَفْسَرْتُ	I	أَنَا
	نَسْتَفْسِرْ	نَسْتَفْسِرَ	نَسْتَفْسِرُ	اِسْتَفْسَرْنَا	we	نَحْنُ
اِسْتَفْسِرْ	تَسْتَفْسِرْ	تَسْتَفْسِرَ	تَسْتَفْسِرُ	اِسْتَفْسَرْتَ	you (m.)	أَنْتَ
اِسْتَفْسِرِي	تَسْتَفْسِرِي	تَسْتَفْسِرِي	تَسْتَفْسِرِينَ	اِسْتَفْسَرْتِ	you (f.)	أَنْتِ
اِسْتَفْسِرَا	تَسْتَفْسِرَا	تَسْتَفْسِرَا	تَسْتَفْسِرَانِ	اِسْتَفْسَرْتُمَا	you (m./f. dual)	أَنْتُمَا
اِسْتَفْسِرُوا	تَسْتَفْسِرُوا	تَسْتَفْسِرُوا	تَسْتَفْسِرُونَ	اِسْتَفْسَرْتُم	you (m. pl.)	أَنْتُم
اِسْتَفْسِرْنَ	تَسْتَفْسِرْنَ	تَسْتَفْسِرْنَ	تَسْتَفْسِرْنَ	اِسْتَفْسَرْتُنَّ	you (f. pl.)	أَنْتُنَّ
	يَسْتَفْسِرْ	يَسْتَفْسِرَ	يَسْتَفْسِرُ	اِسْتَفْسَرَ	he / it	هُوَ
	تَسْتَفْسِرِي	تَسْتَفْسِرِي	تَسْتَفْسِرُ	اِسْتَفْسَرَتْ	she / it	هِيَ
	يَسْتَفْسِرَا	يَسْتَفْسِرَا	يَسْتَفْسِرَانِ	اِسْتَفْسَرَا	they (m. dual)	هُمَا
	تَسْتَفْسِرَا	تَسْتَفْسِرَا	تَسْتَفْسِرَانِ	اِسْتَفْسَرَتَا	they (f. dual)	هُمَا
	يَسْتَفْسِرُوا	يَسْتَفْسِرُوا	يَسْتَفْسِرُونَ	اِسْتَفْسَرُوا	they (m. pl.)	هُم
	يَسْتَفْسِرْنَ	يَسْتَفْسِرْنَ	يَسْتَفْسِرْنَ	اِسْتَفْسَرْنَ	they (f. pl.)	هُنَّ

Answers

Alphabet/Pronunciation

A2 Script

1 correct 1, 3, 5, 6, 8
incorrect 2 ـســـ 4 ـت 7 ـو

2 1 وزير 2 دُكَان 3 مُدِير 4 أدوَار 5 زَمَان 6 آدم 7 دَوري 8 يَزُورُ

3 1 علم 2 بَخِيل 3 يَزُورُ 4 حَصاد 5 رَحَبَ
6 سُمَيَا 7 لَمَعَ 8 غَزَال 9 طَبَخَ 10 جَمَل

A3 Vowels: Long Vowels / Short Vowels

2 1B • 2D • 3A • 4E • 5C

3

1.					2.					3.				
دَ	وَ	يَ	نَ	تَ	مِ	بِ	زِ	سِ	عِ	حُ	رُ	لُ	جُ	قُ

4 long vowel: 1, 2, 5 short vowel: 3, 4, 6

A4 Diacritical Marks: *sukūn*, *shadda*, and *tanwin*

2 1G • 2D • 3A • 4I • 5C • 6K • 7B • 8J • 9L • 10E • 11H • 12F

3

1.					2.					3.				
بَنْك	مِصْبَاح	اِبْنُهُ	مَسْرَح	مِسْوَاك	كُلّ	فَرّ	مَزَّق	جَرّ	دبّ	قَلَمٍ	مُعَلِّمٌ	شَجَرَةٍ	رَجُلٌ	رَجُلاً

4 1 طَويلاً 2 شَهْرٌ 3 رَدَّ 4 قَهْوَةٌ 5 سِتَّة 6 رَمْل

A5 Syllables / Stress

2 1 را/دَّ 2 هُـ/وَ 3 هَـا/ذَا 4 مَا/ذَا 5 يَكْـ/تُبَـ/انِ 6 هِـ/يَ 7 قَا/لُوا 8 عَ/لَى

3 1 *jaddun* 2 *jā'a* 3 *mallāḥun* 4 *y'akulna* 5 *kulluhum* 6 *'almāniyā* 7 *'āṣimatun* 8 *zārū*

A6 Vowels: *alif* ا (1)

2 1 ا 2 ـا 3 أ - إ 4 لا

3

1.					2.				
صباح	مساء	بارد	يدها	رجليها	أكل	إمرأة	أم	أخ	إبن

4 1, 4, 6, 8

A7 Vowels: *alif* ا (2)

2

2.						1.					
كبرى	على	مقهى	ليلى	حبلى	صغرى	رماه	نَبات	مشينا	شعرها	سيارة	مساء

3 1 آهاتٌ 3 آلامٌ 5 آفاقٌ 6 آمالٌ

4 2, 5, 6, 7

A8 Consonants: *hamza* ء (1)

1

3.					2.				1.				
بُؤس	رُؤوس	مَسؤول	مُؤنَث	لُؤلُؤ	عَائِدٌ	جَائِعٌ	نَائِب	مِئَة	إنسانٌ	إجابَةٌ	أُكِلَ	أَبو	أنا

2 1B • 2D • 3E • 4G • 5C • 6H • 7A • 8F

3 1 إيطالِيا 2 سَألَ 3 مُتَأمِلٌ 4 نَائِبٌ 5 مُؤمِنٌ 6 عَائِدٌ 7 اِبنٌ 8 مِئَةٌ

A9 Consonants: *hamza* ء (2)

1 1 أ 2 ء 3 ـؤ 4 إ 5 ـئـ 6 ـأ

2 1 أَبداً 2 سَألَ 3 إنَّ 4 سُؤَالٌ 5 أَكَلَ 6 يَأكُلُ

3

2.							1.						
قارئ	نائب	أخ	أن	تأخر	أب	أملك	ابنة	اكتب	اثنان	اسم	اشتَرَى	البَيت	ابن

A10 Consonants: *bā* ب / *tā* ت / *thā* ث

3 1 ابتث 2 باثث 3 ثتبا 4 تاثب 5 اثاتب 6 بتبثا 7 ثتثبا 8 تاتثب

4 1 = م + ث + ب 2 = ث + م + ت 3 = ت + ب + ث 4 = ب + ك + ت 5 = أ + ث + ا + ث

A11 Consonants: *nūn* ن / *yā* ي

3 1 نَبَتَ 2 بِنتٌ 3 نابٌ 4 أنبَتَ 5 بَنَاتٌ 6 نَبِيٌّ 7 اثنَانِ 8 إناثٌ

4 1C • 2E • 3F • 4A • 5G • 6H • 7B • 8D

Answers

A12 Consonants: *jīm* ج / *ḥā* ح / *khā* خ

3 حَبِيبٌ 2 جَبَنَ 3 حَجَبَ 4 بَحَثَ 5 حُجِبُّ 6 أجَابَ 7 إنتَخَبَ 8 جَاءَ

4 = خ + ي + ب + ة 2 = ح + ب + ة 3 = ج + ن + ة 4 = ح + جّ

= ج + و + ا + ب 6 = ح + ي + ن 7 = خ + ا + ب 8 = ج + ا + ب

A13 Consonants: *dāl* د / *dhāl* ذ / *rā* ر / *zāy* ز

3 أبداً 2 ذَابَ 3 ذُبَابٌ 4 جَدِيدٌ 5 أخَذَا 6 زَيدٌ 7 دَرَاجَةٌ 8 أرزٌ 9 دِيَارُه 10 زِيَادَةٌ

4 1C • 2E • 3A • 4B • 5D

A14 Consonants: *sīn* س / *shīn* ش / *ṣād* ص / *ḍād* ض

3 شَمسٌ 2 شَجَرٌ 3 مِصبَاحٌ 4 ضَعِيفٌ 5 شَارِعٌ 6 الصُبح 7 سَمِين 8 ضَحِكَ 9 شُفِيَ 10 رُسُومٌ

4 1C • 2G • 3H • 4F • 5D • 6E • 7A • 8B

A15 Consonants: *ṭa* ط / *ẓa* ظ / *ʿain* ع / *ġain* غ

3 غَال 2 مَظلُومٌ 3 عِقَابٌ 4 الغُلامُ 5 شَوَارِعَ 6 طَائِرَةٌ

4 = إ + ض + ط + ج + ع 2 = م + ط + ر 3 = ظ + ل + ا + م 4 = ص + د + ا + ع

= غ + ي + ا + ب 6 = س + ق + ط 7 = ع + ب + ر 8 = ظ + ه + ر + ا

A16 Consonants: *fā* ف / *qāf* ق / *wāw* و

3 فَقِيرٌ 2 وَاحِدٌ 3 فِلمٌ 4 أقلامٌ 5 وَقَفَ 6 أبُوهَا 7 شَوَارِعَ 8 فَوقَهُ

4 1G • 2A • 3E • 4F • 5B • 6C • 7D

A17 Consonants: *kāf* ك / *lām* ل / *mīm* م / *hā* ه

3 كُرَةٌ 2 كِتَابٌ 3 هِوَايَةٌ 4 مَسجِدٌ 5 لَونٌ 6 مَكتَبَةٌ 7 قَلَمٌ 8 مُهَذّبَةٌ

4 1D • 2G • 3A • 4C • 5B • 6H • 7F • 8E

Vocabulary

V1 Personal Information

1

1 الهَاتِف 2 اِسمُ 3 الإلِكتروني 4 الوَضعُ

5 الوِلادَة 6 مَكَانُ 7 القَامَة 8 حَالَةُ

2

Character Attributes	Appearance
وُدِّيٌ / مُمِلٌّ / مُتَكَبِّرٌ / ثَرثارٌ	قَصِيرٌ / ذُو شَعرٍقَصِيرٍ / طَوِيلٌ / ذُو شَارِبٍ

3 1C • 2B • 3D

4

الإِسمُ: جَمَال

اِسمُ الأُسرَة: آدَم

تَاريخُ الوِلادَة: 01/07/1976 م

مَكَانُ الوِلادَة: عَدَن

العِنوَان: ص.ب. 29703 عَدَن - اليَمَن

V2 Occupations / Job Locations

1 1C • 2D • 3A • 4B

2 1 مُدِيرَةٌ 2 تَاجِرَةٌ 3 مُهَندِسٌ 4 سِيَاسِيٌّ 5 خَبَازَةٌ 6 بَائِعَةٌ 7 مُعَلِمٌ 8 طَبِيبٌ

3 1 حَلاقٌ / حَلاقَةٌ 2 شُرطِيٌ / شُرطِيَّةٌ 3 بَائِعٌ / بَائِعَةٌ 4 مُعَلِمٌ / مُعَلِمَةٌ

4 1B • 2A • 3C • 4B

V3 Countries / Nationalities / Languages

1 1C • 2B • 3B

2 1A • 2E • 3D • 4B • 5C

3 1 العَرَبِيَةَ 2 إنجِلِيزِيَةٌ 3 الإيطَالِيَة 4 هِندِيٌّ 5 الصُومَالِيَةَ 6 أمرِيكِيٌّ 7 البُرتُغَالِيَةُ 8 صِينِيَةٌ

4 1 مِنْ أمرِيكَا 2 مِنْ إنجِلتَرَة 3 مِنْ إيطَالِيَا 4 مِصر 5 مِنْ رُوسِيَا 6 مِنْ أَسبَانِيَا 7 مِنَ الهِند

V4 Family

1 1 أَخٌ 2 زَوجَةٌ 3 زَوجُ الاِبنَةِ 4 حَمَاةٌ 5 عَمٌّ 6 أُمٌ 7 حَفِيدَةٌ 8 اِبنٌ

2 1 أَخٌ 2 جَدٌّ 3 اِبنُ الخَال 4 اِبنَةُ العَمَّة 5 حَمَاة

3 1 مُتَزَوِجٌ 2 أَرمَلٌ 3 مُطَلَقَةٌ 4 غَيرُ مُتَزَوِجَةٍ

4 1C • 2A • 3B

V5 Recreation / Hobbies

1 1 الغنَى 2 السّيَاحَة 3 السّبَاحَة 4 التّجول 5 لَعب كُرَة القَدم
6 القِراءَة 7 الرّقص 8 الرّسم 9 الرّكض 10 الذّهاب إلَى المَسرح

2 1D, F, H • 2A, C, E • 3B, G, I

3 1C • 2B • 3C

V6 Numbers

1 1. 4 أربَعَةٌ 4. رابعٌ 7 سَبعَةٌ 7. سَابعٌ
2 اثنَانِ 2. ثانٍ 5 خمسَةٌ 5. خامِسٌ 8 ثمَانيَةٌ 8. ثامِنٌ
3 ثلاثَةٌ 3. ثالِثٌ 6 سِتّةٌ 6. سادِسٌ 9 تِسعَةٌ 9. تاسِعٌ

2 1 خمسَة واحِد صِفر أربَعَة ثَلاثَة. 2 ثَمَانِيَة تِسعَة اِثنَان سِتّة سَبعَة

3 A 11, B 14, C 19, D 18, E 15, F 17, G 16, H 13, I 12

4 B ثَلاثُون C أربَعُون D خمسُون E سِتُّون F سَبعُون G ثمَانُون H تِسعُون

5 A واحِدٌ وَثلاثُون B سَبعَةٌ وَسِتُّون C مِئَةٌ واثنَانِ وَأربَعُون D مِئتَانِ وَخمسُون

V7 Time Designations

1

خريف	صيف	ربيع	شتاء
أيلُول / تَشرينَ الأوّل / تَشرينَ الثّاني	حُزيران / تمّوز / آب	آذار / نِيسَان / أيّار	كَانُون الأوّل / كَانُون الثّاني / شَبَاط

2 1C • 2B • 3D • 4A

3 1 بَعدَ الظُهر 2 السّاعَةُ الثّامِنَة 3 السّاعَةُ الثّانيَة عَشرة 4 وَخمسَ عَشرَة دَقيقَة صَباحاً 5 السّاعَةُ الثّامِنَةُ

V8 In Town

1 1C • 2A • 3B • 4D

2 1 المَوَاد الغِذائيَة 2 الأحذيَة 3 مَخبزٌ 4 اللُّعب 5 مَكتَبَةٌ 6 المَلابِس 7 الرِيَاضَة

3 1 مَسجِد 2 ميدَان 3 سُوق 4 المَتحَف 5 جامِعَة

V9 Restaurant / Foods and Beverages

1 1 كَأْسٌ 2 جِعَةٌ 3 حَسَاءٌ 4 نَادِلٌ

2

مَشْرُوبَاتٌ خَالِيَة مِنَ الكُحول	مَشْرُبَاتٌ كُحُولِيَةٌ	تَحْلِيَةٌ
شَايٌ / عَصِيرٌ / مَاءٌ مَعدَنِيٌ / قَهوَةٌ	نَبِيذٌ / بِيرَةٌ	جِيلاتِي / كَعكٌ

3

Down:

1 م ق هـ ى 3 م ا ء م ع د ن ي 6 م ل ع ق ة 7 م ط ع م 8 م ن ا د ي ل 10 س ك ي ن

Across:

2 ق ا ئ م ة ا ل ط ع ا م 4 ج ع ة 5 ج ي ل ا ت ي 9 ن ا د ل

V10 Groceries / Quantities

1 1 طَمَاطِمٌ 2 زُبدَةٌ 3 سُكّرٌ

2 1 رُز 2 خُبزٌ 3 لَحمٌ 4 سَلطَةٌ 5 جُبنٌ 6 طَحِينٌ / دَقِيقٌ 7 زَيتٌ

3 1 قمح نَاعِم 2 طَمَاطم 3 بَصل 4 زَيت زيتُون 5 ملح 6 فِلفل أسود

V11 Clothing / Colors

1

مِقْيَاس	طِرَاز	أَلْوَان
طَوِيلٌ / قَصِيرٌ / كَبِيرٌ / وَاسِعٌ	رَائِعٌ / زَيٌّ شَائِع / أَنِيقٌ / رِيَاضِيٌّ	أَزرَقٌ / أَبيَضٌ / رَمَادِيٌّ / أَحمَرٌ

2 1D • 2A • 3F • 4B • 5C • 6E

3 1 غَيرُ مُنَاسِب 2 خَلَعَ 3 صَغِيرٌ 4 قَصِيرٌ

4 1 حِذَاءٌ 2 تَنُورَةٌ 3 سِروَال 4 مِعطَفٌ 5 بَدلَةٌ 6 طَاقِيَةٌ 7 تِيشَرت

V12 Housing and Furniture

1 1 بَابٌ 2 تلفِزيُون 3 سَرِير 4 نَافِذَةٌ

2 1 غُرفَةُ النوم 2 مَطبَخ 3 مِرآب 4 حَمَام

3

1	2	3	4	5
لِشُقَتِي - غُرَفٍ	غُرفَةُ النَّوم	لِسَرِيرٍ - دُولابٌ	غُرفَةُ العَمَلِ - طَاوِلَةٌ - وكُومبيُوتَر	لِغُرفَةِ الجُلُوس شُرفَةٌ

4 أَرِيكَةٌ / كُرسِيٌّ / سَرِيرٌ / دُولابٌ / تِلفِزيُون / طَاوِلَةٌ

V13 Transportation

1 1B • 2C • 3C • 4B

2 1 طَائِرَةٌ 2 قِطَارٌ 3 سَيَارَةٌ 4 بَاص 5 دَرَّاجَةٌ هَوَائِيَةٌ

3 1B • 2C • 3A • 4D

4 1 تَذكِرَةٌ - غَرَامَةٌ 2 مَوقِفٌ 3 صَعِدَ 4 سَائِقٌ 5 أوقَفَ - نَزَلَ

V14 Body / Personal Care / Health

1

جِسمٌ: أَصَابِعٌ / ذِرَاعَانِ / كَتِفَانِ / أَرجُلٌ

وَجهٌ: أَسنَانٌ / فَمٌّ / أَنفٌ / عُيُونٌ / حَاجِبَانِ / شَفَتَانِ

2 1 شَعرٌ 2 رَأسٌ 3 عُنُقٌ 4 كَتِفَانِ 5 صَدرٌ 6 بَطنٌ 7 أَرجُلٌ 8 أَقدَامٌ

3 1B • 2D • 3E • 4C • 5A

4 1 البَطنِ 2 الصَدرِ 3 مَحمُومٌ 4 الأسنَانِ 5 الحَلقِ 6 صَحِيحٌ

V15 Verbs

1 1 تَكَلَّمَ 2 أَجَابَ 3 كَفَّ 4 أَحَبَّ 5 جَلَسَ 6 اِستَرَاحَ

2 1 أَحَبَّ 2 اِستَطَاعَ 3 أَرَادَ 4 عَمِلَ 5 رَأَى 6 ذَهَبَ 7 فَهِمَ 8 فَعَلَ

3

ك	ك	ج	س	ن	ب	ح	أ	و	ض
س	ر	ع	ل	ح	ث	ث	ا	س	ي
ك	غ	ه	ل	س	ث	ا	ب	ك	ش
ج	ا	م	ا	ش	ض	ك	ق	ت	ي
ل	ع	ف	ك	س	م	ا	ق	ع	غ
ز	ف	ف	ك	ع	ت	س	ط	ا	ق
ط	ب	ض	فّ	و	ك	ط	ظ	و	ا
ن	ح	ص	ط	غ	ك	م	أ	و	ل
ا	ث	ي	ع	ك	س	ج	ش	ع	م

Grammar

G1 Nominal Sentence

1 1 أنَا فَرحانٌ. 2 الطَبِيبُ هُنَا. 3 الغرفةُ واسعةٌ. 4 هَذَا سَلِيمٌ. 5 هَذِهِ المَرأةُ طَبِيبَةٌ.

2

1.			2.		
هُوَ سَمِينٌ	أنَا سَلِيمٌ.	أنتَ طَوِيلٌ	هِيَ طَبِيبَةٌ.	هَذَا قَصِيرٌ.	هَذِه جَمِيلَةٌ.

3

1	2	3	4	5
هَل هَذا سَلِيمٌ؟	هَل هُوَ مِنَ القَاهِرَةِ؟	هَل هَذِه طَبِيبَةٌ؟	هَلِ الغُرفَةُ وَاسِعَةٌ؟	هَلِ الطَبِيبُ هُنَا؟

4 1 أنَا طَالِبٌ. 2 أنَا مِنَ الصُومَالِ. 3 أنَا طَوِيلٌ. 4 أنَا سَعِيدٌ.

G2 Nouns: Gender

1

1.	2.
زَيدٌ / ابنٌ / اِسم / عُمَر / بَيتٌ	أسرَةُ / هَالَة / اِبنَةٌ / حَلِيمَة / القَاهِرَة

2 1 قَاضِي 2 مَحَامِي 3 مُذِيع 4 شُرطِي 5 جُندِي 6 سَائِق 7 مُعَلِم 8 طَبِيب

3 correct 8, 7, 5, 1

incorrect 2 هَالَةٌ طَبِيبَةٌ. 3 عَلِيٌّ طَالِبٌ. 4 مُحَمَدٌ مُهَندِسٌ. 6 خَدِيجَةٌ مُهَندِسَةٌ.

G3 Nouns: Number

1

1.						2.					
سَيَارَةٌ	عَاقِلٌ	رَجُلٌ	جَرِيدَةٌ	حَمَامَةٌ	اِمرَأةٌ	سَيَارَتَانِ	عَاقِلَانِ	رَجُلَانِ	جَرِيدَتَانِ	حَمَامَتَانِ	اِمرَأتَانِ

2

1
A مُرَاقِبُونَ B مَندُوبُونَ C كَاتِبُونَ D مُسلِمُونَ E مُهَندِسُونَ F لَاعِبُونَ G أرضُونَ H مُسَاعِدُونَ

2
A لُغَاتٌ B حُكُومَاتٌ C شَرِكَاتٌ D سَفَارَاتٌ E مَحَطَاتٌ F قَارَاتٌ G سَيَارَاتٌ H طَائِرَاتٌ

3 1E • 2C • 3F • 4A • 5B • 6D

G4 Nouns: Definite Article *al* ال

1 1 الكِتَابُ 2 البَيتُ 3 الثَّلَّاجَةُ 4 الطَّالِبَانِ 5 المُهَندِسُونَ

6 البَابُ 7 المَصَابِيحُ 8 الدُّكَانُ 9 الشُّرطِيَاتُ 10 المَدِينَةُ

2

1.
ت ث د ذ ر ز س ش ص ض ط ظ ل ن

2.
أ ب ج ح خ ع غ ف ق ك م ه و ي

3

1. الرَّبِيعُ / الظِّلُ / الزَّوجَةُ / التِّجارَةُ / الشَّمْسُ / السَّمَاءُ
2. اليَومُ / الكُرْسِيُ / الفَمُّ / القَهْوَةُ / البَابُ / المَطْبَخُ

G5 Nouns: Declension of Singular Forms

1 1B • 2C • 3A • 4C • 5B • 6A • 7C • 8A • 9B

2

1	البَيتُ	البَيتِ	البَيتَ
2	الرَّجُلُ	الرَّجُلِ	الرَّجُلَ
3	المُدِيرُ	المُدِيرِ	المُدِيرَ
4	الطَّعَامُ	الطَّعَامِ	الطَّعَامَ
5	المِلْعَقَةُ	المِلْعَقَةِ	المِلْعَقَةَ
6	الوَرَقَةُ	الوَرَقَةِ	الوَرَقَةَ

3 1F • 2C • 3A • 4E • 5H • 6B • 7D • 8G

4 1 حَقِيبَةً 2 المَكتَبِ 3 الطَعَامُ 4 الشَجَرَة

G6 Nouns: Declension of Dual / Plural Forms

1 1C • 2B • 3C

2

1.	2.	3.	4.
الكِتَابَانِ / القَمِيصَانِ / المَقعَدَانِ / المَتحَفَانِ	الشَرِيطَتَانِ / النَافِذَتَانِ / المَدِينَتَانِ / الرِسَالَتَانِ	الطَالِبَينِ / الوَلَدَينِ / الرَجُلَينِ / المُعَلِمَينِ	المُعَلِمَتَينِ / الطَبِيبَتَينِ / الطَالِبَتَينِ / الشُرطِيَتَينِ

3 1 امَرأَتَانِ 2 المُعَلِمِينَ 3 شُرطِيٌّ 4 المُعَلِمَاتِ 5 المُدِيرِ 6 تُفَاحَتَينِ 7 المُحَرِرُونَ 8 البِنتَينِ

G7 Nouns: Partially Declinable Nouns

1 1A • 2B • 3B

2

1	الهَدِيَةُ	الهَدِيَةِ	الهَدِيَةَ	الهَدِيَتَانِ	الهَدِيَتَينِ	الهَدِيَتَينِ	الهَدَايَا	الهَدَايَا	الهَدَايَا
2	القَرِيَةُ	القَرِيَةِ	القَرِيَةَ	القَرِيَتَانِ	القَرِيَتَينِ	القَرِيَتَينِ	القُرَى	القُرَى	القُرَى
3	الزَاوِيَةُ	الزَّاوِيَةِ	الزَّاوِيَةَ	الزَّاوِيَتَانِ	الزَّاوِيَتَينِ	الزَاوِيَتَينِ	الزَّوَايَا	الزَّوَايَا	الزَّوَايَا
4	البَقِيَةُ	البَقِيَةِ	البَقِيَةَ	البَقِيَتَانِ	البَقِيَتَينِ	البَقِيَتَينِ	البَقَايَا	البَقَايَا	البَقَايَا

3

correct 1, 2, 5

incorrect 3 هَذِه العِمَارَةُ تَحتَوي مَكَاتِبَ كَثِيرَةً. 4 الوَزِيرُ يَعرِفُ رُؤَسَاءَ كُثُرٌ. 6 أَكَلُوا فِي مَطَاعِمَ عَدِيدَةٍ.

Answers

G8 Nouns: Nunation

1 1 ـٌ 2 ـٌ 3 ـٍ 4 ـً 5 ـً 6 ـٍ 7 ـً 8 ـٌ

2 1F • 2D • 3G • 4A • 5B • 6H • 7E • 8C

3 1 تُفَاحَةً 2 شَجَرَةٍ 3 كِتَاباً 4 أصدِقَاءٍ 5 قِطَارٍ 6 أُسُوداً

G9 Nouns: Genitive Constructions

1 1 البَيتِ 2 الطَّالِبِ 3 القِطَارِ 4 النَّومِ 5 الوَزِيرِ 6 سَائِقِ 7 وَزَارَةِ - العَدلِ 8 كِتَابُ - المَعهَدِ

2 correct 2, 3, 5, 7
incorrect 1 بِطَاقَةُ تَهنِئَةٍ 4 مُعظَمُ المَقَاعِدِ 6 شَجَرَةَ التُفَاحِ 8 آخِرَ الطَابُورِ

3 1 غُرفَةُ الأطفَالِ 2 خُبزٌ أبيَض 3 قَائِمَةُ الطَّعَامِ

G10 Personal Pronouns (Independent)

1 1 أنَا 2 هُوَ 3 هِيَ 4 أنتُمَا 5 نَحنُ 6 أنتَ 7 هُم 8 هُمَا

2 1 هِيَ 2 هُمَا 3 هُوَ 4 هُم 5 هِيَ 6 هِيَ 7 هُنَّ 8 هُم

3

2	3	4	5	6	7	8
هُنَّ مُعَلِمَاتٌ	أنتُنَّ تَاجِرَاتٌ	هُمَا مُحَامِيَتَانِ	هُم سَائِقُونَ	انتُمَا شُرطِيَانِ	نَحنُ مُهَندِسَاتٌ	هُمَا جُندِيَانِ

G11 Personal Pronouns / Possessive Pronouns (Attached)

1 1B • 2B • 3C

2 1 ـهَا ـهِ ـكُمَا ـكُم 2 ـهَا ـهُ ـكُمَا ـكُم

3

1	2	3	4	5	6	7	8
هَذَا كِتَابِي	أَخَذتُ مِعطَفَكِ	هَذِهِ غُرَفُكُم	رَأَينَا أطفَالُكُمَا	هَذِهِ سَيَارَاتُنَا	هَذَا حِمَارُهُ	كَتَبُوا رِسَالَتَهُم	هَذِهِ أحَذِيَتُكُمَا

G12 Demonstrative Pronouns

1 1 هَذِه 2 هَذِه 3 هَذَا 4 هَذَا 5 هَذَا 6 هَذِه 7 هَذِه 8 هَذَا

2 1 هَاتَانِ 2 هَذِهِ 3 أُولئِكَ 4 هَذَينِ 5 هَذا 6 هَاتَينِ 7 تِلكَ

3 correct 1, 5, 6, 7, 8
incorrect 2 اشتَرَيتُ هَذَا المِعطَفَ الجَمِيلَ. 3 هَذِه مُحَررَةٌ. 4 تِلكَ أَبقَارِي.

G13 Relative Pronouns

1 1 الَّذِي 2 الَّتِي 3 اللَّذَانِ 4 اللَّذِينَ 5 الَّتِي 6 اللَّذَانِ 7 اللاَّتِي

2 correct 1, 3, 4

incorrect 2 جَاءَ رَجُلٌ يُرِيدُ أن يَتَحَدَّثَ مَعَكَ. 5 رَأيتُ اِمرَأةً حَاوَلَت أن تَتَصِلَ بِكَ. 6 هَذَا هُوَ المَقَال الَّذِي كَتَبْتُهُ.

3

1 الرَّجُلانِ اللذانِ لَقِينَاهُمَا	2 مَعَ الطالِبَينِ اللَذَينِ كَانَا مَعَكَ	3 المَرأتانِ اللَّتانِ كَانَتا تَبِيعَانِ الخُضرَوات
4 الطَالِبَانِ اللذَانِ جَاءا مِن سُوريَا	5 الصَدِيقَانِ اللَذانِ زَارَانِي	6 تَحتَ الشَّجَرَتَينِ اللَّتَينِ زَرَعتُهُمَا

G14 Interrogative Pronouns

1 1 مَنْ 2 مَا 3 مَاذَا 4 مَاذَا 5 مَا 6 مَنْ 7 مَنِ 8 مَاذَا 9 مَا

2 1 مَنْ قَالَ هَذَا؟ 2 مَاذَا أكَلتُم؟ 3 مَاهُوَ عِنوَانُكَ؟ 4 لِمَنْ هَذا الكِتَاب؟ 5 أيَّةِ طَالِبَةٍ تقصُدُ؟ 6 مِنْ أيِّ دُكَانٍ اشتَرَيتَه؟

3 1E • 2D • 3A • 4F • 5C • 6B

G15 Question Words

1 1 كَيفَ 2 كَم 3 لِمَاذَا 4 كَيفَ 5 لِمَاذَا 6 أينَ 7 مَتَى - أينَ 8 مَتَى

2 1 لِمَاذَا تَشتَرِي كُتُباً كَثِيرَةً؟ 2 مَتَى يُمكِنُ أن نَلتَقِيَ؟ 3 أينَ يُمكِنُ أن نَلتَقِيَ؟ 4 كَم السَاعَةُ الآنَ؟

5 مَتَى وَأينَ نَلتَقِي؟ 6 هَل أنتَ مِنْ الولايَاتِ المُتَّحِدَةِ؟ 7 أينَ تَسكُنُ؟ 8 هَل هَذه أختُكَ؟

3 1C • 2D • 3B • 4F • 5A • 6E

G16 Adjectives

1 1 طَوِيلٌ 2 كَبِيرَةٌ 3 ذَكِيٌّ 4 جَدِيدَةٌ 5 ثَرثَارَةٌ 6 حَارٌّ

2 1 بَيضَاءُ 2 صَغِيرَةٌ 3 لَذِيذٌ 4 كَبِيرَةٌ 5 دراسِيَةٌ 6 سَرِيعٌ 7 جَمِيلَةٌ 8 شَاهِقٌ

3 correct 1, 4, 6, 7, 8

incorrect 2 رَجُلٌ وَسِيمٌ 3 فَتَاةٌ مِصرِيَةٌ 5 السَاعَةُ الذَهَبِيَةُ

G17 Adjectives: Comparison

1 1C • 2A • 3A • 4B • 5C • 6B

2 1 أقدَمُ 2 أحدَثُ 3 أسرَعُ 4 أطوَلُ 5 أجمَلُ 6 أصغَرُ

3 1 أذكَى 2 أقدَمُ 3 أحسَنُ 4 أطوَلُ 5 أرخَصُ 6 أكبَرُ

G18 Verbal Sentence

1
2 أَكَلْتُ. I ate.
3 كَتَبَتْ. She wrote.
4 سَقَطْتِ. You (f. sing.) fell.
5 نَجَحتُم. You (m. pl.) were successful.
6 مَزَحْتِ. You (f. sing.) made a joke.
7 قَرَأتُ. I read.
8 لَعِبَتْ. She played.

2 1 نَامَ 2 طَبَخْتَ 3 اشتَرَى 4 ضَحِكَ 5 غَضَبَ 6 كَتَبتُم 7 نَبَحَ 8 شَاهَدنَا

3 1 أَفَتَحْتَ البَابَ؟ 2 هَل وَقَفَ البَاصُ؟ 3 هَل رَجَعَ المُسَافِرُ؟ 4 هَل غَادَرَ القِطَارُ؟
5 هَل فَرَّ الفَأرُ مِنَ القِطَةِ؟ 6 أَفَتَحتِ النَّافِذَةَ؟ 7 هَل جَاءَ زَيدٌ؟ 8 هَل سَافَرتَ إِلَى القَاهِرَةِ؟

G19 Verbs: Infinitive / Past Tense

1 1B • 2C • 3A

2 1 كَتَبتُ 2 سَافَرنَا 3 ذَهَبُوا 4 اشتَرَى 5 لَعِبَتَا 6 نَجَحتُ 7 قَرَأتَ 8 سَافَرنَ 9 طَبَختِ 10 زَارَا

3
2 سَافَرَتْ إِلَى سِينغَافُورة.
3 سَافَرَتَا إِلَى سِينغَافُورة.
4 سَافَرَا إِلَى سِينغَافُورة.
5 سَافَرْنَا إِلَى سِينغَافُورة.
6 سَافَرَ إِلَى سِينغَافُورة.
7 سَافَرنَ إِلَى سِينغَافُورة.
8 سَافَرتَ إِلَى سِينغَافُورة.

G20 Verbs: Present – Indicative / Subjunctive

1 1E • 2C • 3B • 4A • 5D • 6I • 7H • 8J • 9K • 10G • 11L • 12F

2 1 أجلِسُ 2 أَكَلَتْ 3 تذهَبَانِ 4 يَدرُسنَ 5 تَنظُرُ 6 يَسُوقُونَ 7 تَلعَبُ 8 نَطبَخُ

3 1 يَنسَوا 2 تَذهَبِي 3 تَصِلَ 4 نَدرُسَ 5 يَتَأَخرنَ 6 نَكتُبَ

4
Singular 1 أَنَا أقرَأُ كِتَاباً. 2 هُوَ يَذهَبُ إِلَى السُوقِ. 3 هِيَ تَلعَبُ كُرَةَ القَدَمِ.
Plural 1 نَحنُ نَقرَأُ كِتَاباً. 2 هُم يَذهَبُونَ إِلَى السُوقِ. 3 هُنَّ يَلعَبنَ كُرَةَ القَدَمِ.

G21 Verbs: Present – Jussive / Imperative

1 1 لَم يَشربُوا. 2 لَم نَبنِ بَيتاً. 3 لَم تُناقِشنَ. 4 لَم أُنظِفِ الغُرفَةَ. 5 لَم تَزُورَا المَرِيضَ.

2 1 اِفتَحْ, قُمْ 2 قُولِي, كُلِي 3 اُدخُلا, سَاعِدَا 4 اُنظُرُوا, اِرجِعُوا 5 حَاوِلنَ, قِفنَ

3 1 إذهَبْ 2 خُذْ 3 اِتَّصِلْ 4 اِشتَرِ

4 1 اِلعَبُوا 2 تَحَدَّثُوا 3 اِذهَبُوا 4 سَافِرُوا

G22 Verbs: Future / Active and Passive

1 A3 • B5 • C1 • D2 • E4 • F12 • G10 • H11 • I6 • J8 • K9 • L7

2 1 سَوفَ أَنَامُ 2 سَوفَ تُجَهِّزُ 3 سَوفَ تَلعَبُ 4 سَوفَ يَزُورنَا
5 سَوفَ تَأتِي 6 سَوفَ يَبِيتُ 7 سَوفَ نَذهَبُ

3 1 أُقِيمَتْ 2 صُلِّحَتْ 3 يُدهَنُ 4 فُتِحَ 5 طُبِعَ 6 يُعزَمُ 7 سُدَّتْ 8 يُحرَسُ

G23 Verbs: Negation

1 affirmative 1 غَادَرَ القِطَارُ. 2 يَسُوقُ سَيَّارَةً. 4 سَيَتَأخَرُ القِطَارُ.
negative 3 لَن يَتَأخَرَ القِطَارُ. 5 لايَسُوقُ سَيَّارَةً. 6 لَم يُغَادِرِ القِطَارُ.

2 1 لَم نُنَاقِش 2 لايُحِبُّ 3 لَم تَكُن 4 لَيسَت المَدِينَةُ 5 ألاّ تُسَافِرَ 6 لاتَطبَخ 7 لَم أفهَم 8 لَن يَشتَغِلَ

3 1 لَم أقرَأ هَذَا الكِتَابَ المُمتِع.
2 هَذِهِ الجَامِعَةُ لَيسَت قَدِيمَةً.
3 لا تَدخُلُوا مِنْ هَذَا البَاب.
4 لَم يُسَافِر عُثمَان فِي عُطلَةِ الصَيفِ.
5 لايُمكِنُ أن تَدفَعَ بِبِطَاقَةِ الإئتِمَانِ.
6 الكُتُبُ العَرَبِيَّةُ لَيسَت رَخِيصَةً فِي القَاهِرَةِ.
7 الأفضَلُ ألاّ نَذهَبَ لِلتَّنَزُه الآنَ.
8 لَم تَزُوروا مُدُناً كَثِيرَةً.

G24 Verbs: Verb "to be" / Modal Verbs

1 correct 1, 3, 4, 6, 7, 8
incorrect 2 هَذَا لَيس قَلَمُكَ. 5 هَذِهِ السَيَّارَةُ لَيسَت جَدِيدَةً.

2 2, 6 يَجِبُ 4, 5 أَرَادَ 1, 3 أمكَنَ

3 1 يَجِبُ أنْ 2 يُرِيدُ أنْ 3 يُمكِنُ أنْ 4 يَجِبُ أنْ 5 نُرِيدُ أنْ 6 يَجِبُ أنْ 7 يُمكِنُ أنْ 8 يَجِبُ أنْ

G25 Adverbs

1 1C • 2B • 3A

2 1 خَلفَ 2 غَداً 3 بِسُرعَةٍ 4 كَثيراً

3 1 جَيِّد 2 أمسِ 3 دائِماً 4 الآنَ 5 قَليلٌ, بِسُرعَةٍ 6 أمَامَ 7 مُقَابِلَ 8 الخَارِج

4 1 جَاءَتْ أُختِي أمسِ مِنْ دُبَي. 2 فِي وَقتِ الفُطُورِ نَأكُلُ الخُبزَ دَائِماً. 3 السَاعَةُ الآنَ الثَالِثَةُ بَعدَ الظُهرِ.

G26 Prepositions (1)

1 A3 كـ B2 بـ C5 لـ D1 إلَى E4 بـ

2 1 بِـ 2 لِـ 3 بِـ 4 لِـ 5 كَـ 6 لِـ 7 بِـ 8 كَـ

3 2 لَهُمَا 3 لِي 4 لَهُم 5 لَهُنَّ 6 لَنا 7 لَكُمَا 8 لَكَ 9 لَهُ

4 1 لِلمَرأَةِ بَيتٌ. 2 لِلغُرفَةِ شُرفَةٌ. 3 لِلقَميصِ جَيبٌ.
4 لِلبَيتِ بَابٌ خَلفِيٌّ. 5 لِلشَجَرَةِ ثِمَارٌ. 6 لِلسَيَارَةِ لَونٌ أحمَر.

G27 Prepositions (2)

1 1C • 2E • 3D • 4B • 5B • 6A • 7C

2 1 مِنْ 2 عَنْ 3 مِنْ 4 مِنْ 5 مِنْ 6 عَنْ 7 مِنْ

3 1 فِي الفُندُقِ الجَميلِ 2 عَلَى الطَاوِلَةِ الكَبيرَةِ 3 إلَى المَحَطَةِ
4 فِي القِطَارِ 5 فِي الغُرفَةِ الصَغيرَةِ 6 عَلَى الأقدَام

4 1 تُقلِعُ الطَائِرَةُ إلَى الرياض فِي السّاعَةِ الثَالِثَةِ.
2 يُغَادِرُ القِطَارُ إلَى الإسكَندَرِيَةِ مِنَ الرَّصيف5.
3 عِشتُ فِي مَدينَةِ دِمَشق.

Answers

G28 Conjunctions

1 1A • 2B • 3B

2 1 إذَا 2 لأَنَّنِي 3 ثُمَّ 4 لَكِن 5 فَـ

3
1 ذَهَبنَا أنَا وَزوجِي وَإبنَتِي إلَى حَدِيقَةِ الحَيَوَانَاتِ
2 فَرَأينَا أسَداً وَوَحِيد القَرنِ وقُروداً وَثَعَابِين وَطُيُوراً كَثِيرَةً.
3 مَا رَأينَا زَرافَةً ولا فيلاً.
4 ثُمَّ رَجَعنَا بِالقِطَارِ ونَزَلنَا فِي مَركَزالمَدِينَةِ
5 كُنَا نُرِيدُ أن نَذهَبَ إلَى السِينمَا ولِكِن ابنَتِي كَانَت قَد تَعِبَت
6 فَلَم نَذهَب إلَى السِينمَا بَل رَجَعنَا إلَى البَيتِ
7 قُلتُ لِزوجِي إمَا أن تَطبَخَ وَإمَا أن تَغسِلَ المَوَاعِين
8 فَطَبَختُ دَجاجاً ومَعكَرُنَة لأَنَّنا نُحِبُّ الدجَاج.

G29 Numerals

1 1B • 2A • 3A • 4B• 5A • 6B

2 1 A ثَلاثَةٌ 1 B خَمسُ 2 A أربَعَةَ عَشَرَ 2 B أَربَعَ عَشْرَةَ 3 A إحدَى عَشْرَةَ 3 B سَبعَةُ

3
1 وَاحِد وعِشرُونَ + سِتّةَ عَشَرَ = سَبعَةٌ وَثَلاثُونَ.
2 مِئةٌ وثَلاثَةٌ وَخَمسُونَ + سَبعٌ وَسِتُّونَ = مِئتَانِ وَعِشرُونَ
3 ثَلاثُمِئةٍ وَخَمسَةٌ وَخَمسُونَ + مِئتَانِ وَاثنَانِ وَثَلاثُونَ = خَمسُمِئةٍ وَسَبعَةٌ وثَلاثُونَ

4 1 اليَوم الخَامِس 2 الأسبُوع السّابع عَشَر 3 الكِتَابُ التَاسِع 4 الطِفلُ الثّالِث

G30 Word Formation

1 1G • 2E • 3A • 4C • 5B • 6H • 7F 8D

2 3 فَعِلَ 4 يَفْعَلُ 5 فَعَلَ 6 يَفْعِلُ 7 فَعَلَ 8 يَفْعُلُ

3 2 كَتَبَ 3 دَرَسَ 4 كَرُمَ 5 رَفَعَ 6 فَسَرَ

Answers

Communication

C1 Saying Hello / Inquiries into Each Other's Health / Saying Goodbye

1

hello	goodbye
السَّلامُ عَلَيكُمْ! / أَهلاً وَسَهلاً! / مَسَاءَ الخَير. / نَهَارُكَ سَعِيدٌ.	مَعَ السّلامَة! / حظاً سَعيداً! / إِلَى اللِقَاءِ! / أَتَمَنَى لكَ كُلَ الخَيرِ!

2
formal 2 وَعَلَيكُم السّلام 3 حَالُكَ 4 أَنَابِخَيرٍ - أنتِ
informal 2 مَرحَباً 3 حَالُكِ 4 أنتِ

3 1 مَرحَباً / أهلاً وَسَهلاً 2 صَبَاحُ الخَيرِ 3 مَرحَباً / أهلاً وَسَهلاً 4 السّلامُ عَلَيكُم 5 أهلاً وَسهلاً

4 1 بِخَير 2 الحَمدُ لِلّه 3 لابَأس

C2 Introducing Yourself / Someone Else

1 A1 • B6 • C3 • D5 • E2 • F4

2 1 مَسَاءُ الخَيرِ 2 مَالِك 3 وَأنَا أسعَد

3 1 سَعِيد 2 مَالِك عَبد السَتَار - اسمُكِ الكَرِيم 3 فُرصَة سَعِيدَة

4 1 اِسمَحِي لِي بِأن أُقَدِمَ لَكِ نَفسِي. 2 اِسمَح لِي بِأن أُقَدِمَ لَكَ نَفسِي. 3 هَذَا مَالِك / هَذِه مَريَم.

C3 Stating Your Age / Occupation / Address

1
1 عُمرِي ثَلاثُونَ سَنَة. 2 عِنوَانِي: ص. ب.7432 دِيرَة - دُبَي.
3 أَنَا مُهَندِسٌ. 4 أَشتَغِلُ فِي إحدَى الشّرِكَاتِ العَالَمِيَة.

2 1A • 2C • 3B

3 1 مَا هِيَ حِرفَتُكَ؟ 2 كَم عُمرُكَ؟ 3 مَاهُوَ عِنوَانُكَ؟

C4 Stating Your Nationality / Origin / Place of Residence

1 1C • 2B • 3A • 4D

2 1 أمرِيكَا - أمرِيكِيَة 2 الكُويت - كُوَيتِيَة 3 فَرَنسَا - فَرَنسِيّ

3 1 أَنَا أسكُنُ فِي القَاهِرة. 2 أَنَا أُقِيمُ فِي فُندُقٍ. 3 أَنَا مِنْ بَاكِستَان. 4 أَنَا أُقِيمُ عِندَ أَصدِقَائِي

Answers

C5 Talking About Your Family

1 1B • 2C • 3B

2 1 هَل لَكَ إخوَة؟ 2 هَل أنتَ مُتزَوِّج؟ 3 هَل أنتَ مُطَلَّق؟ 4 هَل لَكَ أولاد؟

3

1	2	3
زَيد عَلي مُحمَد - هَالة حَسَن عُثمَان	اِبنَة وَاحِدة - اِبن وَاحِد. اسمُ اِبنَتي - عَبد الرحمَن بِن زَيد.	لِي - خَدِيجة عَلِي مُحَمَد.

4 لِي أخٌ وَاحِد. اِسمُ أخِي عَبد النُور حَسَن.

C6 Apologizing / Asking for Something / Saying Thank You

1

request	thank you	apology
لا يُهِمُك!/لاتُبالِ!/ لاشُكرَ عَلى الوَاجِب!	شُكراً!/أشكُرُكَ!	مِن فَضلِكَ قُل لِي .../ هَل يُمكِنُكَ .../لَو سَمَحتَ!

2 1 لاتُبَال 2 عَفواً

3 1 اَعطِني - هَل بِإمكَانِكَ أن تُعطِنِي 2 قُل لِي - لَو سَمَحتَ أخبِرنِي

C7 Knowledge of a Language / Clearing Up Misunderstandings

1 1 تَعرِفُ 2 تَتكَلَمُ 3 تُجِيدُ 4 أفهَمُ

2 2 جَيّد جِداً 3 جَيّد 4 قَلِيلاً 5 بِشكلٍ سَيّء 6 لا

3 1E • 2B • 3D • 4A • 5C • 6F

C8 Talking About Habits / Preferences / Dislikes

1 1 أُحِبُّ 2 لا أُحِبُّ 3 أُفَضِلُ

2 1 أنَا لا أُحِبُّ المُوسِيقَى. 2 أنَا لا أُفَضِلُ المَسرَحَ. 3 أنَا لا أحِبُّ الرِيَاضَة أبَداً.

3 A1 • B4 • C6 • D3 • E2 • F5

4 1 كَثيراً مَا أُسَافِرُ فِي الصَيف. 2 عَادَةً ألعَبُ كَرَةَ القَدَمِ فِي عُطلَةِ الأسبُوع.

C9 On the Telephone

1 1D • 2F • 3C • 4A • 5B • 6E

2 A1 • B5 • C2 • D4 • E3

3 1 هَلْ يُمْكِنُني أن أتَكَلَمَ مَعَ مونِكا؟ 2 اِسمِي مَالِك. 3 بِأن تَتَصِلَ بِي - مَعَ السّلامَة.

Answers

C10 Arranging to Meet / Making, Accepting, Turning Down Suggestions

1 1D • 2B • 3E • 4A • 5C

2 1 فِكرَة جَيِّدَة! 2 أستَطِيع - أُفَضِّل 3 أينَ - مَتَى

3 1 هَل نَذهَبُ إلَى السينَمَا؟ 2 هَل نُشَاهِدُ مُبَارَاة كُرَة القَدم؟ 3 لَعَلَّكَ تُرِيدُ أن تَذهَبَ إلَى المَسرَح؟

C11 Asking for Directions / Giving Directions

1 1A • 2C • 3A

2 1E • 2F • 3B • 4A • 5H • 6G • 7D • 8C

3 1 كَيفَ الوُصُول 2 الشَارِع - تَوَجَه إلَى اليَسَار 3 مِئة مِتر 4 تَوَجَه إلَى اليَمِين. 5 المَحَطَة

C12 At a Restaurant

1 A1 • B6 • C2 • D3 • E5 • F4 • G7

2 1D • 2C • 3E • 4A • 5B

3 1 شَهِيَّة طَيِّبَة 2 فِي صِحَتِك 3 أُرِيدُ - مِن عَصِيرِ اللَّيمُون 4 الطَعَامُ طَيِّباً 5 قَائِمَة الطَعَام

C13 Shopping

1 1 I would like this dress. 2 I'm just looking (around). 3 How much does this sweater cost? 4 That shirt is too expensive. 5 How much do I owe? 6 Do you have these shoes one size bigger?

2 1D • 2E • 3A • 4B • 5C

3 1 هَذِه - غَالِية جِداً 2 صَغِيرٌ جِداً 3 لاتُعجِبُنِي 4 أجمَل 5 يُعجِبُنِي - جِداً

C14 At a Hotel

1 2, 5, 6

2 1G • 2F • 3B • 4E • 5C • 6A • 7D

3 1 أُرِيدُ غُرفَةً لِشَخصٍ وَاحِد. 2 أُرِيدُ غُرفَةً مَعَ الفُطُور.
3 بِمَاذَا مُجَهزَة؟ 4 أُرِيدُ غُرفَةً لأسبُوعٍ وَاحِد.

C15 Traveling

1 1 تَذكِرَة وَاحِدَة إلَى القَاهِرَة لَوسَمَحتَ. 2 أينَ مَكتَبُ التَذاكِر؟
3 سَوفَ يَتَأخَرُ القِطَار. 4 هَل هَذَا القِطَارُ إلَى القَاهِرَة؟

2
1 مَتَى يُغَادِرُ القِطَارُ؟
2 إلَى أينَ يَذهَبُ هَذَا القِطَارُ؟
3 مِنْ أينَ يُغَادِرُ القِطَارُ؟
4 مَتَى يَصِلُ القِطَارُ؟
5 هَل يَذهَبُ البَاص إلَى مَركَزِ المَدِينَة؟

3 رِحلَة سَعِيدَة!

Arabic-English Mini-Dictionary

The Arabic entries are arranged in alphabetical order, that is, not according to word stem, as is customary in other dictionaries. The verbs are given in the infinitive, which is represented in Arabic by the 3rd person masculine singular past tense form. The nouns and adjectives are given in the singular throughout and—if they have both a masculine and a feminine form—in the masculine. The entries are vocalized only to the extent necessary to distinguish between words with the same basic stem.

ا

August	آب
father	أب
never	أبداً
slower, more slowly	أبطأ
white	أبيَض
All the best!	أتمنى لك كُلّ الخير
to come (be) from	أَتى مِن
to reward	أثاب
trace	أثر
to answer	أجاب
grandparents	أجداد
prettier, nicer	أجمل
stranger	أجنبي
to love	أحب
eleven	أحد عشر
shoes	أحذِية
best / most of all	الأحسن
better	أحسن
to bring	أحضر
red	أحمر
brother	أخ
to inform, impart (news)	أخبر
sister	أخت
to take	أخذَ
end	آخر
green	أخضر
brothers and sisters, siblings	إخوة وأخوات
to raise, educate	أدّب
March	آذار
to want / to want to	أراد
four	أربع
fourteen	أربع عشرة
forty	أربعون
cheaper, lower priced	أرخص
Jordan	الأردن
rice	رُزّ
to send	أرسَل
floor	أرضِية
widower	أرمل
to show, point out	أرى
sofa	أريكة
blue	أزرَق
to disturb, bother	أزعج
Spanish	أسباني
week	أسبُوع
professor	أستَاذ
lion	أسد
family	أسرة
Alexandria	الإسكندرِية
name	إسم
surname	إسم العائلة
teeth	أسنان
to have diarrhea	إسهال
black	أسود
traffic light	إشارة المُرور

إصبُع	finger
أصفر	yellow
أصلع	bald, bare
أضطرّ	to have to, must
أطاع	to obey
إطفائي	fireman
أطفال	children
إطلالة جميلة	beautiful view
أعاد	to repeat
أعاد الاتّصال	to call back
أعجب (ب)	to please
أعزب	single, unmarried
أعطى	to give
إفريقِيا	Africa
أفضل	better, rather
أقام	to hold (a celebration)
أقدام	feet
إقليم	province
أكبرسِناً	older
أكُف	palms (of hands)
أكل	to eat
أكل خفيف	to eat a snack
آلة الحلاقة	razor, shaver
أَلْف	thousand
ألم	pain
ألماني	German
ألمانيَا	Germany
إله	God
إلى	to
إلى أين	where (to)
إلى الأمام	straight ahead
إلى اللقاء	So long!
أم	mother
أمَام	across from / in front of
أمريكا	USA
أمسِ	yesterday
أمطرت السمَاء	to rain
أمكَنَ	to be possible
أمل	hope
الآن	now
أنَا	I
أنت	you
أُنثى	feminine
إنجِلترة	England
إنجليزي	Englishman
إنسان	human, person
أنف	nose
أنيق	elegant
أهلاً وسهلاً	Welcome!
أوتوستراد	freeway, superhighway
أوربَا	Europe
أوقف	to stop
أوقف سيارة في مِرْآبٍ	to park a car
أول	first
أيار	May
أيدي	hands
إيطاليا	Italy
أيلول	September
إيميل	e-mail
أين	where
ابن	son
ابن خَال	cousin (m.) (on the mother's side)
ابن عم	cousin (m.) (on the father's side)
ابنة	daughter
ابنة خَال	cousin (f.) (on the mother's side)
ابنة عم	cousin (f.) (on the father's side)

اِتِّصال خاطئ	wrong number
اِتَّصل	to connect
اِتَّصل هاتفياً	to call, telephone
اِثنا عشر	twelve
اِثنان	two
اِجتِماعي الطبع	sociable, gregarious
اِجتَمَعَ	to meet (each other)
الاحتِفال بِالأَعْيادِ	to party
اِحتفلَ	to celebrate
اِحْمَرَّ	to blush
أُذنان	ears
اسبانيا	Spain
اِستحم	to bathe
استدعى سيارة أجرة	to call a taxi
اِستراح	to rest
اِستطاع	to be able, can
اِستعَار	to loan, lend
اِسْتَفْسَر	to inquire, ask
اِستَقال	to quit, resign
اِستَمرّ	to continue
اِستمع	to listen
استوديو	studio
اِسم	name
اِشارة المرور	traffic light
اِشترى	to buy
اِضطجع	to lie, be situated
اِغتسل	to shower
أُفق	horizon
اِمرأة	wife, woman
اِنتَخب	to choose; to vote
اِنتصر	to win
اِنتَظر	to wait
اِنكَسَر	to get broken

ب

بُؤس	misery, distress
بائع	salesman
بَائعُ الأزهار	flower vendor
بَاب	door
بَاب خَلفِي	rear / back entrance
بار	bar
بَارد	cold
بَاص	bus
باص كهربائي	streetcar
بَاع	to sell
باكستان	Pakistan
بَتاتاً	not at all
بجانِب	next to, beside
بَحثَ	to seek
بخِيل	stingy
بدأ	to begin, start
بدّل (الباص / القطار)	to transfer, change (buses, etc.)
بدلة	suit
بدين	corpulent, stout
البرَازيل	Brazil
برلمان	parliament
بَرلين	Berlin
بريد	post office
بسرور	With pleasure!
بسكويت	cookie
بشرة	skin
بصل	onion
بطاطِس	potato
بطاقة	ticket, card
بِطاقة الإئتِمان	credit card
بِطاقة تَهنئة	greeting card
بَطن	abdomen

بَطيء	slow
بعد الظُهر	in the afternoon(s)
بعد الظُهر	afternoon
بعضكم على بعض	together
بعيد	far
بغداد	Baghdad
بقال	vegetable seller
بَقرة	cow
بَقِية	remainder
بَلد	land, country
بلغ	to reach, achieve
بلوزة	blouse
بِنت	girl
بنت عمة	cousin (f.) (on the mother's side)
بنك	bank
بَنى	to build
بُنّي	brown
بِيئَة	environment
بيبة	pipe
بيت	house
بيت السُلم	stairwell, stairs
بيت شخصي	private residence
بيرة	beer
بيضة	egg

ت

تأخر	to be late
تأمل	to consider, reflect
تَابل	spice, seasoning
تَاجر	businessman
تاريخ الوِلادة	date of birth
تاسِع	ninth
تاسِع عشر	nineteenth
تبع	to follow
تِجارة	industry, trade
تجرِبة	experience
تجول	hiking
تَحتَ	under
تحدث	to discuss
تَحَرَّك	to move, be on the move
تحويلة	detour
تِذكاري	monument
تذكرة	ticket (for transportation)
تذكرة الرُكوب	ticket (for transportation)
تذكرة للذهاب فقط	one-way trip
ترك خبراً	to give a message, tell
تَزوّج	to marry
تسع	nine
تِسع عشرة	nineteen
تِسعون	ninety
تَسوَق	to shop, purchase
تشرين الأول	October
تشرين الثاني	November
تَظاهَر	to (go on) strike
تَعِب	tired
تعجب	to be surprised, wonder
تعلم	to learn
تعلُم اللُغات	to learn languages
تُفاحة	apple
تفضل	You're welcome!
تقاطُع	crossing, intersection
تَكَاتَب	to write (each other), correspond
تكلم	to speak
تلفزيون	TV
تلفزيون مُلون	color TV
تِلميذ	student, pupil
لَوَّثَ	to get (something) dirty

تمر	date (fruit)
تناوَل	to take in, partake (of a meal)
تنزه	to go for a walk
تَنورة	skirt
تَهنئة	felicitation, congratulation
توجه	to turn
تورْتَة (كعك)	tart, torte
تيشرت	T-shirt
التينس	tennis

ث

ثالِث	third
ثالِث عشر	thirteenth
ثامن	eighth
ثامن عشر	eighteenth
ثاني	second
ثاني عشر	twelfth
ثَبات	reliability
ثرثَر	to chatter
ثُعبان	snake
ثِقل	weight
ثَقيل	heavy
ثلاث	three
ثلاث عشرة	thirteen
ثلاثون	thirty
ثلاّجة	refrigerator
ثلج	snow
ثمان	eight
ثمانُون	eighty
ثماني عشرة	eighteen
ثوب	dress
ثور	bull

ج

جَاءَ	to come
جاب	to bring
جاع	to be hungry
جامعة	university
جَانِب	next to, beside
جانب الشارع	side of the street
جبان	cowardly
جبَل	mountain
جبن	to be cowardly
جُبن	cheese
جد	grandfather
جِداً	very
جِدار	wall
جَدة	grandmother
جديد	new
جذّاب	attractive
جرّ	to pull
جَريدَة	newspaper
جُزء	part
جَزر	carrot
جِعة	beer
جفف	to dry oneself
جلّ الغسل	shower gel
جَلسَ	to sit
جمَادى الآخِرة	6th month of Islamic calendar
جمَادى الأولى	5th month of Islamic calendar
جَماعة	group
جمل	camel
جَمِيل	pretty, nice
جنّة	garden
جُندِي	soldier

جِنسِيَة	nationality
جهة	side
جَهَد	to try hard
جهز	to prepare, set up
جَوّ	weather
جواب	answer
جوارب	socks
جَواز سفر	passport
جوهَنِسبَاغ	Johannesburg
جيِّد	good
جيّد جداً	very good
جيران	neighbor
جَيش	army
جيلاتي	ice cream

ح

حائط	wall
حاجِبان	eyebrows
حادّ	spicy
حَادث	accident
حادي عشر	eleventh
حالة التعلِيم	educational background
حالِياً	right now, at the moment
حاول	to try
حُبّ	love
حبة	grain
حُبلى	pregnant
حبيب	darling; favorite
حتى	until
حجّ	pilgrimage
حَجب	to cover
حجز	to reserve
حَدث	to happen, occur
حديقة	park
حديقة الحيَوان	zoo
حِذاء	shoe
حرس	to guard
حرق	to get burned
حزيران	June
حَساء	soup
حساب	check, tab, bill
حصَاد	harvest
حضانة الأطفال	kindergarten
حضر مِن	to come (be) from
حظاً سعيداً!	Good luck!
حَفلة	party, celebration; event
حفلة موسيقى	concert
حفِيد	grandson
حَقيبة	bag
حكُومَة	government
حلّاق	hairdresser
حلْق	throat
حلَق	to shave (oneself)
حُلو	sweet
حلويات	dessert
حليب	milk
حَم	father-in-law
حماة	mother-in-law
حِمَار	donkey
حمّام	bathroom
حَمَامة	dove, pigeon
الحمد لله	Thank God!
حمل	to carry
حوض إستحمام	bathtub
حوض الغسل	sink
حي	part of town, quarter
حيا	to greet

خ

خاب	to fail
خارج	outside, outdoors
خاص	own, special
خَال	uncle (on the mother's side)
خالٍ مِنَ الكحُول	alcohol-free
خالة	aunt (on the mother's side)
خامِس	fifth
خامِس عسر	fifteenth
خباز	baker
خُبز	bread
خُبز أبيض	white bread
خَريطة للمدينة	city map
خرِيف	fall, autumn
خشب	wood
خُضرَوات	vegetables
خطأ	incorrect
خِطبة	engagement
خل	vinegar
خَلع	to undress (oneself)
خَلف	behind
خمس	five
خمس عشرة	fifteen
خمسون	fifty
خيار	cucumber
خياط	tailor
خيبة	failure

د

دائماً	always
دار البلدِية	city hall
دار النشر	publishing house
دُبّ	bear
دباغ	tanner
دُبي	Dubai
دَجاج	chicken
دخلَ	to enter, go in
دخنَ	to smoke
دراجة هوائية	bicycle
دَرْس	instruction, class
درّس	to teach
درَس	to study
دفع	to pay
دفن	burial, funeral
دقيق	flour
دقيقة	minute
دُكان	store, shop
دكان أدوات الرياضة	sporting goods store
دُكان الأحذِية	shoe store
دكان الأطعِمة	grocery store
دكان الملابِس	clothing store
دُكان لِبيع الأزهار	flower shop
دكان لبيع اللُعب	toy store
دلّ	to show
دَلّ عَلَى الطَّريقِ	to show the way
دهن	to put on lotion; to apply paint
دواء	medication
دواجِن	poultry
دورة	round
دوري	cyclical
دوش	shower
دولاب	cupboard, cabinet, armoire
دولاب المطبخ	kitchen cupboard
دولاب غُرفة الجُلوس	living room cabinet

ذ

ذاب	to melt
ذاق	to taste

ذُباب	fly (insect)
ذَبذب	to dangle
ذِراعان	arms
ذَكِي	intelligent, smart
الذِهاب إلى حفلة مُوسيقى	to go to a concert
الذِهاب إلى سينما	to go to the movies
الذِهاب إلى مسرح	to go to the theater
ذَهبَ	to go
ذَهَبي	golden
ذو طابِق واحِد	one-story
ذو طابقين	two-story
ذُوالحِجّة	12th month of the Islamic calendar (pilgrimage month)
ذُوالقَعْدَة	11th month of the Islamic calendar
ذوشارب	with a mustache
ذوشعرطويل	with long hair
ذوشعرقصير	with short hair
ذولحية	with a beard
ذونظارات	with glasses

ر

رأس	head
رَأى	to see
رَئيس	president
رائع	chic
رابِع	fourth
رابع عشر	fourteenth
رَاكِب	passenger
رَبيع	spring (season)
رَبيع الأوّل	3rd month of the Islamic calendar
رَبيع الثّاني	4th month of the Islamic calendar
رجا	to request
رَجَب	7th month of the Islamic calendar
رجع	to come back, return
رَجُل	man
رِجلان	legs
رِحلة سعيدة	Have a good trip!
رُخصة القيادة	driver's license
رَخيص	cheap, low-priced
ردّ	to give back, return
رزين	calm, quiet
رِسالة	letter
رِسالة حُبٍّ	love letter
رسام	painter
رسم	to paint
رُسوم	fee
رَصيف	track (train)
رغِب	to like, be fond of
رغِيف صغِير	roll (bread)
رف	shelf, bookshelf
رفض	to deny, refuse
رقص	to dance
رقم	number; size
رقم الهاتف	telephone number
ركض	to jog
رمادي	gray
رمز البريدي	post office box
رَمضَان	9th month of the Islamic calendar (month of Ramadan fast)
رمل	sand
رمى	to throw
رواق	gallery
روسي	Russian
روسيا	Russia
رومَا	Rome

رِيَاض	Riyadh
رياضة	track and field events
رياضي	athletic, sporty
رِيف	land, country

ز

زار	to visit
زاوِية	corner
زبدة	butter
زحمة	traffic jam
زَرافة	giraffe
زَرع	to plant
زَهرة	flower
زوج	husband
زوج الابنة	son-in-law
زوجان	married couple
زوجة	wife
زوجة الابن	daughter-in-law
زيّ شائع	fashionable
زِيادة	more
زِيارة	visit
زيت	oil (edible)

س

سُؤال	question
سَأل	to ask
سَائق	driver
سابِع	seventh
سابِع عشر	seventeenth
سادِس	sixth
سادِس عشر	sixteenth
سَاعة	hour
سَاعدَ	to help
سَافَر	to travel, go away
ساق	to drive, go (by vehicle)
ساق إلى	to go / drive to
ساق إلى الداخِل	to drive in, enter
ساقَان	legs
سَبب	reason
سبح	to swim
سبع	seven
سبع عشرة	seventeen
سبعُون	seventy
ست	six
ست عشرة	sixteen
سِتَار	curtain
سترة	jacket
ستون	sixty
سجارة	cigarette
سدّ	to block
سِرِّي	secret
سروال	pants, trousers
سرور	pleasure
سَرِير	bed
سَرِيع	fast
السعودية	Saudi Arabia
سَفارة	embassy
سفر	trip
سفينة	ship
سقط	to fall (down)
سقف	roof, ceiling
سكت	to be silent
سُكر	sugar
سكرتير	secretary
سكن	to live, reside
سكن في	to live in, inhabit
سُكوت	silence
سكين	knife

سلام	peace
السلام عليكُم	Peace be with you!
سلطة	lettuce; salad
سَلِيم	healthy
سَمَاء	sky
سمِع	to hear
سمى	to be called / named
سمِين	fat
سنيما	movie theater
سوريا	Syria
سُوق	market, bazaar
سوك أسنانه	to brush one's teeth
سُويِسرا	Switzerland
سيئ	bad
سياحة	travel
سيارة	car
سيارة أجرة	taxi
سِياسي	politician
سَيِّد	Mr.

ش

شارع	street, road
شارع سريع	expressway
شامبانيا	champagne, sparkling wine
شامبو	shampoo
شاهِد	witness
شَاهد	to look (at)
شاي	tea
شباط	February
شِتاء	winter
شجَرة	tree
شجَرة تُفاح	apple tree
شحم الخِنزير	bacon
شَخص	person
شدِيد	strict
شَراشِف	bed linen
شرِب	to drink
شرح	to explain
شُرطة	police
شُرْطِيُّ المُرورِ	traffic policeman
شُرطِي	policeman
شُرفة	balcony
شرِكة	firm, company, concern
شركة عالمِية	international concern
شَرِيط	cassette
شُعاع	radiance
شَعْبان	8th month of the Islamic calendar
شعَر	to feel
شعْر	hair
شفتان	lips
شَفى	to get well, recover
شُقة سكنِية	apartment; residence
شكَر	to thank, say thank you
شُكر	gratitude, thanks
شُكراً	Thank you
شُكراً جزيلاً!	Thanks very much!
شمّ	to smell
شمس	sun
شهر	month
شهِية طيبة!	Bon appétit!
شَوَّال	10th month of the Islamic calendar
شوكة	fork
شيء	anything, something

Arabic–English Mini-Dictionary

ص

صابون	soap
صالُون الحلّاقة	hairdresser's; barber shop
صباح الخير	Good morning
الصبح	morning
صَبْر	patience
صَبَر	to be patient
صَحرَاء	desert
صحيح	healthy
صُداع	headache
صدر	breast, chest
صَدِيق	friend
صعِد إلى	to board, get on
صُغرى	smallest
صغير	small
صَف	school class
صَفَر	2nd month of the Islamic calendar
صِفر	zero
صلّح	to repair
الصندوق	checkout, cashier's desk
صَور	to photograph
صُورة	photo, picture
صوف	wool
الصُومال	Somalia
صيدلي	pharmacist
صيدلِية	pharmacy
صيف	summer
الصِين	China

ض

ضحِك	to laugh
ضَرب	to strike, hit
ضَعِيف	weak
ضِفدَع	frog
ضوء	light
ضيف	guest
ضيق	narrow, tight

ط

طائرة	airplane
طابق	floor, story
طابور	(waiting) line
طاقِية	cap
طَالِب	(college) student
طَاوِلة	table
طِب	medicine
طَبَاخ	cook
طَبخ	to cook
طبَق	plate
طَبِيب	physician, doctor
طحين	flour
طرد صغير	package
طَريق	way, avenue
طَريقة	means
طَعام	food, meal, dish
طعام العشاء	dinner
طعام الغذاء	lunch
طِفل	child, baby
طلاق	divorce
طلب	to order
طماطِم	tomatoes
طمع	greed
طُوفان	storm
طول القامة	size, height
طَويل	big, long
طويلاً	(for a) long (time)
طَير	bird

ظ

ظُفر	fingernail
ظِل	shadow
ظُلام	darkness
ظنّ	to think, believe
الظُهر	noon, midday
ظَهر	reverse, back (side)

ع

عائلة	family
عادة	normally, as a rule
عاش	to live
عاشِر	tenth
عاصِمة	capital (city)
عاقل	wise
عالِم	scientist
عامِل	worker
عبَر	to cross
عِتاب	reproach
عجُز	behind, backside
عدل	justice
عربي	Arabic
عُرس	wedding
عَرفَ	to know
عرّف	to introduce, introduce oneself
عرق	to sweat
عزف	to make music, play an instrument
عزَم	to invite
عشر	ten
عِشرون	twenty
عصِير	juice
عصير اللّيمون	lemon juice, lemonade
عُطلة	vacation
عُطلة الأسبوع	weekend
عطلة الصيف	summer vacation
عفواً!	Excuse me!
عقيقة	name-giving ceremony
عقِيم	sterile
عُلبة	box, packet
عَلّق	to hang
عَلّم	to teach, instruct
عَلَم	flag
علِم	to know
عَلى	on
عَلى الأقدام	on foot
على الأقل	least
على زي الحديث	fashionable
على طول	along
عمّ	uncle (on the father's side)
عمارة عالية	multistory; high-rise building
عمة	aunt (on the father's side)
عُمر	age
عَمِل	to work
عمل	work, job
عند	at, with
عُنق	neck
عَنكبُوت	spider
عِنوان	address
عنى	to mean
عِيد	Eid (holiday)
عُيون	eyes

غ

غادر	to leave, depart, go away
غالٍ	expensive
غذاء	food, nourishment
غرام	gram

غرامة	punishment
غُرفَة	room
غُرفة الأطفال	children's room, nursery
غُرفة الجلوس	living room
غُرفة العمَل	workroom, study
غُرفة النوم	bedroom
غُرفة لِشخص واحد	single room
غُرفة لِشخصين	double room
غزال	gazelle
غسل	to wash (oneself)
غُصن	branch, twig
غضب	anger, annoyance
غَضِب	to be angry
غَضبَان	angry
غُمُوض	uncertainty, ambiguity
غنى	to sing
غِياب	absence
غيرمُناسب	to not fit

ف

فَأر	mouse
فارِغ	free, vacant
فاكِهة	fruit
فَتح	to open
فَتى	young man
فَرّ	to race
فَرَانكفورت	Frankfurt
فَرِح	happy
فَرَح	happiness; luck
فرشة الأسنان	toothbrush
فُرصة سَعِيدة	Pleased to meet you!
فرقة المطافي	fire department
فرنسا	France
فرنسي	Frenchman
فسخ	to annul
فِضة	silver
فُطور	breakfast
فعل	to do, make
فقط	only
فقِير	poor
فَكر	to think
فِكرة	thought, idea
فلافِل	falafel
فلفل	pepper
فلفل أحمر	paprika; (bell) pepper
فِلم	film
فَم	mouth
فن الرسم	painting
فنجان	cup
فُندُق	hotel
فهم	to understand
فوق	over
في البيت	at home
في الرّيف	in the country
في العطل الأسبوعِية	on the weekend
في المدينة	in town / in the city
في صحتك!	Cheers!
فِيل	elephant

ق

قائمة الطعام	menu
قارئ	reader
قَارة	continent
قَارُورَة	bottle
قاس	to try on
قَاضِي	judge
قَال	to say
قام	to rise, get up

القَاهِرَة	Cairo
قبضَ	to hold (fast), retain
قبل	before (in terms of time)
قبو	cellar, basement
قبِيح	ugly
قديم	old
قَرأ	to read
قرابة	relatives, kin
قِرد	ape, monkey
قُرص	slice
قرص	tablet, pill
قرية	village
قِشطة	cream
قِشطة رائبة	sour cream
قِشطة مخفوقة	(whipping) cream
قصِير	short
قضى العُطلة في	to vacation in
قَضية	occasion; matter
قِطَار	train
قِطة	cat
قلب	heart
قَلَم	pen, ballpoint
قَلِيل	little
قليلاً	a little
قُماش	fabric, cloth
قمر	moon
قَميص	shirt
قهوة	coffee
قيمة	to cost

ك

كأس	glass
كأس نبيذ	wineglass
كاتِب	writer
كان	to be
الكانتين	canteen, staff cafeteria
كانون الأول	December
كانون الثاني	January
كَبُرَ	to age, grow
كُبرى	biggest
كبير	big, old
كِتَاب	book
كَتَب	to write
كتِفان	shoulders
كَتمَ السِرّ	to keep secret
كَثير	much
كثيراً ما	frequent, often
كثِيف	thick
كُرة	ball
كُرة السَلة	basketball
كرة الطائرة	volleyball
كُرة القدَم	soccer
كُرسي	chair
كُرنب	cabbage
كره	to hate
كَسَّر	to beat to pieces
كسر	to break something (one's leg, arm)
كُشك لِبيع الصُحف	newspaper stand / kiosk
كعك	cake
كفّ عن	to stop, cease
كلّ	all, everything
كلب	dog
كِلِمَنجَارُو	Kilimanjaro
كم	how much
كُمبيوتر	computer
كَمل	to complete, make ready

كنبة	armchair
كنزة	pullover, sweater
كَنيسة	church
الكويت	Kuwait
كيف	how, as
كِيلو	kilo
كِينيا	Kenya

ل

لُؤلُؤ	pearl
لا	no
لا أحد	no, none, not any
لاتُبال	Don't mention it!
لاشَيْءَ	nothing
لاعِب	player
لايُهمك	It doesn't matter.
لَبس	to wear
لبن	yogurt
لِتر	liter
لُجوء	asylum
لحظة	second
لحظة لوسمحت.	Just a minute, please.
لَحم	meat
لحم بقر	beef
لحم خروف	lamb
لحم خِنزير	pork
لحم ضأن	mutton
لحم مُجفف	dried meat
لحم معز	goat meat
لَذيذ	delicious, tasty
لطيف	nice
لَعِب	to play
لعب على آلة الكمبيوتر	to play computer games
لعب كُرة السَلة	to play basketball
لعب كُرة القدم	to play soccer
لعل	perhaps, maybe
لُغة	language
لفظ	pronunciation
لِقاء الأصدِقاء	to meet friends
لَقيَ	to meet
لكن	but
لماذا	why
لمع	to shine
لندن	London
لو	when, if
لوسمحت!	Excuse me! / please
لون	color
لون البشرة	skin color
لون الشعر	hair color
لون العُيون	eye color
لي	to mean
ليبيا	Libya
ليس	not
ليل	night
ليمون	lemon

م

مِئة	one hundred
مئتان	two hundred
مُؤمن	believer
ماء	water
ماء معدني	mineral water
ماذا	what
ماعجب	to not like
مالح	salty
ماليزيا	Malaysia
مَبنَى	building

مِرآة	mirror
مُرَاقِب	observer
مرة أخرى	again
مِرحاض	toilet
مرحباً	Hello!, Hi!
مرطب لِلبشرة	lotion
مركز	center
مَركز المَدينة	center of town
مُروءة	virtue, sense of honor
مريض	patient (medical)
مريض	sick, ill
مَزح	to make a joke
مزّق	to tear to pieces
مسؤول	responsible
مساء	evening
مساء الخير	Good evening!
مُسَاعِد	assistant
مسبح	swimming pool
مُستَشفَى	hospital
مسجد	mosque
مسرح	theater
مسرحية	play (stage)
مسك	to touch
مُسكِرات	alcoholic
مِسواك	toothbrush
مشاة	pedestrian
مَشَاهِد	spectator
مُشاهدة التلفزيون	to watch TV
مشاهدة فِلم	to see a film
مُشاهدة كُرة السَلة	to watch basketball
مُشاهدة كُرة القدم	to watch soccer
مُشاهدة مسرحِية	to see a play
مَشرق	east

مُتأخر	late
مَتجر عام	department store
متحف	museum
المَتْحَفُ الشَّعْبِيُّ	national museum
مترو	subway, metro
مُتزوج	married
مُتكبر	arrogant
متى	when
مُجتهِد	hardworking, industrious
مجزرة	butcher's shop
محَامِي	lawyer, attorney
مُحرر	editor
مُحرَّم	1st month of the Islamic calendar
محطة	stop (bus, streetcar)
محطة الباص	bus station
محطة القِطار	train station
محل الخياطة	tailor shop
محموم	to run a temperature, have fever
مخبز	bakery
مخرج	exit
مُدة طَويلة	for a long time
مدح	to praise
مدخل	entry, entrance
مدرسة	school
مُدير	director, manager
مدينة	city, town
المدينة القَديمة	old town
مدينة كيب	Cape Town
مُذيع	newscaster, reporter
مَرّ	to pass, go past
مُرّ	sour
مرأب	garage

radiant	مُشرِق
beverage, drink	مشروبات
project	مَشرُوع
comb	مِشط
to comb one's hair	مشّط
to be busy	مشغُول
problem	مُشكِلة
sunny	مُشمِس
interesting	مُشوِق
to run	مشى
lamp	مِصباح
Egypt	مصر
Egyptian (*adj.*)	مصري
Egyptian (*noun*)	مصري
elevator	مصعَد
factory, plant	مَصنع
press photographer	مصور صُحُفي
airport	مطار
kitchen	مطبخ
canteen kitchen	مطبخ كبير
rain	مطر
restaurant	مَطعم
divorced	مُطلق
strike, demonstration	مُظاهرة
umbrella	مظلة
unfortunately	مع الأسف
Goodbye!	مع السلامة
together	مَعاً
toothpaste	معجون الأسنان
exhibition	معرَض
knowledge	معرِفة
coat	مِعطف
most	مُعظم
spaghetti, noodles, pasta	مَعكرونة
teacher	مُعلِم
language teacher	مُعلِمُ اللغة
meaning	مَعنى
institute, institution	مَعهد
Morocco	المغرِب
singer	مُغن
across from, opposite	مقابِل
newspaper article	مَقال
snack, appetizer	مقبلات
Mogadishu	مَقدِيشو
seat	مقعد
coffeehouse, café	مَقهى
place	مكان
place of residence	مكان السكن
place of work	مكان العمَل
place of birth	مكان الوِلادة
office	مَكتَب
ticket window (transportation)	مكتَبُ التذاكر
bookstore, library	مكتبة
to stay	مَكث
dresses, clothes	ملابِس
men's clothing	ملابس الرِجال
women's clothing	ملابِس النِساء
underwear	ملابس داخِلية
sailor	ملاّح
crossing, intersection	ملتقى الطُرق
salt	مِلح
sports field, playing field	ملعب
stadium	ملعب مدرّج
spoon	مِلعَقة
to have	ملك
colored	مُلوَن

one million	مليون
entertaining	ممتع
crosswalk	ممرّ المشاة
nurse	مُمرضة
rainy	مُمطر
rain jacket	ممطر
boring	مُمل
Who's speaking?	منِ المُتكلِم؟
please	من فضلك
who	منْ
napkin	مناديل المائدة
to fit; to be suitable	مُناسب
discussion	مُناقشة
scholarship	مِنحة دِراسية
representative (parliamentary)	مَندُوب
towel	منديل
polite	مُهذب
important	مُهم
occupation, profession	مِهنة
engineer	مُهندِس
traffic, transportation	مُواصلات
music	موسيقى
topic	موضوع
employee	مُوظف
bank employee	مُوظف في بنك
appointment	موعد
stop (bus, streetcar)	موقف
parking place / lot	موقف السيارات
field	ميدان
port, harbor	ميناء

ن

representative	نَائب
canine tooth, eyetooth	نابٌ
successful	نَاجح
waiter	نَادل
people	ناس
skyscraper	نَاطِحَاتُ السَحَابِ
window	نَافِذة
to discuss	ناقش
to sleep	نَام
plant	نَبات
to grow (up)	نَبتَ
to bark	نَبح
prophet	نبي
wine	نبيذ
success	نَجاح
slender	نحيف
date palm	نخل
to get off, get out	نزل
to forget	نَسيَ
activity	نشاط
to publish	نشَر
to recommend	نصح
half	نصف
to butt, ram	نَطحَ
to look, look around	نظر
glance, look	نظرة
to clean	نَظفَ
clean	نَظيف
detour	نقطة تفرع
Austria	نمسا
ant	نَملَة
Good afternoon!	نهارُك سعيد
April	نيسان

ه

هاتف	telephone
هبط	to land
هجر	to emigrate
هَدِيَة	gift
هَذا	this, this one (m.)
هَذه	this, this one (f.)
هُنَا	here
هناك	there
الهِند	India
هَندسة	engineering
هُو	he
هِواية	hobby
هولندة	Holland
هوية	ID card
هِيَ	she

و

وأنا أسعد	likewise
وَاجبَات المَنزِل	homework
واحِد	one
والِدا الزوج	parents-in-law (husband's parents)
والِدا الزوجة	parents-in-law (wife's parents)
والِدان	parents
وجبَة	dish (food)
وجبة الخضروات	vegetable dish
وجبة السمك	fish dish
وجبة اليوم	table d'hôte
وجبة لحم	meat dish
وجع	to hurt
وجه	face
وَحيد القَرن	rhinoceros
وُدي	friendly
وراء	behind
وَرقَة	paper, sheet of paper
وَزير	minister
وسيم	good-looking
وَصل	to arrive
الوضع العائلي	marital status
وقت	time
وقت الإقلاع	time of flight departure
وقت مُبكِر	too early
وقت متَأخَر	too late
وقف	to stand
ولد	son, boy

ي

اليابان	Japan
يَجبُ	to have to, must
يجوز	to be allowed to, may
يَد	hand
يَسار	(on / to the) left
يَمين	(on / to the) right
يوم	day
اليَوم	today
يوم الإثنين	Monday
يوم الأحد	Sunday
يوم الأربِعاء	Wednesday
يوم الثُلاثاء	Tuesday
يوم الجمعة	Friday
يوم الخَميس	Thursday
يوم السبت	Saturday
يوم الميلاد	birthday